RIPE WAS
THE DROWSY HOUR

Also by J. E. Chamberlin

THE HARROWING OF EDEN:
White Attitudes Toward Native Americans

J.E. CHAMBERLIN

RIPE WAS THE DROWSY HOUR

THE AGE OF OSCAR WILDE

A CONTINUUM BOOK
THE SEABURY PRESS · NEW YORK

1977
The Seabury Press
815 Second Avenue
New York, New York 10017

The lines by Hart Crane are reprinted from "Chaplinesque" from *The Complete Poems and Selected
Letters and Prose of Hart Crane,* edited by Brom
Weber, with the permission of the publisher, Liveright Publishing Corporation, New York. Copyright
1933, © 1958, 1956 by Liveright Publishing Corporation. "The Motive for Metaphor," by Wallace Stevens, is reprinted from *The Collected Poems of Wallace Stevens,* by permission of Alfred A. Knopf, Inc.
Copyright © 1947 by Wallace Stevens.

Printed in the United States of America

**Library of Congress Cataloging in Publication
Data**
Chamberlin, J E   1943–
Ripe was the drowsy hour.
(A Continuum Book)
Includes bibliographical references and index.
1. English literature—19th century—History and
criticism. 2. Arts, Victorian. 3. Wilde, Oscar, 1854–
1900—Biography. 4. Authors, English—19th cen-
tury—Biography. I.Title.
PR461.C45   820'.9'008   77–8072
ISBN 0–8164–9308–1

FOR MY PARENTS

Ripe was the drowsy hour;
The blissful cloud of summer-indolence
    Benumb'd my eyes; my pulse grew less and less;
Pain had no sting, and pleasure's wreath no flower . . .

*   *   *

O, for an age so shelter'd from annoy,
    That I may never know how change the moons,
        Or hear the voice of busy common-sense!

JOHN KEATS, "ODE ON INDOLENCE"

CONTENTS

PREFACE

This is a book about Oscar Wilde, and about the age in which he lived. There is a persistent artificiality about the definition of any age, for reality does not often display the kinds of coherence that satisfy the orderly imagination. But the age which Wilde prevailed upon was characterized by remarkably identifiable attitudes and dispositions, and by remarkably distinctive personalities. In turn, certain individuals tended to exemplify the habits and beliefs, and to precipitate the controversies, which flourished during the latter half of the nineteenth century.

Wilde and many of his circle quite consciously strove to make the life they led imitate the structures of the imagination which they admired, and thereby to give a recognizable coherence to their age and an aesthetic meaning to their lives. What follows is an attempt to understand that coherence and the ways in which it may be recognizable, and to explain that meaning and the ways in which it was perceived as aesthetic. To this end, the book consists of a series of differently structured reflections, linked together by common themes and by the presence of Wilde himself—which is to say, by a common focus on the age of Oscar Wilde. I refer to the period in this manner because Wilde came to a highly visible social, intellectual and artistic position at a point and in a way that illuminates many of the sustaining features of the art and life of the age.

It was a period during which the life of individuals became increasingly a part of the life of ideas, as the life of the mind and spirit regained something like legitimacy, and flaunted its new status in the revived expressions of social and aesthetic artifice. To an unusual degree, the *forms* of expression were recognized as having an independent validity and as providing a kind of common currency between quite different realms of thought and feeling. The rituals of religious belief and those of aesthetic response were linked with the rituals of social intercourse and economic initiative, for example, and it was generally agreed that some new understanding of man's activities resulted from this new kind of scrutiny.

The age of Oscar Wilde was not exclusively defined by its eccentric personalities, of course, nor by its provocative thoughts and contrived mannerisms, nor even by its astonishing social, artistic, intellectual and spiritual allegiances—though none of these can be ignored, and many are splendidly picturesque. There is much written on many aspects of the age, but the age was more than the individual fragments of truth that such studies tend to display. There are biographies of Wilde, by a wide variety of writers of diverse interests, talents and intentions; there are studies of the period, and of its art, its religion, its science, its politics, its social conditions, its taste in furniture; there are critical assessments of Wilde's work, varying from the most insincere and superficial to the most earnest and diligent. Coffee tables shudder under the load, and amateurs and professionals alike sport with Wilde's life and art.

I have tried to do something rather different which, I hope, may lead towards a clearer assessment of Wilde's career, of its place in the nineteenth-century scheme of things, and of the art and intellectual life of the period itself. However arbitrary our sense of the age of Wilde, the coherence that we invent or discover in the period is not accidental, but derives quite directly from the ideas that informed the beliefs and the believers that we wonder at, and from the forms of thought and action that characterize the thinkers and actors who constitute our ostensible subject. Wilde used to insist that our sense of the coherence of an age depends upon the way in which we perceive its abstract and ideal qualities, and I think his instinct was sound in that respect. Furthermore, and in any event, the ways in which such coherence is derived are more than historical curiosities, for they are to a considerable extent continuous with the ways in which we still derive a sense of our own culture, our own age. Finally, Wilde's age was a time in which talk of the fusion or confusion of life and art was endemic; one of Oscar's celebrated aphorisms was that life imitates art far more than art imitates life. It is therefore somewhat surprising that writers on Wilde and on the period continue to take a serious look at life while neglecting to combine this with a serious look at art, and at the principles and attitudes which informed both. I have tried to restore some of this balance, and in particular the apparent critical solemnity of Chapter Four—"Whatsoever Things Are Comely"—is a hostage to the fortunes of that more balanced perspective.

The age of Oscar Wilde was a remarkably interesting time; and Wilde was one of its most brilliant and complex representatives. This book displays some of the things that made the age interesting and, indeed, remarkable; it discusses some of the ways in which Wilde was both representative, and quite too utterly Oscar. Some of the material in chapter one first appeared in a different form in my essay, "Oscar Wilde and the Importance of Doing Nothing," in *The Hudson Review*, Vol. XXV, No. 2 (Summer, 1972).

I am grateful to many friends and colleagues for assistance and encouragement while I was working on this book. In particular, I would mention Frederick Morgan, who as editor of *The Hudson Review* has given me the best sort of encouragement and advice, for which I am deeply grateful. Mr. William E. Conway and the staff of the William Andrews Clark Memorial Library in Los Angeles were especially courteous during my final revision of the proofs, when I was in the midst of another project. Justus George Lawler and Margot Shields have been very considerate editors, and I appreciate their many helpful words and deeds. Most of all, I have benefitted from the suggestions of my wife Jane, whose uncommon patience and intelligent criticism made this book possible.

RIPE WAS
THE DROWSY HOUR

CHAPTER ONE

A GRAIL OF LAUGHTER OF AN EMPTY ASH CAN

The game enforces smirks; but we have seen
The moon in lonely alleys make
A grail of laughter of an empty ash can,
And through all sound of gaiety and quest,
Have heard a kitten in the wilderness.

HART CRANE, "CHAPLINESQUE"

"He is to be called Oscar Fingal Wilde," his mother said in the autumn of 1854, when the baby was a month old. "Is not that grand, misty and Ossianic?" His father, William Ralph Wills Wilde, was a distinguished eye and ear surgeon, who was knighted in 1864 in recognition of his achievements as Medical Census Commissioner. He was a Protestant Dubliner of erratic ambitions, who pursued both his vocation and his hobbies—natural history, ethnology, Irish antiquarian lore, and women—with enthusiasm and a considerable return, including numerous degrees, diplomas and memberships, a hospital which he converted from a stable, the authorship of twenty books, and at least three natural children. He earned much, spent much, was generous to a fault, displayed exceptional talents, and cared little for the niceties. A popular joke went: "Why are Sir William Wilde's nails black? Because he scratches himself." George Bernard Shaw described his early impression of him as "Beyond Soap and Water, as his Nietzschean son was beyond Good and Evil."

Dr. Wilde's interest in things Irish naturally included the nationalism that was especially lively following the potato famine, when the Young Ireland Party provided a focus for revolutionary patriotism. The party published a weekly, *The Nation*, in which some particularly seditious verse and prose appeared under the pen name of "Speranza"; one of Speranza's articles, a call to arms to the young men of Ireland, contributed to the suppression of *The Nation* in 1848 and to the prosecution of its editor Charles Gavan Duffy. Speranza became a well-known figure, achieving notoriety by confusing the jury sufficiently to procure Duffy's acquittal when she cried out in court that she was responsible, not he; and her real name, Jane Francesca Agnes Elgee, was widely recognized. William Wilde met her, and they were married in 1851.[1]

Rather grand, misty and Ossianic herself, she was given to poses, claiming descent from Dante (Elgee being a corruption of Alighieri, it was said), and more immediately (and accurately) from the Irish novelist Reverend Charles Robert Maturin, whose Gothic romance *Melmoth the Wanderer* (1820) was admired by writers such as Byron, Balzac, and Baudelaire. Her histrionic deportment—"soaring," as she claimed, "above the miasmas of the commonplace"—was widely applauded, both because of its entertainment value and because of her genuinely likable nature. Her literary ambitions proved more enduring than her political ones, and her social aspirations outflanked them all, as she made her house a centre for all those of any interest whatsoever, especially those in the height of fashion, who passed through Dublin; and she entertained in a manner appropriate to what Oscar once referred to as her "society for the suppression of virtue."

Oscar was born in 1854, to a father who was somewhat preoccupied, and a mother who, at the time, wished for literary and social fame and a daughter. He was the second child and became a favourite with his mother. His brother William, two years his elder, had his mother's journalistic instincts and his father's philandering ways, and spent and drank his way to death in 1899. He and Oscar were not close for most of their adult years, perhaps in part because of their competitive desire for public (and their mother's) attention. Oscar's sister, Isola Francesca, was born in 1858 and died at the age of nine, leaving Lady Wilde inconsolable and Oscar deeply grieved.

Oscar's arrival in this world was fairly inauspicious in itself, though it coincided with events of considerable, if distinct, importance: the Crimean War began, and the dogma of the Immaculate Conception was defined. They provide a usefully eccentric context within which to consider the period during which Wilde grew up and became such a celebrated, then reviled, and finally neglected figure. It was a period of pervasive ideological commitments, by far the most powerful of which in England were to various forms of political imperialism, social liberalism and religious evangelicalism. Uniting all of these was an emphasis upon conduct, upon national or ethical or moral "salvation" by works. Each one of these enthusiasms presumed certain beliefs, of course, but there was a sense of consequence, a sense that the enterprise mattered for reasons which went beyond any individual belief, that united these aspirations in a kind of impervious earnestness. Thus, imperialism became (in the mind and art of Kipling, for example) a missionary endeavour. And thus, one of the most celebrated results of the Crimean War turned out to be a social reform, in the shape of improved health care in England. All of these enterprises had another common element, which was their implicit acceptance of a more active role for a central or state authority, or whatever body it happened to be that dispensed and organized the distribution of whatever variety of truth it happened to have a monopoly on. This element, which ran counter to the individualist enthusiasms of the century, became increasingly pervasive as the century drew to a close, and eventually moved into a curious sort of alliance with the collectivist political thought of many of the idealist philosophers, and with the socialist economic programs of many of the materialist thinkers. It was to this monolithic solidarity that Wilde addressed many of his remarks during the 1880s and 1890s, even (or especially) when he agreed with some of the evangelical enthusiasms upon which they were based. The Crimean War gave an early focus to this pattern of allegiances and an early impetus to a political and social attitude of great consequence and resolute zeal.

The dogma of the Immaculate Conception, on the other hand, had a more symbolic relationship to the attitudes and aspirations which were important to Wilde. His dogged iconoclasm led him (along with many of his contemporaries) at least nominally to embrace everything that ran counter to the major tenets of evangelical thought. Against an ignorantly literal reading of the Bible, he would place the intelligently provocative "higher" and comparative criticism that had become popular on the continent; against the promise or threat of an afterlife of rewards and punishments, he wrote about the futility of punishment, however certain, as a deterrent to crime or evil; against the celebration of the present life as a preparation for the next, he became a leading advocate of the celebration of the present moment for its own sake. These were, in a sense, secular rebellions, however they may have been based on what some took to be sacred conditions. The one notable focus for specifically religious dissent was provided by the (to many common-sensical Englishmen) utterly irrational appeal of Roman Catholicism, which combined broadly catholic doctrines to which any Christian might adhere with specific dogma that tested belief in strenuous ways. The dogma of the Immaculate Conception was one of the first, and one of the most obvious, of those which appeared to be designed to separate the flock quite decisively, and it provided something of a touchstone for Wilde's own religious disputations in the 1870s, at a time when the Anglican community was itself seriously divided between those who wished for a more ritualistic (and thereby more Roman Catholic) basis for worship and those who wished to celebrate along more methodically evangelical lines. In the middle were those who wondered whether any middle ground should or would be left.

And so, in 1854, the struggles for various kinds of ascendancy, with the spirit rallied in various kinds of ways, achieved a certain clarity. The Crimean War itself was not especially significant except to those interested in mismanagement, and in the development of the considerable modern technology which was deployed there. But it did represent the reaffirmation of a principle of British interests, and it did so in a manner that laid the foundation for the wars that followed—such as the Afghan War (1878–79) and the Zulu War (1879)—and for the obsessive concern with foreign policy that characterized the second half of the nineteenth century in Britain. This obsession created a curious calm in domestic political affairs which allowed indulgence in frivolous social pleasures and which mitigated against some of the serious social reforms that were needed, though there were brief intense flurries of reform legislation and royal commissions. A war with Czarist Russia was an ever-present possibility, at times an imminent threat, all through Wilde's lifetime, and the 1870s in particular were years of deep ideological division about the nature of national responsibility, for which the troubled 1790s and 1930s possibly provide the only appropriate comparison. The furious chauvinism of the Boer War (1899) brought the era to a fitting climax, even as the last decade of the century witnessed an increasingly polarized debate on the domestic front between those who advocated socialist reform and those who wished to retain their traditional privileges. There were, as well, differences of opinion about almost everything else that mattered. On the one hand, for example, an array of public laments could be heard over England's failure to fulfil her moral obligations (to the Armenians, say, who were being slaughtered by the Turks). On the other hand, there was a relentless series of enthusiastic poetic and prosaic celebrations of England's imperial mission, whether in Asia, Africa, India or Canada:

> From Gib to Vancouver, from Thames to Yukon,
> The live air is loud with you—*Storm along, John!*[2]

John Bull stormed along through the second half of the century, as the Great Exhibition of 1851 and the Crimean War initiated imperial enthusiasms that were saluted by Queen Victoria during her Grand Review of the Fleet on her Diamond Jubilee in 1897.

There were other social consequences of significance that flowed from the main preoccupations of the age. In particular, there was a curious community of interests which developed between the middle and the working class, as the one supported foreign intervention (war with Russia during the 1870s, for example) on the grounds that it would protect and might even enhance England's commercial interests, while many of the radicals of the working (and intellectual) class commended the principle of such action as a defence of freedom against Czarist tyranny.[3] One of the consequences of this implicit alliance was that the social unrest which political theorists of various persuasions would find it convenient to discover was not nearly as prevalent or as powerful as had been predicted earlier in the century. Furthermore, the perception of a community of interests, however differently conceived, produced a solidarity among the barbarians and philistines whom the artists of Wilde's aesthetic persuasion sought to flaunt and bewilder, a solidarity which was much greater and much less exclusively bourgeois than is sometimes admitted.

There were, needless to say, voices speaking against the conventional enthusiasms and allegiances. William Morris turned towards socialism during the 1870s and wrote his "Manifesto to the Working Men of England," calling on them to recognize their distinct interests and ignore the sabre-rattling politicians. And before a decade was past, various socialist groups were becoming very irritating to the authorities with their open-air meetings in Trafalgar Square. But at the same time, the music hall was ringing with a new word and an old instinct:

> We don't want to fight, but by Jingo if we do
> We've got the ships, we've got the men,
> We've got the money too . . .[4]

Tennyson had laid the ground rules in "Maud" (written mainly during the Crimean War), which later writers such as Rudyard Kipling, Rider Haggard, John Buchan, W. E. Henley and William Watson adopted and modified according to their own interests.

It is easy to oversimplify the instinct of these writers and to miss the ironies and qualifications which pervade their work; and it is quite true, for example, that Henley might be said to have differed from Wilde more in personality than in principle. But a point that is as often ignored is the effective function which they performed of outlining a new logic of societies—a sociology—describing social groupings in an empirical way, emphasizing common interests and patterns of behaviour, rather than using philosophical or ethical premises to support the social analysis.[5] It was, in short, descriptive logic which tended towards simple, empirically verifiable distinctions; the sort of characterization that lumps together people who wear hardhats or speak with certain accents. However laughable, it was upon such simple Coriolan divisions between "them" and "us" that so much of Wilde's work and so many of his poses depended. Those who appeared earnest and diligent, who praised sincerity and probity, or submerged their individual identity in popular and gross enthusiasms, were answered with the praise of indolence and insincerity, with arguments in favour of deception and illusion, and with a celebration of the necessity of a new and higher individualism.

This kind of response to conventional pieties, and ingenuous grouping according to superficial social patterns of behaviour, is no less apparent in any other age than in Wilde's, but the importance of it as far as Wilde was concerned is that it defined his dissent from contemporary virtues and aspirations. He did not, of course, confine himself to a simple opposition to wars; indeed, he supported at least one call to arms and would reflect that although "it is often said that force is no argument, that, however, entirely depends on what one wants to prove." But the wars and imperial enthusiasm of the time gave cohesion to social forces and values which have been analyzed as quite complex but which, in terms of their expression and effect, had a remarkable simplicity, a coherence which was immensely useful to Wilde as he wandered along on his polemical way.

The Crimean War, then, was symbolic of one kind of development and one kind of coalescence; and there was, throughout the century, a continuing debate about the character of social energies, and the direction into which they should be channeled—whether towards individual or collective action, aesthetic or material improvement, ideological or imminent revolution, cultural or military development. But of at least equal importance was another issue, pertaining not to secular but to sacred allegiances. One aspect, concerning atheism or agnosticism and its adherents, did not immediately involve Wilde, though it certainly filled the pages of what John Morley, editor of the *Fortnightly Review* from 1867–1882, called the "new Reviews . . . [the] powerful pulpits where heretics were at least as welcome as orthodox,"[6] and filled the seats of not a few halls and churches. The relentless rationalism of those who proclaimed an agnostic creed was not especially congenial to those of Wilde's circle who cultivated exquisite sensations, and who viewed any attempt to bring the mind and soul together as all very well provided one did not neglect the body. But there was one religious controversy—centering around the difference between Protestant and Roman Catholic belief—in which Wilde

felt extremely involved. In part, his interest in religious dispute
was a reaction to the somewhat weary Protestantism which was a
facet of Irish life at the time,[7] and in part it was a response to the
fashionable enthusiasm for Catholicism which prevailed at Oxford
when Wilde arrived there, just three years after dissenters were
first admitted to the M.A. degree in 1871.[8] For some years there
had been a movement, strongly supported by E. B. Pusey and H.
P. Liddon among others, for a union of the Churches of England
and Rome. It was finally laid to rest when the Roman Catholic
Church accepted the doctrine of Immaculate Conception. This,
together with the decrees of the first Vatican Council (which
included the definition of Papal Infallibility) in 1869–1870,
seemed publicly to define the nature of belief that Roman Catholicism represented; it was a belief that increasingly attracted adherents and elicited debate. In 1870, for example, John Henry Newman published his *Grammar of Assent*, a subtle introduction to
Catholic belief, and Matthew Arnold his *St. Paul and Protestantism*, in which he suggests that the word God is a convenient sign
for "that stream or tendency by which all things seek to fulfil the
law of their being."[9]

Wilde was very much influenced by the sectarian religious controversies of the time; they conditioned his thinking on aesthetic
as well as theological matters, for he became convinced that the
assent that one gives to creeds of any sort is controlled almost
equally by the form of the ritual and by the temperament of the
individual. He was enough of a Protestant to accept the validity
of the divine Word as it revealed itself to each individual; he was
sufficiently inclined towards Catholicism to accept that the individual was not always capable of assessing the meaning and import
of such spiritual revelation, however valid. Visiting at the home
of Frank Miles in 1876, Wilde remarked with obvious enthusiasm
on the discussions he had had with Dean Miles, who was "a very
advanced Anglican and a great friend of Newman, Pusey, Man-
ning, Gladstone and all English theologians . . ."[10] In the same
letter he recommended the reading of *Pomponio Leto*, an account
of the Vatican Council; and he spoke of going to Rome itself "to
test the whole matter." But although Wilde himself toyed with
the possibility of "going over" at this time (he was finally converted on his death bed), he was wise enough to realize that only

clerics become Cardinals, and that neither his inclinations nor his talents were especially suited to divine orders. It should be added that he dallied with Freemasonry as well, and mastered the rituals very quickly; this too was eventually dropped, but he must have taken to it fairly seriously while he was at Oxford, if only for social reasons, for he left the lodge some quite handsome silver settings to remember him by.

Wilde's other interests during his early years appear not to have been unusual, except that his accomplishments in classical studies were exceptional. Along with many of his contemporaries, and with parents who genuinely thought that a wider public than family and close friends might wish the benefit of their opinions, Oscar took to print quite quickly. It is, in this regard, important to realize that periodical literature constituted a major influence at this time, and attracted a diligent if eccentric readership. In providing a forum it often courted heretical opinions on subjects both sacred and profane; it was not unusual to have included, in the same publication, a wide variety of material from the most specialized to the most general. It was assumed that educated readers would be interested in what educated writers had to say and, since it was a time in which "new approaches" to almost every subject flourished, it was also assumed that the manner if not the matter of a piece would probably provide some interest. Fiction appeared in periodical form throughout the age, and illustrations began to be quite the fashion. Finally, the world of universities and essays and books and reviews was almost shamelessly incestuous, and terribly sure of itself; the great periodicals of the age became rather like cultural meeting places in which one would dare to say almost anything, and to think it important. The only world which matched it for effrontery was that of politics. These worlds were linked both to each other and to the patrician world, a world which gave the ideas of leisure and of cultivated controversy meaning and function in the order of things. This would change quite rapidly, however, until by the end of the century journalism (like politics) had become a different kind of popular enterprise, to be ruled over by men such as Alfred Harmsworth (later Lord Northcliffe), whose policies often seemed to be determined by his notion that readers like "a good hate".

Wilde's early appearances were, if not indicative of his genius,

at least symptomatic of his interests and of the milieu in which
he furthered them. In November, 1875, he published in the *Dublin University Magazine* a translation of the chorus of cloud maidens in Aristophanes' *The Clouds*. Aside from formulaic references
to springtime Bacchanal dances and pleasures, there is nothing
particularly striking about the poem; but it may serve as a small
reminder of Wilde's considerable classical scholarship. He had
already been publicly thanked by John Pentland Mahaffy, his
Trinity College (Dublin) tutor, for "having made improvements
and corrections all through" Mahaffy's *Social Life in Greece from
Homer to Menander* (1874), and he was capable of reasonably
informed criticism of a wide variety of works on classical subjects.
Mahaffy's book was especially distinctive because it provided the
first reasonably straightforward account of homosexual relationships in ancient Greece, phrased in judiciously classical measures.
Another passage in the book which may have appealed to (or
indeed bear the marks of) Wilde occurs when Mahaffy speaks of
the religious divisions in Ireland, and refers especially to the apocryphal Protestant distrust of Roman Catholics "whose religion [is]
full of lies." Not quite willing to dismiss the matter, Mahaffy
speculates that "the pure Celt, who is always a Catholic, has less
regard for truth than the Protestant, with his touch of Saxon
breeding." It was a fine cue for the "grand, misty and Ossianic"
Oscar, who would later lament over "The Decay of Lying".

Wilde's work at Oxford, such as we know it, was not without
originality, and certainly was not lacking in ostentatious scholarship. When he left Oxford in 1879 he had some correspondence
with Macmillan's publishing house about translating some
Herodotus and editing some Euripides, with an encouraging response which he did not follow up. Wilde's later use of Hellenic
art and culture as a touchstone was by no means uninformed, and
his reputation as a man of formidable classical learning was widespread, especially among the younger generation whom he courted
and whose opinion and adulation he liked so much to hear. Much
of his commentary on classical matters has about it the air of
sanctimony that abounded in an age which was witnessing the
decline of classical learning, but his recommendation of, say, the
Greek Anthology as "necessary for a complete understanding of

the Greek spirit" and his defence of the references in *The Picture of Dorian Gray* to Suetonius' *Lives of the Caesars* and Petronius Arbiter's *Satyricon* as books which should be familiar to "the most ordinary of scholars" were probably genuine. (At least, he could argue that several years earlier he had advised the readers of the *Pall Mall Gazette* that Suetonius was one of the few authors who must be read; Plato and Keats, he continued, must be re-read.)[11] It should be emphasized that this was a splendid period for Greek scholarship and study in particular. Heinrich Schliemann's discoveries at Troy and Mycenae took place and were quickly published during the 1870s, and in 1877 (while Wilde was on a trip to Greece with Mahaffy) Olympia was excavated, and the *Hermes* of Praxiteles discovered. It was a good time to be a good classical scholar.

Whatever measure is taken of his classical learning, "Oscar Fingal O'Flahertie Wills Wilde, as he signed himself in early days and filled two lines of paper doing it, was a personality even in 1874."[12] He soon dropped his middle names, on the grounds that "a name which is destined to be in everybody's mouth must not be too long. It becomes so expensive in the advertisements." He developed with fastidious care his abilities as a conversationalist and storyteller—he tended to prefer the monologue—and by the time his years at Oxford were spent he had become widely known as a dinner guest of wit and charm. His description of Lord Henry Wotton's talk at dinner in *The Picture of Dorian Gray* undoubtedly reflected his ambitions, if not quite his accomplishments.

> He played with the idea, and grew wilful; tossed it into the air and transformed it; let it escape and recaptured it; made it iridescent with fancy, and winged it with paradox. The praise of folly, as he went on, soared into a philosophy, and Philosophy herself became young, and catching the mad music of Pleasure, wearing, one might fancy, her wine-stained robe and wreath of ivy, danced like a Bacchante over the hills of life, and mocked the slow Silenus for being sober. Facts fled before her like frightened forest things. Her white feet trod the huge press at which wise Omar sits, till the seething grape-juice rose round her bare limbs in waves of purple bubbles, or crawled in red foam over the vat's black, dripping, sloping sides. It was an extraordinary improvisa-

tion. . . . He was brilliant, fantastic, irresponsible. He charmed
his listeners out of themselves, and they followed his pipe laugh-
ing.[13]

Wilde—"so indolent, but such a genius"—was an individual
about whom there was often fierce disagreement, but never any
disputing his brilliance in conversation, or his irresponsibility. He
developed considerable social skills, to be sure, and he had considerable social ambitions; but the wit and irreverence which he
brought to his conversation had, for him, a more serious place in
the scheme of things. Wilde instinctively felt, and developed
much of his critical approach on the premise, that wit preserves
all that is individual and egotistic in man, and that man's highest
accomplishments depend upon its preservation. (It was this function of wit, with reference both social and aesthetic, that Freud
discussed so often in his writings.) Wilde, in fact, admired the
pose which was a part of the exercise of wit and fancy, seeing in
the dilettante or the dandy a gesture of incomparable value, a
defense against the fanaticism as well as the tedium of the serious
and the earnest. He carried this to its logical and ironic conclusion,
basically by insisting on the interdependence of the serious and
the frivolous, the earnest and the insincere, and by advocating the
cultivation of the idle fancy in a way that confounded his critics.
They were prepared for him to be like Johnson's Rasselas, a pleas-
ure-loving dilettante in a walled garden, for they could dismiss that
as an adolescent phase, an imaginative kindergarten. But they
were by no means prepared for him to suggest that this cultivation
of the fanciful and the beautiful for their own sake alone must be
an inseparable part of the cultivation of a better society, and even
of a more productive one. The dreamers, as far as Wilde was
concerned, were of no use at all if they insisted on dreaming on
the mountaintop. They must do their dreaming in the market
place, for it is there that they are most irritating, and there that
the contagion can spread.

One of Wilde's delights in later years was discovering the writings of the Chinese sage and mystic Chuang Tzŭ, one of the
founders (along with the legendary Lao Tzŭ) of the Taoist tradition of Chinese thought, which had been made available to English readers by Herbert A. Giles. In a review of Giles' translation,
Wilde noted that the sage

spent his life in preaching the great creed of Inaction, and in pointing out the uselessness of all useful things. "Do nothing, and everything will be done," was the doctrine which he inherited from his great master Lao Tzŭ. To resolve action into thought, and thought into abstraction, was his wicked transcendental aim. Like the obscure philosopher of early Greek speculation, he believed in the identity of contraries [a phrase which Giles used for a chapter title in his translation]; like Plato, he was an idealist, and had all the idealist's contempt for utilitarian systems; he was a mystic like Dionysius and Jacob Böhme. . . . In fact, Chuang Tzŭ may be said to have summed up in himself almost every mood of European metaphysical or mystical thought, from Heraclitus down to Hegel.[14]

This "great creed of Inaction," as Wilde called it, embodies an insight which he felt to be of the very highest order, whether applied to artistic or social concerns. "When we have fully discovered the laws that govern life," he wrote, "we shall realise that the one person who has more illusions than the dreamer is the man of action. . . . In the sphere of action a conscious aim is a delusion"; and action should therefore be recognized as "the last resource of those who know not how to dream."

England during Wilde's life was very much a place of last resource, a place populated by practical people, proud of their pragmatism, who followed Carlyle down the path of hard and diligent toil, and who fondly remembered that Edmund Burke had classed industrial stinks and stenches with the sublime. The ascendancy of the manufacturing and commercial class that followed the Reform Bill of 1832, the new Poor Law of 1834 (which, by insisting on centralized relief, made "the only available relief less desirable than the worst employment"), the defeat of those who agitated against the Poor Law as well as of those who cried for a People's Charter, and the free trade enthusiasm which led to the repeal of the Corn Law (thereby removing the duty on grain, and at least nominally returning the economy to the perils of "laissez-faire"), together these created an England that moved into the 1850s and 1860s fairly convinced of the work and efficiency ethic that was associated in Europe with a bourgeois mentality. Even the 1870s, despite the serious economic depression, were years in which energy and action were called upon, as England waged war with the Zulus abroad and in due course with

sodomy and lesser vices at home. Public health and housing clear-
ance legislation occupied much time, and the intermittent
thoughts of the nation were on serious problems and their earnest
solutions.[15]

To this England, Wilde spoke with audacious flippancy, realiz-
ing that the survival (not to mention the ascendancy) of an aesthetic spirit depends upon a continual confrontation with its
contrary. He suggested to a serious age that "dulness is the coming
of age of seriousness"; to a diligent age that "industry [by which
he meant diligence] is the root of all ugliness"; and to an age that
celebrated honest toil that "the first duty in life is to be as artificial
as possible." The most available source of this artificiality, this
beauty, this delightful play of thought and feeling, is to be found
in art, and in the stylized forms of life which we usually associate
with highly formalized manners and dandified behaviour that
conspicuously defies conventions in the interests of emotional or
intellectual expression. Furthermore, as Wilde saw clearly, the arts
and certain forms of social behaviour and disengagement protect
one's individuality, one's emotions and ideas—two most danger-
ous and most precious assets—from contamination by practical
pursuits, and perhaps from contamination by the new gospel that
would be propounded somewhat ironically by men like Oswald
Spengler, who wrote in his introduction to the *Decline of the West*
(1918) that

> if the influence of this book leads men of the new generation to
> turn from poetry to technology, from painting to the merchant
> marine, from epistemology to politics, they are doing what I desire.
> One could wish nothing better for them.

The idea of art as performing a psychological and social function was hardly new, but the nineteenth century took it up with
the particular enthusiasm that followed naturally from the "ordering" of the arts that had taken place in the eighteenth century and
the interest in romanticism that developed at the same time. The
confusion that seemed to prevail in these years reflected not so
much a doubt about what art does, but about the way in which
it does it. Running through the commentaries of the period was
a basic distinction, which represented one of the most celebrated,

and certainly one of the most intransigent dichotomies in art—
that of form and content, style and subject. Both are necessarily
incorporated in a work of art and, although inseparable in a genuine aesthetic experience, are ordinarily separated for the purposes
of analysis.

The analysis of art has never been a simple matter, but some
fairly simple distinctions have often been made between certain
kinds of motivation that result in certain kinds of art. Wilde
himself tended to follow a romantic line, and assume that art
satisfies individual (as distinct from social) needs. On that assumption, art is an expression of an excess of creative energy over that
which is necessary simply to cope with the demands of living; it
is a function both of the need to give imaginative coherence to
one's environment, and of the need to establish a relationship with
something extraneous and thereby to confirm one's sense of one's
self, and achieve some form of self-consciousness. These functions
are related, of course, primarily in that both are responses to what
Wallace Stevens termed the "rage to order," what early twentieth-
century psychologists called *Gestaltungsdrang,* or what Wilde
called "egotism," which oppose an individual (or cultural) energy
creative of some order to the anarchy of the world outside the self.
Thus, on one level, geometric designs appear on primitive shelters;
and, on another, elegiac, pastoral and witty metaphysical poems
are written. Wilde's cavalier version (which illustrates, almost
accidentally, the familiar model of the mind as a mansion) is that
"egotism, which is so necessary to a proper sense of human dignity, is entirely the result of indoor life. . . . Nature is so indifferent,
so unappreciative."

Insofar as the form that is created bears the stamp of a determining personality, the element of style will be foremost, and an
ordering rather than an imitation of nature will be the norm. "My
own experience," wrote Wilde,

> is that the more we study Art, the less we care for Nature. What
> Art really reveals to us is Nature's lack of design, her curious
> crudities, her extraordinary monotony, her absolutely unfinished
> condition. Nature has good intentions, of course, but, as Aristotle
> once said, she cannot carry them out. When I look at a landscape
> I cannot help seeing all its defects. It is fortunate for us, however,

that Nature is so imperfect, as otherwise we should have had no art at all. Art is our spirited protest, our gallant attempt to teach Nature her proper place.[16]

These "spirited protests" in which Nature is taught her proper place are nothing other than attempts at "civilizing" one's environment, of insisting on a human rather than a natural order; William Blake's comment that "Natural Objects always did and now do weaken, deaden and obliterate Imagination in Me" is an especially provocative version of this notion. In broader terms, the terms to which Wilde turned his attention and which informed his social posturing and his aesthetic affectations, this becomes the suggestion that "to be natural is to be obvious, and to be obvious is to be inartistic." Speaking of the lily and the sunflower, the two emblems of the aesthetic movement in England which he popularized in the early 1880s, Wilde noted that "we love ... these two lovely flowers [because they] are in England the two most perfect models of design, the most naturally adapted for decorative art—the gaudy leonine beauty of the one and the precious loveliness of the other giving to the artist the most entire and perfect joy."[17] An important point behind such easily parodied affectations was that a sense of form and style—an aesthetic sense—was a conditional as well as a consequence of a truly civilized life, and that an appropriate style was both the effect and the cause of the imaginative realization of a distinct identity and a purified language. It was an easy step to affirm the priority of the imagination by holding up decoration as a pure example of an imaginative excess over what is useful or necessary, and to suggest that

the art that is frankly decorative is the art to live with. It is, of all our visible arts [at least], the one art that creates in us both mood and temperament. Mere colour, unspoiled by meaning, and unallied with definite form, can speak to the soul in a thousand different ways. The harmony that resides in the delicate proportions of lines and masses becomes mirrored in the mind. The repetitions of pattern give us rest. The marvels of design stir the imagination. In the mere loveliness of the materials employed there are latent elements of culture. Nor is this all. By its deliberate rejection of Nature as the ideal of beauty, as well as of the imitative method of the ordinary painter, decorative art not merely prepares the soul for the reception of true imaginative work, but develops in it that sense of form which is the basis of creative no less than of critical achievement.[18]

Wilde's attention to decorative detail became a part of the spirit of the age—an age that witnessed a revival of interest in the manners and graces, as well as the architecture, of the Georgian period—as architects such as R. Norman Shaw (whose most famous building was the New Scotland Yard [1889]) moved towards elegant proportion and E. W. Godwin developed a modified Japanese style of furniture and decorative design.[19] With fashionable (though not always creative) concern, people attended to interior decoration and design; William Morris and Company are remembered, to be sure, but they had nothing like a monopoly on public interest. There was always the bizarre, such as Whistler's notorious transformation of Frederick Leyland's dining room into the "Peacock Room"; more in the normal run of the avant-garde, there was the work of Godwin, who renovated the house at 16 Tite Street (to which Wilde moved with his wife Constance after their marriage in 1884) and created a room there painted in shades of lacquered white and grey, the furniture all white except for a red lampshade. This room, or at least its reputation, had a considerable influence on C. R. Mackintosh, the great Glasgow craftsman who himself was a pioneer of modern interior design. The great German arts and crafts movement of the early part of the twentieth century, which came to a flowering in the Bauhaus, was fundamentally indebted to the work of the English artists and craftsmen of this period, and a sense of this legacy continued through the 1920s.[20] The instinct behind the interest in decorative values was an instinct to surround oneself with beautiful forms, with rooms and houses and costumes and conversation and manners that reflected and, in turn, created an artistic sensibility. There was a continuity and an interdependence among social forms that was, it was quite seriously believed, very precious; letting one's attention to detail in matters of dress or design or conversation slip was the beginning of a slide down a slope that might lead to the disintegration of society. So much depended upon style and form. As Lady Bracknell advises Cecily in *The Importance of Being Earnest,* there are distinct social possibilities in your profile. The two weak points in our age are its want of principle and its want of profile. The chin a little higher, dear. Style largely depends on the way the chin is worn. They are worn very high, just at present.

And to the unfortunate Jack Worthing, who is trying to explain his origins—he was found in a handbag in the cloakroom at Victoria Station—Lady Bracknell is explicit about the consequences of such unforgivable lapses in social decorum:

To be born, or at any rate bred, in a handbag, whether it had handles or not, seems to me to display a contempt for the ordinary decencies of family life that remind one of the worst excesses of the French Revolution. And I presume you know what that unfortunate movement led to?[21]

Such lapses as Jack Worthing's are extreme examples, and negative ones. The positive side was the more easily explicated, and was associated with nothing less than imaginative and cultural survival, the defence of the self against natural inclinations, utilitarian enthusiasms, or the sordid demands which were inseparable from bare human existence. The art and artifice of a self-conscious age were, in short, a means of rising above the human condition, or at least above its common denominator; they were, practically speaking, useless, which made them psychologically and imaginatively invaluable, for they freed the psyche from its imprisoning obligations. The most imprisoning obligation of all was the obligation to be natural. It was difficult enough ignoring this injunction in daily life without having to deal with it in art, and it therefore became very much the conventional wisdom to reject all that was tainted with the offensive odour of naturalness and candour. By this new orthodoxy, art was celebrated for "the telling of beautiful, untrue things"; truth becomes "entirely and absolutely a matter of style" for (as Browning said), "the histrionic truth is in the natural lie"; and "the only beautiful things" are agreed to be "the things that do not concern us." In social terms, since sincerity is the counterpart in ethics to imitation in aesthetics, insincerity becomes, according to Wilde, a means by which we can multiply and consequently develop our personalities.[22] As Lord Illingworth says in A Woman of No Importance, "taking sides is the beginning of sincerity, and earnestness follows afterwards, and the human being becomes a bore." Set against boredom there was exquisite variety, new experiences, subtle moods—the things which art could offer. Art offered beauty as its essential quality; it offered truth, as simply "one's last mood." And it served no purpose other than to make life worth living.

> Art is useless because its aim is simply to create a mood. It is not meant to instruct, or to influence action in any way. It is superbly sterile, and the note of its pleasure is sterility. If the contemplation of a work of art is followed by activity of any kind, the work is either of a very second-rate order, or the spectator has failed to realise the complete artistic impression.
>
> A work of art is useless as a flower is useless. A flower blossoms for its own joy. We gain a moment of joy by looking at it. That is all that is to be said about our relations to flowers. Of course man may sell the flower, and so make it useful to him, but this has nothing to do with the flower. It is not part of its essence. It is accidental. It is a misuse.[23]

Being properly affected by this superb sterility, we are engaged by the form and disengaged from the content of a work of art. For example, when watching a tragedy we experience, according to as ancient an expert as Aristotle, a purging of the emotions as a consequence of aesthetic involvement in the play. In Wilde's terms, this process of catharsis becomes a "rite of initiation" into the mysteries of a particular artistic form—in this case tragedy—rather than a surrogate for killing one's wife like Othello, or sleeping with one's mother like Oedipus. The standards of this art are that it is useless, that it is its own evidence, and that it is consistent with itself and sufficient unto itself. Occasionally life produces its own work of art, such as Phipps, the butler in *An Ideal Husband*, who is described as "a mask with a manner," and who is said to represent "the dominance of form." But generally, the only link between Art and Nature, except for incorrigible sentimentalists such as Wordsworth, is, in Wilde's opinion, "a really well-made buttonhole."

One consequence of the premise that art is hermetic and never expresses anything but itself, is the paradox that art is the only means by which thoughts and feelings and beliefs can find expression without ever having to "pay the price" of that expression. Art embodies the truth, and avoids the consequences. Furthermore,

the subject of a work of art is first and foremost the artist's
awareness of himself—his self-consciousness, just as the style of a
work of art is the artist's *expression* of himself—his personality.
Together, they constitute what Walter Pater called the "virtue"
by which a work operates aesthetically. Since an artist's awareness
of himself is often much less precise or available than his personality, his art may become obscure. Wilde's reaction to Browning was
typical of his treatment of obscurity in poetry, and of his sensitivity
to the new literature:

> There is something curiously interesting in the marked tendency
> of modern poetry to become obscure. Many critics, writing with
> their eyes fixed on the masterpieces of past literature, have ascribed
> this tendency to wilfulness and to affectation. Its origin is rather
> to be found in the complexity of the new problems, and in the fact
> that self-consciousness is not yet adequate to explain the contents
> of the Ego.[24]

This is not an apology for incompetence, though Wilde recognized that kind of obscurity also, and used to say that "to be
intelligible is to be found out." Rather, it leads inevitably to the
paradox that "only the great masters of style ever succeed in being
obscure," and provides an insight into

> the great truth that Art's first appeal is neither to the intellect nor
> to the emotions, but purely to the artistic temperament, and
> . . . this temperament, this "taste" . . . being unconsciously guided
> and made perfect by frequent contact with the best work, becomes
> in the end a form of right judgment.[25]

Years later, Pablo Picasso noted that

> from the point of view of art there are no concrete or abstract
> forms, but only forms which are more or less convincing lies. That
> those lies are necessary to our mental selves is beyond any doubt,
> as it is through them that we form our aesthetic view of life.[26]

When Wilde got sentimental, he could write dramatically to
Robert Ross how

> on the other side of the prison-wall there are some poor black
> soot-smirched trees that are just breaking out into buds of an
> almost shrill green. I know quite well what they are going through.
> They are finding expression . . .[27]

But in his clearer moments, Wilde knew of the artistic disaster that inevitably results when the poor black soot-besmirched people of the world try to find expression directly in art, without converting their passion into the counterfeit currency of art—his own *Ballad of Reading Gaol* is, as he recognized, a schizophrenic poem for this very reason. For the truths which art has to offer are not agonized and honest; they are essentially unserious, and insincere —only then will the agony and honesty shine through.

What Wilde proposed, in short, was that the brutish seriousness of action and sincerity be transcended by the genial spirit of the artist. Friedrich Schiller's theory of play is the application of this idea to the arts, and Oscar himself often performed in a manner that had all those elements of incongruity that the dada artists of the twentieth century ritualized. In one particularly entertaining incident

> Prince Leopold of Belgium, accompanied by Mrs. Liddell, the wife of Canon Liddell, Dean of Christ Church, and Miss Alice Liddell, the Alice of *Alice in Wonderland*, came to hear the choir singing [in Magdalen College chapel] under Sir William Parratt's expert direction. It was Wilde's duty to read the First Lesson. He went up to the lectern, turned over the pages, and began in a languorous voice to recite the Song of Solomon. The Dean of Arts, the Rev. Henry Bramley, promptly swooped down from his stall and, thrusting his beard into the reader's face, exclaimed in a tone of concern, "You have the wrong lesson, Mr. Wilde. It is Deuteronomy XVI."[28]

"Poor Oscar," commented G. T. Atkinson, who recalled the incident, "he was so thoroughly enjoying himself."

This is, as it were, a profane example of what was for Wilde essentially a sacred function, in which the truths of art were the litany of a new worship of beauty and truth. Art was recognized as supplying a critique of the bondage imposed by serious endeavours of any kind, and the one sure way of keeping the spirit, of keeping what is humane and individual, alive. It was an indispensable function, especially in what Wilde referred to as an "age in which people are so industrious that they become absolutely stupid." The arts free the spirit from the constraints of both mundane and moral obligations; and the aim of art is in a sense "emotion for the sake of emotion," while the aim of life and society and religion is emotion for the sake of action. Thus, on the one level, Tom Sawyer and his friends can enjoy white-washing the fence, since they are not constrained by the obligation to do it; and on another level—the imaginative level of the arts—we can enjoy watching the death of Romeo and Juliet since we are not inhibited by the obligations of the actual, but on the contrary are freed by the artistic form, the perfect inconsequence of which delights us.

Those who were philosophically inclined, and with an Hegelian bent, such as Wilde, realized that although the pleasure and imaginative freedom which is an aspect both of the style and the content of art—and more generally of inaction or indolence—consists in avoiding the pernicious consequences of social and moral obligation, yet this same sense of pleasure and freedom exists only in the context of that which would cancel it. In other words, the state of mind which art or "cultivated idleness" encourages is sustained by the fact that one is conscious of what is being denied. To take an example from another sort of activity, there is no fun (or function) in "conspicuous consumption" unless one remembers as well as forgets that it is wasteful. And anyone watching a production of *Othello* would miss much of the experience of the play if unaware of both the reality as well as the artificiality of Desdemona's murder. Wilde, with his talk of truth and lying, nature (or life) and art, joy and sorrow, rang the changes on this theme, and in so doing continued a romantic preoccupation with the character of the imaginative and the real, disbelief and belief, the dream and the waking vision. Wordsworth and Coleridge and Keats—Keats above all—wrote with these paradoxical relationships continually in mind, and it was this quality in Keats, along with the sensuous charm and the profuse imagery of his verse, that endeared him to the poets of Wilde's time.

Wilde's interest in Keats was deep and abiding, as he recognized in his work (and in his life) the instincts which he felt to be of central importance. Keats celebrated strategies of escape, and recognized the imagination as the most capable vehicle, though he did—in the tradition of the prototypical Romantic martyr Thomas Chatterton (with whose life Wilde as well was fascinated)[29]—find himself "half in love with easeful death." His ambition for "a life of sensation rather than of thought" provided a model for the enthusiasms of the apostles of aestheticism, and the music of his poetry charmed an age that perceived all art as aspiring (more or less) towards the condition of music. His medievalism reinforced what became by the middle of the century an epidemic interest in medieval subjects, both as an escape and as a benchmark against which to measure the decline of civilized values and institutions. And there is little doubt that

> the medieval cult, in all its forms, witnessed to the strain of living and thinking in a society where facts, theories and principles must have seemed to many sensitive people like an unintelligible whirl of atoms.[30]

Keats' acceptance of intensity and artifice as conditions of imaginative assent; his suggestive portrayal of "la belle dame sans merci"—one of the more memorable "femmes fatales" in romantic literature; his perception of the artist as necessarily a victim; and his celebration of the contemplative (not to say indolent) aspect of poetic creativity—of poetry as "Might half slumbering on his own right arm"... all of this provided inspiration for writers and artists in the nineteenth century.[31] Perhaps most important of all, at least to Wilde, was Keats' perception of the union of beauty and truth as elements of style, and the union of joy and sorrow as functions of the subject matter of art—his perception, in his own words, that "Beauty is Truth, Truth Beauty" and that "in the very temple of Delight / Veil'd Melancholy has her sovran shrine."

Wilde's earliest public demonstration of his attachment to Keats took the form of an article and a poem which appeared in the *Irish Monthly* for July, 1877. He praised the "Prince of Beauty slain before his time, a lovely Sebastian killed by the arrows of a lying and unjust tongue," and wrote in his poem of "the youngest of the martyrs . . . /Fair as Sebastian, and as foully slain." The poem was entitled "Heu Miserande Puer," a phrase from Virgil's *Aeneid* (Book VI)—a translation of the phrase as "Child of a nation's sorrow" was praised ten years later by Wilde—and although the title was afterwards changed to "The Grave of Keats," Wilde's sense of the place which Keats occupied in relation to the philistine as well as to the aesthetic presumptions of the age was clear. There was a heroism in Keats's life as well as art which was of immense imaginative potential; it provided a model for a role that the artist or outcast might adopt, as well as an example of a relationship between life and art upon which the values of both depended. Keats, who once said he would "die content" if he could "upset the drawling of the blue stocking literary world," was dead of tuberculosis before he was twenty-six, while the world droned on. Shelley, who was adept at mythmaking, turned Keats' death into a sacrifice on the altar of jealous, stupid orthodoxy. (Wilde himself, in a gesture of almost grotesque melodrama—which nonetheless confirmed his perception of an affinity between his fate and Keats's—took the Christian name Sebastian when he came out of Reading Gaol to go into exile on the continent, joining it to that of the demon martyr Melmoth, the grimly comic hero of Maturin's gothic tale.)

Keats's early death, and his ill treatment at the hands of the critics of his day, took on a legendary quality. But it was a grim legend, as Aubrey Beardsley—the one artist of the age who had followed Keats's steps most closely—knew only too well, and as Wilde instinctively recognized. Beardsley, like Keats, died in his twenty-fifth year (1898) of tuberculosis. "Really," he had once remarked to Ada Leverson, Oscar's "Sphinx," "I believe I'm so affected, even my lungs are affected."[32] This was the final legacy of Keats—a sense of the comic, turned by the late century into gallows humour. It was, of all things, Wilde's supreme talent; as he lay dying, he remarked of the wallpaper in his Paris hotel room, "It is killing me. One of us had to go."

Keats was Wilde's favourite poet, and a symbol of attitudes to which he would later give his own signature. In the meantime, and especially during his Oxford years, he was developing his own interests and a sense of the milieu in which he would further them. In 1877 he wrote (once again in the *Dublin University Magazine*) a notable review of the first exhibition at the new Grosvenor Gallery that Sir Coutts Lindsay had established. Wilde's piece consisted of an enthusiastic display of rather undigested critical responses to particular painters and was heavily dependent upon contemporary Oxford methodologies. In particular, Wilde modelled his approach upon the critical attitudes which Walter Pater had recently set forth, as well as the moral enthusiasms of John Ruskin, by which Wilde (despite his later disclaimer) was much affected.

There were several painters of interest with works on exhibit, including G. F. Watts, John Everett Millais, Alma Tadema, Holman Hunt, Edward Burne-Jones, Walter Crane, Frederic Leighton, Alphonse Legros, and W. G. Wills, a cousin of his father's whose paintings and plays Oscar was inclined to praise excessively. But the artist whose work aroused the greatest stir was James Abbott McNeill Whistler, who was responsible for what Wilde referred to as "the most abused pictures in the whole Exhibition." Wilde himself was sceptically amusing in his review of the "colour symphonies" of Whistler (whom he rather ambiguously glorified by loaning him Heraclitus' reputation as the "dark one"); he remarked with reference to the *Nocturne in Black and Gold: The Falling Rocket*[33] and a companion "nocturne" that "these pictures are certainly worth looking at for about as long as one looks at a real rocket, that is, for somewhat less than a quarter of a minute."

Wilde and Whistler shared many opinions about the arts— among them, as Wilde maliciously noted, the opinion that Whistler was "one of the very greatest masters of painting." Both men developed styles of life and deportment that were conspicuously precious, and both paid great attention to the art of conversation. In each case, there was something of defiance as well as of defence in the poses, passions and principles that were ostentatiously displayed. Their relationship developed after Wilde moved to Tite Street, Chelsea, in 1880. Whistler had a studio there, next to the White House, his former home, which he had lost in a bankruptcy sale in 1879. Wilde shared rooms, at a place they called Keats House, with the artist Frank Miles. Both the White House and Keats House (like Wilde's later home after his marriage at 16 Tite Street) were designed or decorated by the talented Edward Godwin, who in life and in death was an apt symbol of this Chelsea circle. After his first wife died, he set up house with Ellen Terry, who later (in 1878) became Henry Irving's perennial leading lady at the *Lyceum,* and to whom Wilde wrote three sonnets. When they parted ways, Godwin married Beatrix, the daughter of sculp-

tor John Birnie Philip. She, in turn, married Whistler after Godwin's death, which was itself an occasion for a bizarre funeral
procession from London to Northleigh, near Witney, in Oxford-
shire. From the nearest train station the coffin was transferred to
an open farm wagon; the mourners "Trixie," Whistler, and Lady
Archibald Campbell climbed aboard, and when lunch time came
along they spread out the picnic they had prepared on the coffin,
while the wagon lumbered along towards Godwin's final earthly
home.[34]

Whistler and Wilde were well matched. Ellen Terry called
them "the most remarkable men I have known," and she had
known many. Their relationship, aside from its Chelsea circus
character, was a nervous one always, at first punctuated by amusing raillery and then, within a few years, by nasty recrimination.
Wilde, who by the end of the decade was becoming quite successful, dealt magisterially with one whose "only thoroughly original
ideas . . . have had reference to his own superiority as a painter
over painters greater than himself."

Whistler's view was that Wilde had plagiarized his best ideas,
as well as the all too imitable form in which it was Whistler's
fashion to phrase them; there was some truth to the accusation,
but rather more paranoia. Certainly, Wilde learned much from
the "Butterfly," as Whistler signed himself, about how to turn a
phrase or return an insult, and their ideas about the importance
of doing nothing and discussing everything coincided nicely.
There was a delightful perfection about many of Whistler's remarks; Wilde gave them his own personality, and thereby transformed them—for which Whistler, understandably, was not entirely grateful. But Wilde found Whistler's accusations tedious,
and in "The Critic as Artist" he carried his rebuttal a step further
by suggesting that accusations of plagiarism

> proceed either from the thin colourless lips of impotence or from
> the grotesque mouths of those who, possessing nothing of their
> own, fancy that they can gain a reputation for wealth by crying out
> that they have been robbed.

Whistler, who was bankrupt and somewhat out of the limelight,
drew caricatures for his own lonely delight of Oscar as a pig, and
a jockey, and with the famous Whistlerian top hat and stick; later,

on learning that Wilde was at work on a play (after his release from jail), Whistler suggested "The Buggar's Opera" as a title. He published (in 1890) his advice *On the Gentle Art of Making Enemies*, a chronicle of Whistler's own career as an habitual if usually quite elegant scrapper. One of Whistler's greatest contributions to the period was in the design and layout of this particular book. Grant Richards called it "one of the supreme achievements of the age," and there is no doubt that it had a significant influence on the books of the 1890s.

In a celebrated attempt to venture into Wilde's territory, and publicly to proclaim his views on art, Whistler gave his famous Ten O'Clock Lecture at Prince's Hall in 1885. (It was delivered at that unusual hour in the evening in order not to interrupt dinner.) In his lecture he pronounced, as Wilde described it, "the panegyric of the Philistine," by declaring that art is necessarily elitist, and that anybody—such as John Ruskin, the Preacher "appointed", the priest of the Philistine—who confounds art with education is, for want of a better word, a fool.

Ruskin had set the stage for such vituperation; his own response to Whistler's contributions to the Grosvenor Gallery exhibition took the form of some advice to Sir Coutts Lindsay, which was published in *Fors Clavigera* in July, 1877.

> For Mr. Whistler's own sake, no less than for the protection of the purchaser, Sir Coutts ought not to have admitted works into the gallery in which the ill-educated conceit of the artist so nearly approached the aspect of wilful imposture. I have seen, and heard, much of Cockney impudence before now; but never expected to hear a coxcomb ask two hundred guineas for flinging a pot of paint in the public's face.

Whistler, in a righteous rage, sued Ruskin for libel, claiming £1,000 damages. The only good which came out of it was a selection of Whistlerian responses to impudent questions. Asked by counsel for Ruskin (who was ill, and descending rapidly into the insanity from which he never recovered) if "the labour of two days, then, is it that for which you ask two hundred guineas?" Whistler answered, "No, I ask it for the knowledge of a lifetime." (One of the witnesses who appeared on Whistler's behalf was the painter W. P. Frith, whose painstaking and precise representation of

"The Railway Station" once prompted Wilde to ask "Is it all done by hand?" Frith's detailed portrayal of the artistic celebrities of the day in his "Private View of the Academy" [1881] included Wilde, in a very prominent and professorial pose.)

Whistler won his suit; damages assessed were one farthing. This kind of judgment was in fact not that unusual; a decade earlier, Mary Josephine Travers was awarded damages amounting to one farthing when she alleged that Sir William Wilde, Oscar's father, had raped her after lessening her resolve with chloroform, in a libel suit brought against Lady Wilde, who had written an abusive letter to the girl's father. Some time later, George Bernard Shaw suggested that Whistler should have claimed on the basis of loss to his commercial rather than artistic reputation, for "that sort of thing can be understood by lawyers." Costs for each side in the case of Whistler versus Ruskin were put at £386.12s.4d., plus of course attorneys' fees. Within a short space, Whistler was bankrupt.

There should have been a lesson there for Wilde, perhaps about libel suits and English law and the inability of wit to carry the day in court. Some years after Wilde's death, Bertrand Russell remarked that

> the Chinese constantly remind me of [him] in his first trial when he thought wit would pull one through anything, and found himself in the grip of a great machine that cared nothing for human values.[35]

In his essay, "Pen, Pencil and Poison," Wilde described the "curious courage" of forger and poisoner Thomas Griffiths Wainwright in bringing an action in the Court of Chancery against several insurance companies. Wilde referred to Wainwright's "courage" with good reason, for the companies he sued had failed to pay to himself and his wife insurance claims of £18,000 on the death of Mrs. Wainwright's sister, whom Wainwright himself had in fact poisoned. Wilde, Whistler and Wainwright each displayed a similar sort of curiously suicidal daring. In Whistler's case, as *The Times* implied in an editorial the day after the trial, he was flaunting his apparently negligent method of "knocking off" a painting against the accepted virtues of hard work and diligent attention to technical processes. The scrupulous manner of Pre-Raphaelite painting (such as had in the main been shown at the Grosvenor Gallery) was acceptable to such orthodox opinion, however much the matter might disturb; but impressionist insistence upon impulsive and momentary creativity was felt to be unacceptably subversive. Paul Klee remarked a few years later, in an equally earnest environment, that "one wonders if such people have ever read the Book of Genesis, and contemplated God's impulsive creation of the world."

As Whistler's creative affectations and Ruskin's critical biases were being judged in a court of law, Wilde's own affectations of negligent charm and enigmatic wit were becoming celebrated in their own right. He had provided the model for a character (Charles Davenant) in a novel (*Mirage*, 1877) by George Fleming (pseudonym of Julia Constance Fletcher), a character who wears "his hair rather long, thrown back, and clustering about his neck like the hair of a medieval saint," who speaks "with a peculiarly distinct enunciation . . . like a man who made a study of expression," who listens "like one accustomed to speak," and who affects languid tones and enigmatic statements.[36] When Wilde won the Newdigate Prize "for the best composition in English verse" at Oxford in early June 1878 for his poem *Ravenna*, he had it published later that month with a dedication "to his friend George Fleming." The previous year he had sent her copies of Pater's essays on "Demeter and Persephone" and "Dionysus", by which he set considerable store. These essays had appeared in the *Fortnightly Review* during 1876 and, although it was Pater's *Studies in the History of the Renaissance* (1873) that Wilde later said had "such a strange influence over his life," these shorter "Greek Studies" were also highly regarded by Wilde and may have had a more profound effect on him than has yet been recognized.[37] Wilde sent Pater his "first art-essay," the Grosvenor Gallery review, and received a nicely complimentary reply which paved the way for a meeting between the two later the same year and for the curious discipleship that followed. Wilde's *Poem in Prose* called "The Disciple," which concludes with the pool at which Narcissus worshipped himself confessing that "I love Narcissus because, as he lay on my banks and looked down at me, in the mirror of his eyes I saw ever my own beauty mirrored," may well be the best testimony both to the nature of this particular relationship and to the more general question of the various and often quite enigmatic patterns of worship which Wilde inspired or in which he indulged.[38]

Wilde's instincts during these years were inclined to an individualism of a flagrant sort, an individualism which combined the roles of priest, poet and prophet in one compulsive pose. He was priest of a new religion, worshipping beauty (and therefore truth); he was poet in a new court, in which craftsmanship was most highly prized and the doctrines of an aesthetic royalism were vigorously proclaimed; and he was prophet of a new order, whose rituals were conspicuously defiant. Like all prophets, he was the object of a great deal of scorn. His self-conscious posturing became a part of his nature and was reinforced by his belief in the aesthetic value of artifice and what one might call creative deceit. In a final irony, it was the Marquess of Queensberry's accusation that he was *"posing* as a somdomite"—Queensberry could not spell nearly as well as he could spit—which precipitated the libel action that Wilde brought and the criminal prosecution of Wilde which followed Queensberry's acquittal.

Yet whether we decide that it is a pose, a passion or a principle which informed Wilde's life and art, we must still come to terms with his significant influence on and his remarkable embodiment of the cultural values and artistic habits of his age. Perhaps Jorge Luis Borges touched the right note when he remarked that Wilde

> was much more than an Irish Moréas; he was a man of the eighteenth century who sometimes condescended to play the game of symbolism. Like Gibbon, like Johnson, like Voltaire, he was an ingenious man who was also right.[39]

Wilde's attachment to his native Ireland was real, if somewhat undercut with irony. Coming from what he referred to as "a nation of brilliant failures," and from a Dublin that was referred to even by many of the most nationalistic Irish men and women of the period as a cultural bog, he nonetheless was influenced by the popular cant that set Celtic inspiration and imaginative charm above Teutonic stability and common sense. And throughout his

life he was, as Bernard Shaw remarked, "at root a very Irish
Irishman, and as such, a foreigner everywhere but in Ireland."
During his years at Oxford, he was often back and forth across the
Channel; but there was something rather final about the journey
when Wilde left Ireland in December, 1878, shortly after learning
of the engagement (and marriage on December 4) of the love of
his early life, Florence Balcombe, to Bram Stoker, who had become Henry Irving's business manager at the Lyceum in October,
and who later wrote the pot-boiler *Dracula*. Wilde returned to
Ireland only briefly, and only twice. Much later, he remarked that
the two turning points of his life were when his "father sent him
to Oxford, and when society sent [him] to prison." Richard Ellmann, whose studies of Wilde are among the most perceptive,
suggests that the first was an "initiatory" moment; and he places
considerable emphasis on another such moment, Wilde's apparent introduction to active homosexual activities (with Robert
Ross) in 1886. I am not at all convinced of this epiphanic chronol-
ogy but, if one is to be sketched, I would suggest that his all but
final departure from Ireland at the end of his Oxford years (during
which he spent much time on Irish soil), the particular circumstances attending and following his departure, and the milieu into
which he plunged in London, constitute a complex of events
which give a focus to much that he later would display more
explicitly.

His years at Oxford were particularly important, for they
confirmed some and denied other things that were central to his
temperament and to his emotional and intellectual needs. Especially, they prepared for his attachment to London, and his separation from Ireland. During the spring and summer of 1876, much
happened to the young Wilde. His father died in April, and the
specter of financial difficulties arose, never quite to depart. (One
of his final comments to Ross was that he was dying as he had
lived, beyond his means.) In July he received word of his First in
Classical Moderations (Mods)—he took a First in Literae
Humaniores (Greats) two years later—and he spent much time
that summer with Frank Miles, an artist and son of the rector at
Bingham, Nottinghamshire. While in his company, he met Lord
Ronald Gower, a sculptor and writer of charm and perverse incli-

nations, who probably provided something of a model for Lord Henry Wotton, Dorian Gray's "seducer."[40] In August of that year, while waiting for Miles to join him for a fishing excursion, he met Florence Balcombe.

However one looks upon their relationship, it clearly affected Wilde deeply. It is often passed over as a youthful romance, and so it was; but Oscar was twenty-one when he met her, and not unaquainted with life. The two years he courted "Florrie" were, as he told her, "the sweetest years of [his] youth," and it is abundantly clear that her decision to marry someone else was a considerable shock to him. Over two years later he was asking Ellen Terry surreptitiously to give some flowers to Florrie for her to wear on her first stage appearance (as a priestess in Tennyson's verse play *The Cup*):

> I should like to think that she was wearing something of mine
> . . . that anything of mine should touch her. Of course if you think
> —but you won't think she will suspect? How could she? She thinks
> I never loved her, thinks I forget. My God how could I![41]

It seemed clear to Wilde when he first became involved with Florrie that they could not at present marry, for neither had money and he had no immediate prospects; and it is all too easy to imagine the pose of insouciance that he may have adopted for the sake both of his Oxford attachments and his own self-respect. Indeed, by the spring of 1878, things looked rather dismal for him and he contemplated the awful possibility of "doing some horrid work to earn bread."

Florrie had not let Oscar know of her engagement before his return to Dublin in November. Wilde was deeply upset at the news, and his dejection most probably precipitated his move to London, away from depressing Dublin and into a world of social activity and aristocratic association that clearly fascinated him, and that provided much of the material that he later transformed into his fiction and plays. In this world, money mattered—indeed, not only determined but in ways constituted social relationships as well as cultural standards.[42] And in this world relations became confused, and ambitions clouded. His relations with Florrie were broken, and Wilde appeared almost surprised by how important and unrealized the relationship had been to him. His relations with Frank Miles in London were eventually problematic, though the circumstances are unclear. They quarrelled and went separate ways before too long, probably over the winter of 1880–81; there is some hint of a developing homosexual relationship between them in the early London years, and certainly Rev. Miles became quite distressed at the influence that he feared Oscar might have over his son Frank when he read the poems that were intended for publication in Wilde's 1881 volume. It is clear that, at the least, there were some unsettling matters in the relationship between the two. A few years earlier, in the course of a letter to his friend William Ward, Wilde had referred to his "two great gods, Money and Ambition." There is, needless to say, something facetious about such a claim, but it is nonetheless true that money especially came to occupy a central if tedious place in Wilde's thoughts during the two decades during which he pursued his ambitions. Wilde's plays, with the partial exception of *Salomé*, were about society, and therefore about money; his prose fiction is either premised upon or turns around the availability of money. His critical essays play with the idea of a kind of civilized leisure that money alone could secure. Wilde's later years were taken up with an obsession about money, and the company he kept during the period that led up to his conviction for gross indecency was in part bought company. Into this world he went from Oxford, well schooled in its manners and mores, with less than innocent expectations, and conscious that disappointment is a condition of life. Without making too much of the fact, it is worth pointing out that Wilde's string of academic and modestly social successes through until 1878 was beginning to run out. Florrie had gone to Stoker; by the spring of 1879, Oscar's intermittent hopes of a Fellowship at Magdalen had proven empty, and his essay (on "The Rise of Historical Criticism") written for the Chancellor's Essay Prize failed (as did all the other entries) to win the award. One part of Wilde always held very dearly the ancient idea that a competitive forum (such as the rival Greek rhapsodists entered) provided the only true test of talent or genius, and he must from time to time have wondered about his ambitions.

The next few years were spent in cultivating what he referred

to as the "beautiful people"—especially the "Professional Beauties," such as Lily Langtry and Lady Lonsdale—and in perfecting
his pose. Even his regrets were the product of artifice:

> To drift with every passion till my soul
> Is a stringed lute on which all winds can play,
> Is it for this that I have given away
> Mine ancient wisdom and austere control?
> Methinks my life is a twice-written scroll
> Scrawled over on some boyish holiday
> With idle songs for pipe and virelay,
> Which do but mar the secret of the whole.[43]

It is easy to make quick work of Wilde's self-conscious posturing in
a poem such as this one, the rather programmatic "Hélas." Wilde
thought it a characteristic poem and may have been right, for it
certainly has provided sport for critics. One of its earliest bows was
inauspicious enough; Oliver Elton led the Oxford Union to refuse
an inscribed presentation copy of the volume of *Poems* (1881)
which it introduced.[44] The volume (which was published at the
author's expense) had a limited success, being criticized mainly for
its derivative (and to a certain extent its licentious) quality. Yet
what is clear in what Wilde wrote and what he did during these
years is that, although not by any means a great poet, he had a poet's
instincts and sense of artifice and the kind of staggering effrontery
that leads the artist to worry about losing his "soul's inheritance"—
as Wilde worries at the end of the poem—as though it mattered, as
though it were a public as well as private benefaction.

It was this kind of audacity that led to the pose of aestheticism
that is so often associated with the early 1880s, and with the name
of Wilde. Recently back from India, Rudyard Kipling shuddered

> But I consort with long-haired things
> In velvet collar-rolls,
> Who talk about the Aims of Art,
> And "theories" and "goals,"
> And moo, and coo with womenfolk
> About their blessed souls.[45]

Max Beerbohm gave a more affectionate portrait of the time in
an essay entitled simply "1880" which appeared in *The Yellow
Book* in 1895.

I have often felt that it would have been nice to live in that bygone epoch when society was first inducted into the mysteries of art and, not losing yet its old and elegant *tenue*, first babbled of blue china and white lilies, and of the painter Rossetti and of the poet Swinburne. It would have been a fine thing to see the *tableaux* at Cromwell House or the Pastoral Plays at Coombe Wood, to have strained my eyes for Connie Gilchrist, and danced all night long to the strains of the Manola Valse. The period of 1880 must have been delicious . . .

The period of 1880 and of the four years immediately succeeding it must always be memorable to us, for it marks a great change in the constitution of society. . . . The tragic fall of Disraeli . . . Gladstone . . . Parnell . . . young Randolph Churchill . . . Charles Bradlaugh. . . . While these curious elements were making themselves felt in politics, so too in society were the primordia of great change. The aristocracy could not live by good breeding alone. The old delights seemed vapid, waxen. Something new was wanted. And thus came it that the spheres of fashion and of art met, thus began the great social renascence of 1880.

But it remembered that long before this time there had been in the heart of Chelsea a kind of cult of Beauty. Certain artists had settled there, deliberately refusing to work in the ordinary official way, and "wrought," as they were wont to put it, "for the pleasure and sake of all that is fair." Swinburne, Morris, Rossetti, Whistler, Burne-Jones, were of this little community. . . . Beauty had existed long before 1880. It was Mr. Oscar Wilde who first trotted her round. This remarkable youth, a student at the University of Oxford, began to show himself everywhere, and even published a volume of poems in several editions as a kind of decoy to the shy artificers of Chelsea. The lampoons that at this period were written against him are still extant, and from them, and from the references to him in the contemporary journals, it would appear that it was to him that Art owed the great social vogue she enjoyed at this time. Peacock feathers and sunflowers glittered in every room, and curio shops were ransacked for the furniture of Annish days, men and women, fired by the fervid words of the young Oscar, threw their mahogany into the streets. A few smart women even dressed themselves in suave draperies and unheard-of greens. Into whatever ballroom you went, you would surely find, among the women in tiaras and the fops and the distinguished foreigners, half a score of comely ragamuffins in velveteen, murmuring sonnets, posturing, waving their hands. "Nincompoopiana" the craze was called at first, and later "Aestheticism" . . .

I fancy it was a red-chalk drawing of a girl in a mob-cap, signed "Frank Miles, 1880," that first impelled me to research. To give an accurate and exhaustive account of the period would need a far less brilliant pen than mine.[46]

While cartoonist George du Maurier introduced two aesthetes, Postlethwaite and Maudle, to readers of *Punch*, the editor Frank Burnand was writing *The Colonel*, a spoof of Wilde and his circle, which opened in London in early 1881, with Beerbohm Tree in the title role. Parodies and burlesques abounded, but the most celebrated was Gilbert and Sullivan's comic opera *Patience*, produced by Richard D'Oyly Carte and opening in April of 1881. By the end of the year it was on stage in D'Oyly Carte's new theatre the Savoy, the first theatre and the first play to have the benefit of electric lights. The two principle characters, Reginald Bunthorne and Archibald ("I am a very narcissus") Grosvenor, represented the "fleshly" and the "idyllic" poet; the reference to Wilde himself was generalized, though it was Bunthorne who was usually identified as the most specific. The entire group of worshippers of the beautiful, and especially the Pre-Raphaelites, were included in the satire,[47] for they all were identified with those whose ambition was, in Wilde's words, to "live up to their blue china".

> If you're anxious for to shine in the high aesthetic line
>   as a man of culture rare,
> You must get up all the germs of the transcendental terms,
>   and plant them everywhere.
> You must lie upon the daisies, and discourse in novel phrases
>   of your complicated state of mind,
> The meaning doesn't matter if it's only idle chatter
>   of a transcendental kind.

It was to publicize *Patience* and to make some money that Wilde went on tour in America, at the invitation of D'Oyly Carte. Wilde sailed on Christmas Eve, in 1881; the captain of the ship, who did not like him, said later that he wished he had "that man lashed to the bowsprit on the windward side." Wilde, for his part, found the Atlantic "a disappointment." But the tour was a considerable success, if only in that it gave Wilde an opportunity to develop his rhetorical talents in the wilderness. He lectured on what he identified as a renaissance of art in England, on aesthetic principles of decoration and design, on the philistine and barbaric impediments to the new golden age of which he was a prophet—

he did seem rather to enjoy the wilderness, it might be added—
and on particular topics, such as Irish poets of '48, to particular
audiences.

He sailed back to England a year later, leaving from New York
on December 27. ("Don't you keep Christmas?" Wilde was asked
several years later by Charles Brookfield, when Oscar scheduled a
rehearsal of *An Ideal Husband* for Christmas day. "No, Brookfield," replied Wilde. "The only festival of the Church I keep is
Septuagesima. Do you keep Septuagesima, Brookfield?" "Not
since I was a boy." "Ah, be a boy again!") After a three-month
sojourn in Paris during which he made the acquaintance of many
of the leading French artists and writers, and worked on a poem
(The Sphinx) and a play *(The Duchess of Padua),* he returned to
England and fussed about the production (ultimately disastrous)
of his play *Vera, or the Nihilists* in New York (and paid a short
visit there in August of 1883 to watch the play sink into its richly
deserved oblivion after a week). He then began a year or more of
lecturing in Britain on "The House Beautiful," "Personal Impressions of America," "The Value of Art in Modern Life," and
"Dress," among other topics—a suitable witness to the evangelical
and entrepreneurial enthusiasms which he castigated. By November he was engaged to Constance Lloyd; they were married the
following May.

The next few years were reasonably domestic, though even—
or perhaps especially—domesticity received a quite distinct and
fashionably Wildean accent. His financial situation was precarious; he had gone into the marriage with moderate assets, but also
with a considerable debt, certainly well over £1,000. His new wife
was, on her family's own admission, neither frugal nor adept in
money matters; and both of them were inclined to attach more
importance to the virtues of fine display than to those of thrift.
Two children were born—Cyril in 1885 and Vyvyan in 1886—
and Oscar, always willing to "be a boy again," entertained them
with kindness, vivacity, and unfailing fancy. He sang and read
Jules Verne, Stevenson, and Kipling to them; he recalled or made
up fairy stories; and he played with them often. His own books of
fanciful tales, *The Happy Prince and Other Tales* and *A House of
Pomegranates,* were published in 1888 and 1891 respectively; at

the time of the publication of the first he remarked to Richard Le Gallienne that

> it is the duty of every father to write fairy tales for his children. But the mind of a child is a great mystery. It is incalculable, and who shall divine it, or bring to it his own peculiar delights? You humbly spread before it the treasures of your imagination, and they are as dross. For example, a day or two ago, Cyril yonder came to me with the question, "Father, do you ever dream?" "Why of course, my darling. It is the first duty of a gentleman to dream." "And what do you dream of?" asked Cyril, with a child's disgusting appetite for facts. Then I, believing, of course, that something picturesque would be expected of me, spoke of magnificent things: "What do I dream of? Oh, I dream of dragons with gold and silver scales, and scarlet things coming out of their mouths, of eagles with eyes made of diamonds that can see over the whole world at once, of lions with yellow manes, and voices like thunder, of elephants with little houses on their backs, and tigers and zebras with barred and spotted coats . . ." So I laboured on with my fancy, till, observing that Cyril was entirely unimpressed, and indeed quite undisguisedly bored, I came to a humiliating stop, and, turning to my son there, I said: "But tell me, what do you dream of, Cyril?" His answer was like a divine revelation: "I dream of pigs," he said.[48]

When the contents of Wilde's house were sold at the scandalously disorganized dispersal by public auction on April 24, 1895, which was forced by Lord Queensberry (under bankruptcy laws) to settle the creditors, two of the last lots in the sale catalogue included "a rabbit hutch", " a quantity of toys" and the author's signed copy (No. 2) of the large paper edition (75 copies) of *The Happy Prince*, which he used to read from to his boys at bedtime.

Wilde's relations with his wife during this period appear to have been reasonably happy, though sometime during 1886 it is claimed that syphilis which he had contracted in his youth and believed (on medical advice) to have been cured was discovered to be still active, and he was forced to discontinue sexual relations with Constance. Apparently, he then turned to active homosexuality and he slowly began to display the suicidal obsession with perverse pleasures that led him to the dock.

During the mid 1880s, however, while his family life still retained some semblance of order, Wilde attempted in several quite mundane ways to solve his seemingly perpetual financial problems. (He once advised that "it is only by not paying one's bills that one can hope to live in the memory of the commercial classes.") Lecturing and reviewing brought in something; and in 1885 he even wrote his friend George Curzon for a recommendation towards getting him a position as one of Her Majesty's Inspectors of Schools. In 1887, he took over the editorship of *Lady's World* (he had the name changed to *Woman's World*), which he held for two years. Again, money became an acute problem, and continued to be so even when his income became considerably greater during the 1890s, as his plays attracted enthusiastic audiences.

He was, in addition to attending to some of his obligations, extremely active during this period. "The Portrait of Mr. W. H." was written and appeared in *Blackwood's Magazine* in 1889. His one novel, *The Picture of Dorian Gray*, was finished early in 1890 and published in *Lippincott's Magazine* in July of that year. It caused a major sensation, and a lengthy debate ensued about the morality of art and the ethical sympathies of the artist. Wilde, to his not entirely genuine dismay, found himself answering the close to libellous criticisms of Charles Whibley (reviewer for *The Scots Observer*—later *The National Observer*—which was edited by Wilde's former friend W. E. Henley), as well as other scarcely less venomous comments from other quarters.[49] The novel appeared in book form in 1891 and was well received by a more appreciative audience. Lionel Johnson's Latin praise, a parody of the liturgical hymn, was perhaps the most extravagant, and also among the most explicit; it was not published until after Johnson's death in 1902.

> Benedictus sis, Oscare!
>
>   . . .
>
> Hic sunt poma Sodomorum;
> Hic sunt corda vitiorum;
> Et peccata dulcia.[50]

1891 was a year of some sort of grace for Wilde, and his work flourished. "The Soul of Man Under Socialism" was published in February (alongside Grant Allen's "The Celt in English Art", in which "the modern aesthetic movement in England" was described as "due above everything to Celtic initiative," and a connection established "between the decorative revival and the Celtic upheaval of radicalism and socialism"). *Intentions,* Wilde's major volume of critical essays, appeared in May, though all of the essays in it had been previously published in slightly different forms.[51] *Lord Arthur Savile's Crime and Other Stories* appeared in book form in July, *A House of Pomegranates* in November, *The Duchess of Padua,* a play (in imitation of Shelley's *The Cenci*) which he wrote for Mary Anderson in 1882–83, was finally produced in New York as *Guido Ferranti;* and late in the year, in Paris, Wilde wrote *Salomé. Lady Windermere's Fan* was written in 1891 and produced the following February, as Wilde's career as a playwright began to take shape. In response to the shouts for the author when the curtain fell on the opening night of *Lady Windermere's Fan,* Wilde appeared on stage smoking a cigarette—a piece of "insolent effrontery," one critic said—and delivered himself of a brief speech:

> Ladies and Gentlemen, I have enjoyed this evening *immensely.* The actors have given us a *charming* rendering of a *delightful* play, and your appreciation has been most intelligent. I congratulate you on the *great* success of your performance, which persuades me that you think *almost* as highly of the play as I do myself.

In June of 1892, *Salomé* was banned by the Lord Chamberlain on the grounds that it portrayed biblical characters; the law which was brought to bear dated back to Reformation attempts to prohibit Catholic mystery plays and had little to do with the proverbial Mrs. Grundy's real reasons.[52] The prohibition was expected, but it was nonetheless a blow, since Sarah Bernhardt was rehearsing the title role for a production that she had arranged. (It was eventually first produced in Paris in 1896, while Wilde was in prison.) *A Woman of No Importance* was written during the late summer and produced the following spring (1893); *Salomé* was published in French early in 1893, then translated into English (by Alfred Douglas, with "schoolboy faults" later corrected by Wilde) during the summer and fall at the same time as Wilde was writing *An Ideal Husband.* The publication of *Salomé* in English, with illustrations by Aubrey Beardsley, took place in February of 1894; it was a fragile alliance, not made easier by a rivalry between

Beardsley and Douglas, for Beardsley wanted to translate the play himself. Wilde did not like the illustrations; he thought them "too Japanese, while my play is Byzantine." Beardsley, on his part, maliciously caricatured Oscar in four of them, including the frontispiece in which Wilde's features are clearly those of "The Woman in the Moon." Beardsley was well on his way towards his own version of Wilde's dandyism—"on one occasion [he] apologiz[ed] for appearing even more wan than usual by explaining that he had caught a cold by inadvertently leaving the tassel off his cane."[53]

In June of 1894, *The Sphinx*, a long poem purportedly begun at Oxford and finished in Paris in 1883, was published. This volume, designed and illustrated by Charles Ricketts, was one of the most striking examples of the fine work in book design, decoration, illustration and binding done during the 1890s. Ricketts and his friend Charles Shannon were involved in the design of most of Wilde's books (with the notable exception of *Salomé*) from 1889.

Later in 1894, Wilde wrote *The Importance of Being Earnest,* his incomparable comic masterpiece. As 1895 came around, Wilde had two new plays opening within as many months: *An Ideal Husband* on January 3, at the Haymarket Theatre, and *The Importance of Being Earnest* on February 14, at the St. James Theatre. Then, on February 28, he found the card "For Oscar Wilde posing as a somdomite" which Lord Queensberry had left ten days earlier at Oscar's club. Wilde obtained a warrant for the arrest of Queensberry, who was charged with criminal libel. When it became clear that serious incriminating evidence might be provided against Wilde in Queensberry's defence, the prosecution withdrew—entering a plea of justification for the use of the word "posing"—and Queensberry was acquitted. But he was far from through, for having spent a considerable amount of time and money (but not by any means all of his rancour) dredging up evidence against Wilde, he turned it over to the Director of Public Prosecutions. Wilde was arrested on April 5, and charged with committing acts of gross indecency with various specified male persons. His first jury disagreed, but the second convicted him and he was sentenced to two years' hard labor on May 25.

There was something distractingly exhibitionist about Wilde's sexual preoccupations, especially from the early 1890s until his arrest. Although his intimate association with Lord Alfred Douglas (whom he met in 1891 through Lionel Johnson) precipitated his public disgrace, it is important to remember that it was Wilde's (un)discriminating purchase of boys with beautiful profiles that brought him two years with hard labour. It was Wilde's love for and infatuation with Douglas that led to court, for it was this attachment that infuriated Douglas's father, the (eighth) Marquess of Queensberry, and provoked him into what Wilde charged was a libellous statement. Queensberry was a vicious and somewhat unbalanced man who had wrecked his own household long before; but his hatred of Wilde, who was sixteen years older than his son, was probably not so very much different in some respects from what any unsympathetic parent might have felt, considering especially his son's infuriating insults to·him (which included sending him a telegram with the message "What a funny little man you are") and given the public way in which Oscar and Bosie flaunted their relationship. (After all, Rev. Miles—who was not, like Queensberry, a vicious fool—had exercised his righteous indignation on Wilde for the possible influence of a book of his poems—and the kind of character responsible for them—on his son, who was two years older than Oscar. The difference in Queensberry's case was that he detested his son as well as his son's companion.) In any event, Wilde's relationship with Douglas brought him to court, as the accuser; his relationships with numerous young boys who were procured for him by various people for quite specific and illegal homosexual purposes put him on the defence and brought him to prison, after Queensberry's paid muckrakers had discovered enough to turn the legal tables on him. There is nothing even remotely heroic or enlightening about this aspect of Wilde's behaviour; he chose, quite simply, to enter the market in a pitiful trade in order to satisfy the excess of his desires (though it is of course arguable that he was forced to do so by a society that would not explicitly countenance any homosexual attachments). His love for Douglas was genuine and he defended it with dignity:

"The Love that dare not speak its name" in this century is such a great affection of an elder for a younger man as there was between David and Jonathan, such as Plato made the very basis of his philosophy, and such as you find in the sonnets of Michelangelo and Shakespeare. It is that deep, spiritual affection that is as pure as it is perfect. It dictates and pervades great works of art like those of Shakespeare and Michelangelo. . . . It is in this century misunderstood, so much misunderstood that it may be described as the "Love that dare not speak its name," and on account of it I am placed where I am now. It is beautiful, it is fine, it is the noblest form of affection. There is nothing unnatural about it. It is intellectual, and it repeatedly exists between an elder and a younger man, where the elder has intellect and the younger man has all the joy, hope, and glamour of life before him. That it should be so, the world does not understand. The world mocks at it and sometimes puts one in the pillory for it.

Wilde's eloquent speech, delivered in response to cross-examination at the Old Bailey after he had been held in prison without bail for a month, ignores the fact that it was not his affection, however noble, for Alfred Douglas that placed him there, but his resorting to telegraph boys and grooms. One of the more appalling aspects of the appalling trials was the extent to which the judicial system displayed its willingness to view the actions and evidence of the various people involved in a different manner according to their station in society. And for all of their hideousness, there was something disturbingly egalitarian about Wilde's trials; one can understand the mob dancing in the street when the final verdict was given.[54] His punishment was wretchedly inappropriate and murderously vengeful, but it had, in the end, very little to do directly with his love for Douglas.

Yet, of course, it had everything to do with it as well. Wilde's explanation of the moral of *The Picture of Dorian Gray* might apply as well to himself as to his hero, "that all excess, as well as all renunciation, brings its punishment." The excessive displays in which Wilde and Douglas indulged were at least in part—not a large but a central part—prompted by the same motivation that made the artist indulge his love of artifice, or of beautiful forms, or of intense experiences. But Wilde's reflection much later was perhaps more appropriate, if not truer, for it emphasized his loss of the ability to choose, his loss of will, in a way that echoed almost

exactly the kinds of descriptions that the psychological critics of
the decadence such as Paul Bourget were giving a few years earlier
when they spoke of the "problem of the will," and that European
(especially Scandinavian) novelists such as J. P. Jacobsen and So-
phus Schandorph were portraying in their moving demonstrations
of the significance that Hamlet held for the age. Wilde, in coming
to terms with his infatuation with Douglas, decided in a Coleridgean lament, that he made a

> gigantic psychological error. I had always thought that my giving
> up to you in small things meant nothing: that when a great mo-
> ment arrived I could reassert my willpower in its natural superior-
> ity. It was not so. At the great moment my will-power completely
> failed me. In life there is really no small or great thing. All things
> are of equal value and of equal size. My habit—due to indifference
> chiefly at first—of giving up to you in everything had become
> insensibly a real part of my nature. Without my knowing it, it had
> stereotyped my temperament to one permanent and fatal mood.[55]

Wilde was released from prison on May 19, 1897; he left for
Dieppe by the night boat the same day, and spent the next three
and a half years until his death late in 1900 on the continent. The
time in prison had been hard on him, both physically and men-
tally; conditions were dreadful, and the sentence of hard labour
was a vindictive flourish that almost destroyed him. He survived,
even in some measure prevailed, but he came out badly shaken,
almost shattered. He wrote little during the years left to him, and
worried a lot—about money, his family, his health. He had good
reason to worry about them all, but an element of paranoia all too
often prevailed and caused a number of rifts with long-suffering
(though to be sure often quite meddlesome) friends. His wife had
obtained a deed of separation from Wilde, and changed her name
and the children's to Holland (a family name on her side). The
children had been placed under the joint guardianship of herself
and Adrian Hope. Constance Wilde's affection for Oscar was
remarkably true and permanent, as her letters amply demonstrate,
and she tried to be kind to him after his release. Well-meaning
friends interfered time and again, with plans for a partial reconciliation, or a meeting, or even a moderate understanding; as a
result there were some bitter feelings on both sides during the

short time left until her death in 1898. Wilde saw neither his wife nor his children after 1895.

His famous letter to Alfred Douglas, written in early 1897 at Reading Gaol and published after his death as *De Profundis,* was one of the more astonishing products of his grueling years in jail; and his letters on prison conditions sent to the London press after his release are among the more horrifying of his revelations of what he went through. *De Profundis* is a powerful tract, a moving indictment of himself as well as of Douglas, and a harrowing Christian apologetic, written in the slough of despond. Wilde's only other literary accomplishment of these last years was *The Ballad of Reading Gaol,* published in 1898, exactly a century after one of its obvious models, *The Rime of the Ancient Mariner.*

The story of Wilde's life has been told an almost intolerable number of times, but seldom well. Robert Ross, his devoted friend and literary executor, and the most logical contemporary biographer, did not try, in part because he remembered Wilde's comment that "every great man has his disciples, and it is always Judas who writes the biography." But there were other Judases, more adept; and Wilde's greater fear that a legion of Guildensterns would survive to talk over the grave of Hamlet was even more fully realized.

It was only on the continent that Wilde even occasionally escaped the biographical Guildenstern, the provincial Rosencrantz, the minor Judas. England wished that Wilde, reclaimed by civilization (through the good offices of Reading Gaol) like some bog that had recently been drained, would turn to the editing of prayers for those at sea. Europe, on the other hand, blossomed forth with editions (usually pirated) of nearly all of his works, and saw new truths where others had seen only trash; or, as Hart Crane wrote of Charlie Chaplin, saw "the moon in lonely alleys make / A grail of laughter of an empty ash can."

Wilde's popularity was indisputable. *The Picture of Dorian Gray* was translated into Czech, Danish, Dutch, Finnish, French, German, Italian, Polish, Russian and Swedish by 1906; and into Greek, Hungarian and Yiddish by 1912. It was not just in literary circles that Wilde was known. The Swiss painter Paul Klee took the trouble to memorize the entire Preface to *Dorian Gray* and long passages from *De Profundis;* and the Russian artist Wassily Kandinsky quoted Goethe and Wilde together in support of the major proposition in his influential book *The Art of Spiritual Harmony,* published in 1912. "The Soul of Man Under Socialism," another favourite among the Masters of the Bauhaus such as Klee, Kandinsky, and Oscar Schlemmer, had its passionate devotees in Czarist Russia; Richard Strauss modelled his opera after Wilde's *Salomé.* Thomas Mann praised Wilde's work extravagantly, likening him to Nietzsche; and André Gide was influenced by him more than he cared to admit. His influence on twentieth-century criticism has been immense, and his life and art have fascinated successive generations of those who respect the creative imagination.

Despite the obvious, not to say irresistible, temptation to follow Wilde's own lead and reflect that he spent his genius in his life and only his talent in his art, it has not been his life alone that has attracted lasting attention. For his art at its best was, in his words,

> the great primal note by which I had revealed, first myself to myself, and then myself to the world; the real passion of my life; the love to which all other loves were as marshwater to red wine, or the glow worm of the marsh to the magic mirror of the moon.[56]

And speaking of his art, Wilde naturally included his criticism; naturally, for he thought that the highest criticism,

> being the purest form of personal impression, is in its way more creative than creation, as it has least reference to any standard external to itself, and is, in fact, its own reason for existing, and, as the Greeks would put it, in itself, and to itself, an end.[57]

But Wilde's life and his art (or criticism) are not easily separated. Indeed, it is one of the chief accomplishments of Wilde's writing that he relentlessly insists on that interrelationship between life and art which is germane to the preservation of both. This interrelationship obtains in the true and humane values of each, and is very fragile. Often, in both his life and his art, Wilde did not immediately recognize when these values were in jeopardy; and then, when he did, it was on at least one occasion too late. But it was as well quite the fashion to be late, and Oscar liked to lead the fashion. He began, as he liked to say, as a lion in a den of Daniels. He ended by being thrown to the Christians.

CHAPTER TWO

THE AGE OF OSCAR WILDE

For each age is a dream that is dying
Or one that is coming to birth.

ARTHUR O'SHAUGHNESSY, "ODE"

"I was one who stood in symbolic relations to the art and culture
of my age," reflected Oscar Wilde with pride and regret. He was
born in 1854, and died in 1900; and he became what a contemporary called an "astonishing, impudent microcosm" of his time.[1]
There is something mutual about Oscar and his age, and if we
would understand one we must to some extent understand both.
Misunderstanding the past for present convenience is an occupa-
tional hazard, some would say a creative talent, but with reference
to Wilde and his time it is a foolish mistake. This is especially true
with reference to the years in which Wilde first became conscious
of the age in which he lived, the years of his education in Dublin
and Oxford, and in the social world of London, during the 1870s.
At the end of that decade Wilde himself warned "that any attempt to isolate [what he called the contemporary English Renaissance of Art] in any way from the progress and movement and
social life of the age that has produced it would be to rob it of its
true vitality, possibly to escape its true meaning."[2]

Growing up and becoming educated in this period of the nineteenth century was, in many ways that we have long since lost, a
fairly straightforward business; the doubt and despair that we so

often associate with the Victorian age were more acutely the affliction of a generation previous to Wilde's, and to a certain extent of the generation which followed. For Oscar and his contemporaries there was a certain fashionable scepticism that intermittently became something of an intellectual obligation; but often enough the mood was tranquil and the accepted sense of progress contributed a relative stability. Perhaps this situation was reinforced by the stabilities of the classics, with which no one of any pretensions would be unfamiliar; certainly the material prosperity that had settled over the land like beneficent soot from the urban industrial centers appeared to have created a settled calm and to have put the lie to doomsters such as that "Calvinist without a theology" Thomas Carlyle, who had predicted that industrialism and democracy would bring disruption in their wake. Being Irish might constitute something approaching instability, but even that was arguable. For everyone who claimed, as did the historian J. A. Froude, that Celts were congenital liars and sycophants, there was a Matthew Arnold celebrating the Celt as a possessor of magic and melancholy, "sociable, hospitable, eloquent, admired, figuring away brilliantly."[3]

There was, indeed, a sense in the air that life was there to be lived, and that the life of the mind and the spirit especially held wonderful possibilities. The confidence of the scientists and philosophers, the politicians and the historians, the theologians and the aestheticians, was a remarkable feature of the time, and provided a stimulus to those (such as Wilde) who gave pride of place to art and culture.

The early 1870s saw several changes that, especially looking back over the previous decades, encouraged this kind of confidence—Darwin's recently popularized evolutionary scheme (first published in 1859) did, after all, have its affirmative side, at least on the speculative level. But on the practical side as well there was notable progress: there were education reforms, such as the passing of the Elementary Education Act, the abolition of religious tests at Oxford and Cambridge, and the opening of a women's colleges at Cambridge, and later at Oxford; the trade union movement was legalized; and the secret ballot was established. On a more leisurely plane, lawn tennis was patented, and in 1877 Wimbledon added it to croquet on its banner; cricket had splendid innings during this period, when W. G. Grace was in his prime . . . and white flannels became standard sporting dress. Others had a different notion of what evolution meant; 1874 saw the beginnings of renewed agitation for Irish "Home Rule," initially under the auspices of Isaac Butt (who was better known to the Wildes as counsel for Charles Gavan Duffy and Mary Travers). For the next twenty years, no Irish man or woman could be quite indifferent; indeed, the politicians—and especially the fiery C. S. Parnell —saw to it that few Englishmen could avoid the issue. Science was very much in the forefront, of course, and provided convenient analogies for almost every point of view. Darwin himself, and his popularizers such as Herbert Spencer, were widely read; in related fields, European research and study was being continuously translated as important figures like Ernst Haeckel were brought to the attention of English readers. The great James Clerk-Maxwell published his study on *Electricity and Magnetism* in 1873. Wilde was well acquainted with and (as his notebooks show) deeply fascinated by scientific developments; and public discussion was lively, and informed, on many topics of surprisingly modern aspects.

It is quite easy to discover the effect of such changing conditions in Wilde's writing and in what is reported of his conversation during those years: the feeling of a new age of prosperity and reform and intellectual advance was in the air, and the optimism which coincided with this stimulated Wilde's brief career in the early 1880s as the apostle of beauty and the evangelist of the "house beautiful."

Oscar's own sartorial style[4] as he moved into the new social circles that radiated out for him from Oxford must have been influenced by the return of Benjamin Disraeli to the Prime Ministership in 1874. Disraeli was an inveterate and accomplished dandy—not, perhaps, as inveterate or accomplished as his model from the 1830s, Alfred Count d'Orsay, but nonetheless one whose flamboyant arrogance in dress and conversation made him a notorious figure, known in some disagreeable circles as "the Jew d'esprit." Wilde had been an admirer of Disraeli's novels in his school days, a not insignificant inclination when one considers how unin-

terested he was in the English novel in general; he reserved his
greatest enthusiasm for the masters of the French novel, especially
Balzac and, to a lesser degree, Flaubert. It is worth noting, perhaps, that this disinterest in novels was something of a fashion;
Disraeli himself confessed to Lady Londonderry in 1857 that "I
have never read anything of Dickens except an extract in a newspaper," and pompously asserted that "when I want to read a novel,
I write one." Matthew Arnold, for all his concern over the "condition of England," waited thirty years before he read *David Cop-
perfield*. Wilde himself was not greatly taken by Dickens in his
earlier years, though he did request a set of his novels while in
prison in 1896.

The years following Dickens' death in 1870 constituted an
important period for the novel, and it was an immensely popular
literary form, as the records of publishers, the circulating libraries
and the booksellers show,[5] as does Wilde's own dutiful reviewing
in the 1880s. Trollope continued to write energetically and produced an average of nearly a novel a year during the 1870s. George
Eliot, whose reputation belongs more to the twentieth than to the
nineteenth century, published *Middlemarch* in 1871, and although her influence was in many ways restricted to those with
more severe moral enthusiasms than Wilde affected, she was
called "the greatest living writer of fiction" by Walter Bagehot in
1864 (in an essay on Sterne and Thackeray, who had died in 1863).
George Meredith—of whom Wilde wrote, "as a writer he has
mastered everything except language: as a novelist he can do
everything, except tell a story: as an artist, he is everything except
articulate"—was developing an immensely loyal following. R. L.
Stevenson, a "delicate artist in language" as Wilde called him, was
becoming popular, though his greatest success, *Treasure Island*,
did not appear until 1883. When Wilde wrote to Ada Leverson
from Holloway Prison (where he was awaiting trial in 1895) asking
for some books, he mentioned only "some Stevensons—*The Master of Ballantrae* and *Kidnapped*"; later, from Reading Gaol, he
requested other Stevenson volumes. One hopes that this was a
sense of his predicament prevailing over his taste.

Nonetheless, and despite our judgments, the sensational novel
had a wide contemporary appeal. Wilkie Collins' *The Woman in*

White had begun the vogue in 1859, that year of many new directions,⁶ although the occult had received sensational treatment in Bulwer Lytton's novel *Zanoni* (1842), the heroes of which provided a model for the fictional characters of Madame Blavatsky's celebrated *Isis Unveiled* (1877). When George Moore was writing his autobiographical *Confessions of a Young Man,* he described his first "echo-augury" (a kind of de Quincean epiphany)⁷ as occurring when in 1862 he came across "a novel the world is reading," Mary Elizabeth Braddon's *Lady Audley's Secret.* Charles Reade moved from *The Cloister and the Hearth* (1861) —which Wilde ranked as an artistic masterpiece with Thackeray's *Henry Esmond* and Flaubert's *Salammbô*—to a career of very popular journalistic melodrama and theatrical enterprise. There was an audience for sensationalism, an audience that Wilde could not help himself appealing to when much later he wrote *The Picture of Dorian Gray,* which first appeared in *Lippincott's Monthly Magazine* in the company of such classics of the genre as Arthur Conan Doyle's *The Sign of Four.*

New writers such as Henry James (who Wilde said "writes fiction as if it were a painful duty"), Thomas Hardy and George Gissing were beginning their careers, and the 1870s saw novels by each. Disraeli published *Lothair* at the beginning of the decade, displaying in it what Froude called "the perfect representation of patrician society in England . . . in its most brilliant period, like the full bloom of a flower which opens only to fade." The decade closed with the appearance of Disraeli's last novel, the charmingly retrospective *Endymion.* When the eccentric Alfred Orage was preaching the revival of Disraeli's (taken from Coleridge's) "Tory democracy" in the early years of the twentieth century, he lamented in particular what Wilde called the "unimaginative realism" of so many nineteenth-century novelists, and praised Disraeli (and Lytton) as "the two English novelists who aimed highest, though . . . they fell short in actual achievement. Their heroic characters were at least planned on the grand scale."⁸

The advocacy of various concepts of aristocratic heroism and anti-egalitarian leadership was a commonplace of nineteenth-century thought, in a tradition beginning with the Byronic hero and Carlyle's hero-worship through the Darwinian principles of natural selection and Herbert Spencer's notion of the "survival of the fittest" to the superman of Nietzsche and the somewhat fascist "modern utopia" of H. G. Wells. By the early 1870s, the protagonists of the old school of strenuously individualistic political, social and spiritual thought—men such as F. D. Maurice, Charles Kingsley, Walter Bagehot and J. S. Mill—were dying off, but their precepts certainly lived on to inform the succeeding generation and its debate about culture and anarchy, progress and degeneration. There were significant attempts to turn the tide, and to redefine the nature of evolutionary conflict to admit a much greater degree of co-operative enterprise to balance the bluntly intense individualism of the day. The periodicals of the 1880s and early 1890s—the same periodicals in which Wilde was writing—provided a forum for many of the most intelligent and persuasive examples of this kind of argument, but in general the disconcerting possibilities for individual, social and cultural disintegration promoted the cause of the more hierarchical and heroical models. In this manner, Mill's espousal of an intellectual aristocracy or clerisy provided a point of contact for an unlikely agreement between, for example, the Conservative Disraeli and the Liberal Gladstone, both of whom argued against any kind of egalitarian enthusiasm that would "reduce civilized society to human flocks and herds," and recognized that "it is not the love of equality which has carried into every corner of the country the distinct undeniable popular preference, wherever other things are equal, for a man who is a lord over one who is not."[9]

One consequence of this sort of social instinct was to encourage the deliberate and conspicuous spurning of the orthodox, and in particular of the dull (usually dismissed as bourgeois) standards of respectability or conformity, by those who wished to proclaim or to represent the intellectual, ethical or artistic aristocracy that the age inspired. It was as if the values of individuality and originality were being celebrated by the conspicuous display of the unique and the unorthodox in just the manner that a later age would celebrate the values as well as the insecurities of a particular social and economic order by the practice of ostentatious consumption of luxury commodities. In the realms of art and intellect, Arthur Symons argued, rejecting Tolstoy's call for a democratic art, "there at all events the stultifying dead-weight of equality must for ever be spared to us." Symons, writing these words in 1898, was the spokesman for a younger generation, one which had learned its lesson perfectly. Contemporaries, such as his close friend W. B. Yeats or his roommate at Fountain Court in the Temple during these years, Havelock Ellis, would both have agreed, arguing respectively for a creative freedom of mystical and sexual, as well as artistic, expression. When Whistler, in Wilde's words, "read the Commination Service over the critics" by proclaiming in the most extravagant terms an elitist doctrine of the artist as exile and outsider, he was invoking one of the more ubiquitous moods of the age. The creative individual, suggested Wilde elsewhere,

> like the mystic, is an antinomian always. To be good, according to the vulgar standard of goodness, is obviously quite easy. It merely requires a certain amount of sordid terror, a certain lack of imaginative thought, and a certain low passion for middle class respectability.[10]

Another consequence of the emphasis on individualism, no less important but much less obvious than the enthusiasm for flagrant unorthodox display, was the inclination to perceive the life of any notable individual in terms of its embodiment of certain values and beliefs, or in terms of its representative importance. "Humanity manifests itself in each age in great men," proclaimed Pater. Wilde's consistent interest in the nature of personality, and in the dependence of any worthwhile individualism upon a *realized* personality, flowed from such assumptions. The determinants of great personalities were eagerly and by the end of the century quite routinely analyzed as part of any critical study of historical or cultural phenomena. This kind of analysis turned in two directions: the negative line emphasized how, since (in John Dryden's phrase) "great wits are sure to madness near allied," excessive individualism may lead to degeneracy and insanity. By the late 1880s, this kind of argument had rather alarming currency, provided in part by the investigations into the psychology of artistic genius undertaken by Paul Bourget in France and Havelock Ellis in England, and by the studies of criminal psychology by Cesare Lombroso which Ellis translated in 1891.[11] The affirmative version of this analysis recognized the constructive possibilities in unorthodox and creative behaviour and followed a line, partly indebted to Herbert Spencer, that saw the development from homogeneity to heterogeneity, achieved if necessary by mutation, as a mark of evolutionary progress. Wilde himself, prompted by the general evolutionary fascination with pathological conditions and unusual forms, became very interested in the nature of insanity and the "science of the abnormal" during the 1870s, and read a variety of books on the topic.

The focus of the general interest was, in the main, more usually on the processes of individuation than on its products, and this interest anticipated Darwin and his apostles. Critics such as Charles Augustin Sainte-Beuve and Hippolyte Taine had provided a basis for identifying race and environment as the chief determinants of individuality and of the thoughts and actions by which it was displayed, and many writers of the time extended this methodology. Ernest Renan's *La Vie de Jesus*, published in 1863, was perhaps the foremost example of an analysis which proceeded from psychological, social and broadly cultural premises to clarify the nature and development of a unique personality, and it was remarkably influential.[12] But it was only one of many studies of

> remarkable epochs of mental advance when the soul seems to receive a fresh impetus, and rushes onward to the light, [and which] are always found illuminated by the name of some *one* great man; for all history shows that individuals alter the world, not the masses. These are the men to whom power is given to pierce the depths of human sympathy, and touch the springs of human thought. Their object is always mental freedom; for thought must precede action as light preceded creation. . . . And it is strange, though a sure proof of the innate grandeur of the soul of man, that no great flame of enthusiasm ever yet was kindled in the world for anything that concerned merely the physical bettering of [the] human condition.[13]

This description by Wilde's mother of contemporary attitudes towards "World Leaders" is imbued with the myth of progress. (The occasion was a review of Frazer Corkran's wisely forgotten poem, "Time in Dreamland.") There is also implicit in her rhapsody an acceptance of the notion that an individual may stand in uniquely symbolic relations to the art, culture and social history of his or her age. No one in the nineteenth century was entirely untouched by a fascination with the ways in which this might be so.

On the lighter side, it was the era of the potted biography— "cheap editions of great men," Wilde called them, which "rob life of much of its dignity and its wonder, [and] add to death itself a new terror." Many of these biographies were of literary and artistic as well as political or historical figures, as heroes of various complexions were recognized to embody a symbolic relationship to their own age and its descendants. When Wilde picked "two of the most perfect lives I have come across in my own experience" in one of his numerous catalogues of great personalities, he chose the French poet Paul Verlaine and the Russian anarchist Prince Peter Alexeievitch Kropotkin. His final choice was the same as Renan's.

As a kind of corollary to the celebration of great men there was an inclination to celebrate seminal works, which were praised for capturing the essence or spirit of the particular movement or attitude that one embraced.[14] Gerard Manley Hopkins said that he had been in a tremble ever since reading Wordsworth's "Immortality Ode"; Wilde said that he never got over the death of Lucien de Rubempré, in Honoré de Balzac's *Illusions Perdus*. For Wilde's generation in particular, French writers and a few of their specific works were most likely to represent the special symbolic relationship to the age that everyone was anxious to discover. Théophile Gautier, with a celebrated novel (*Mademoiselle de Maupin* [1835] called by Mario Praz the "Bible of the decadence") and a volume of poems *Emaux et camées* (1852, 1863), had announced the creed of a new aesthetic religion which soon had many devotees.[15] The basis of Gautier's belief was in art as an autonomous activity, independent of normal categories of experience (as well as of moral censure), and celebrated for its own sake. Gautier emphasized the anti-utilitarian function of art— what Wilde called "the beautiful, sterile emotions that art excites" —and drew attention to the perverse and the unnatural as both expansions of the spirit and defences against the mundane, while all the time insisting on the importance of fine craftsmanship and imagistic precision. Along with Charles Baudelaire, he affected a "dandyisme" that was both an affirmation of the values of the artificial (as against the natural) and a denial of the useful and the commonplace.

Baudelaire's volume of poems, *Les Fleurs du Mal* (1857), was in its way as influential as any single book of the century; Victor Hugo praised its author for "inventing a new shudder". Algernon Charles Swinburne, who introduced Baudelaire's works to English readers, spoke of its

> perfect workmanship [which] makes every subject admirable and respectable. Through the chief part of this book he has chosen to dwell mainly upon sad and strange things—the weariness of pain and the bitterness of pleasure—the perverse happiness and wayward sorrows of exceptional people. It has the languid and lurid beauty of close and threatening weather—a heavy, heated temperature with dangerous hot-house scents in it; thick shadow of cloud about it, and the fire of molten light. It is quite clear of all whining and windy lamentation; there is nothing of the blubbering and shrieking style long since exploded. The writer delights in problems, and has a natural leaning to obscure and sorrowful things. Failure and sorrow, next to physical beauty and perfection of sound or scent, seem to have an infinite attraction for him.[16]

The publication of *Les Fleurs du Mal* coincided with the appearance of Gustave Flaubert's *Madame Bovary*. The government brought action against both authors for offending public morals. Flaubert, whom Wilde called his "master" and who, along with Keats and Pater, he reckoned the only writers who had influenced him, was successfully defended.[17] Baudelaire lost, perhaps because he advised his lawyers to base his defence on the "terrible morality" of the poems taken as a whole. Another volume of the period which also met with suspicion was Walt Whitman's *Leaves of Grass*, the first version of which appeared in 1855. Its celebration of the unity of the whole man and the problem it posed to its Coriolan readers by its advocacy of a "democratic art" fascinated such writers and critics as Wilde, Ellis, and John Addington Symonds. A later poet, Richard Howard, commemorating a hundred years after the visit of Wilde to Whitman in Camden, New Jersey in 1872, has Oscar say to Walt that

> I can conceive of no Bible worthy, save
> yours and Baudelaire's, to prepare mankind
> for an identical body and soul. *Leaves
> of Grass, Flowers of Evil:* our sacred botany.[18]

It was another French writer, Joris-Karl Huysmans, who wrote a novel that became a sacred text all on its own—*À Rebours* (1884), the story of the elegantly perverse and decadent Des Esseintes. It provided the prototype for the "poisonous book" that Dorian Gray received from Lord Henry Wotton, a book

> written [in] that curious jewelled style, vivid and obscure at once, full of *argot* and of archaisms, of technical expressions and of elaborate paraphrases, that characterizes the work of some of the finest artists of the French school of *Symbolistes.* There were in it metaphors as monstrous as orchids, and as subtle in colour. The life of the senses was described in the terms of mystical philosophy. One hardly knew at times whether one was reading the spiritual ecstacies of some medieval saint or the morbid confessions of a modern sinner.[19]

It was a book of immense importance, a "breviary" (as Symonds called it) for the "decadent" writers and artists of the time. In an age in which French novelists in particular tended to swim in schools it was *sui generis,* and for Huysmans it marked a significant departure from the "realism" which his mentor Emile Zola was promoting.

Yet, when all is said, the only writer who towered above categories and above his contemporaries was Balzac. For Wilde his stature was incomparable; he could be spoken of with Shakespeare without apology. His appeal was complex and compelling, and Wilde revered him as he revered no other writer of his century.

In 1844, Balzac wrote that

> four men [in the nineteenth century] will have led immense lives: Napoleon, Cuvier, O'Connell, and I wish to be the fourth. The first lived the life of Europe; he inoculated armies upon himself. The second embraced the globe. The third incorporated a people. I shall have carried an entire society in my head.[20]

Wilde referred to this with delight at Christmas in 1888, when a young poet named Yeats was a guest for dinner. His enthusiasm was largely prompted by the inclusion of Daniel O'Connell; as his mother's devoted son, he could scarcely avoid sharing her devotion to Irish causes, and O'Connell was in any case being loudly acclaimed a half a century after Balzac wrote—especially by the proponents of Home Rule. (In 1889, for example, there was a long article in praise of O'Connell by William Gladstone in the *Nineteenth Century,* in the company of Wilde's "The Decay of Lying".) But the significance of the *kind* of statement that Balzac made does not depend upon the specific names, but upon the possibility of recognizing in individuals "the total character of their effective energy." Wilde's wry comment to Yeats was that "we Irish are too poetical to be poets; we are a nation of brilliant failures." And yet failure, like anything else, can bear the impress of a distinct individuality; the dilemma as it presented itself to Wilde and his age was how such an individuality can be achieved in the context of bewildering experiences, diverse impressions, and a sense that the human will is less than fully able to realize its function.

By the end of the nineteenth century German philosophy and its English interpreters had taken over this dilemma as its almost exclusive subject, and through the writings of Hegel, Schopenhauer and Nietzsche had given it quite specific interpretations. Georg Friedrich Hegel was popularized in England in the 1860s by a group which included F. D. Maurice at Cambridge and the influential classicist Benjamin Jowett, Master of Balliol College at Oxford.[21] William Wallace gave a series of lectures at Oxford in 1873 which were published the following year as a prolegomena to a study of Hegel's logic, and this volume was widely read (and used extensively by Wilde). Jowett's lectures (attended by Walter Pater, among many others) developed correspondences in the thought of Plato, Hegel and Darwin; the idea that every condition has implicit in it a contradiction (between freedom and necessity, say, in human affairs) which must be resolved in some reconciliation is a requisite for progress in the logic and metaphysics of all three. Detachment or alienation from this process of dialectical resolution is a pernicious condition, according to this scheme, and Oxford philosophy in particular did its best to guard against such a calamity. Many Oxford students in the 1870s claimed that for a long period they never saw Darwin except through Hegelian bifocals.

Arthur Schopenhauer's *The World as Will and Idea* was translated by R. B. Haldane (who, as a Liberal Member of Parliament was especially kind to Wilde while he was in prison) and J. Kemp in 1883. In it the helplessness of mankind, caught in a world of haphazard conflict and ceaseless flux, informed the pessimism that was inseparable from Schopenhauer's philosophy, though his advocacy of art as a redemptive pursuit offered something of an alternative. Wilde amusingly described Schopenhauer as his mother's

> last pessimist, [who] says the whole human race ought on a given day, after a strong remonstrance *firmly but respectfully* urged on God, to walk into the sea and leave the world tenantless, but of course some skulking wretches would hide and be left behind to people the world again I am afraid.[22]

Friedrich Nietzsche began to appear in English late in the century, in 1896; Havelock Ellis, who was one of his earliest and most articulate exponents, described him as one who

> desired to detach the "bad conscience" from the things that are merely wicked traditionally, and to attach it to the things that are anti-natural, anti-instinctive, anti-sensuous.[23]

Nietzsche was himself indebted to Schopenhauer, but quickly passed to a denunciation of traditional categories of moral experience, and a celebration of creative energy "beyond good and evil." Sigmund Freud, born two years after Wilde, would not read Schopenhauer or Nietzsche in his early years because he recognized the similarity of their ideas to his own. J. M. Kennedy, one of the best of the chroniclers of the period, called Nietzsche, somewhat curiously, a second Disraeli; a more common association, made by Arthur Symons and W. B. Yeats, was with William Blake.

It was Blake who had provided inspiration for many of the most notable poets of this period, especially the poets of the Pre-Raphaelite Brotherhood (such as Dante Gabriel Rossetti, his sister Christina Rossetti, and William Morris) who saw in him a precursor, and the mercurial Algernon Charles Swinburne, who recognized a genius. Swinburne in particular was very much the rage in the 1870s; he had, as Wilde later wrote, "set his age on fire by a volume of very perfect and very poisonous poetry," the volume of *Poems and Ballads* which he published in 1866. Ralph Waldo Emerson, who was not as easily set alight, described Swinburne (in print) in 1874 as "a perfect leper and a mere sodomite." Wilde's enthusiasm, along with that of most of his contemporaries, waned considerably as Swinburne declined into a nicely reactionary versifier, but it is worth recalling Wilde's remarks in a letter to the *Daily Telegraph* in 1892 that "in this century, in England . . . we have had only two great plays—one is Shelley's *Cenci,* the other Mr. Swinburne's *Atalanta in Calydon* (1865), and neither of them is in any sense of the word an actable play."

Wilde also praised the unactable plays, and more especially the unfathomable poems of Robert Browning, who, by the 1870s was becoming a venerable figure, a perfect symbol for those who wished to advance an aristocracy of the artistic temperament and dismiss those who looked to poetry, as Symons put it, "for the solace of an afternoon cigar." Browning's notorious obscurity did, of course, have its drawbacks; after *Sordello* appeared in 1840, Jane Carlyle said that she had read it through without being able to ascertain whether Sordello was a man, a book or a city. It was with the volume of *Dramatis Personae* which appeared in 1864 that he achieved his first public success, and the publication of *The Ring and the Book* in 1868 established him with Tennyson as a poet of the first rank. Tennyson's four *Idylls of the King,* which appeared in 1859, had put the poet laureate (successor to Wordsworth) on the pedestal somewhat earlier; a decade later he published four more idylls under the title of *The Holy Grail.* Wilde (in 1876) valued Tennyson's *In Memoriam* (1850) especially highly, setting it next to *Hamlet* and a work he described as "much the greatest work in our literature . . . *intense* in every way," Elizabeth Barrett Browning's *Aurora Leigh.*

William Morris, the astonishingly energetic and talented artist, craftsman and socialist, published his *Earthly Paradise* between 1868 and 1870. It was an event which enhanced his already considerable reputation to the point where his work was compared to Tennyson's most recently published idylls. The utopian inspiration of Morris's work found an ironic counterpart in Samuel Butler's *Erewhon* (1871), while his debt to Thomas Carlyle and John Ruskin linked these two great though quite different zealots to a

generation of heroic socialists. To a considerable extent, popular
English socialism was essentially utopian and idealistic, at least in
its initial phase. Its greatest popular utopian text—Edward Bel-
lamy's *Looking Backward*—came in the next decade (1887),and
its American provenance gave even greater spirit to Wilde's assertion that "England will never be civilized until she has added
Utopia to her dominions". Morris's *News from Nowhere* appeared
in 1890–91.

The one considerable and very un-utopian political event of the
1870s was the bitter struggle between Disraeli and Gladstone over
the question of what to do about the matter of Turkish atrocities
in Bulgaria. It was an old question of whether *realpolitik* should
yield to humane considerations, whether "the permanent and
important interests of England" should be set aside for a moral
crusade. Wordsworth had argued the case in his tract on the
Convention of Cintra; Gladstone carried the same brief and argued it fiercely in one of the most famous political pamphlets in
British history, "The Bulgarian Horrors and the Question of the
East." Within a month of its appearance on September 6, 1876,
it had sold 200,000 copies. How to judge the diplomatic and
political consequences of the eventual settlement of the interna-
tional dispute is still unclear a century later; but Gladstone's stirring call was certainly crystal clear at the time.[24] Even Wilde, who
was not given to political interests, wrote a poem on the subject,
which he sent to Gladstone, along with a request for some advice
on how to get it published; in thanking Gladstone for his kind
words in reply, he sent him another poem, this time on "Easter
Day" in Rome.

Wilde was at Oxford when he wrote to Gladstone. He had
matriculated on October 17, 1874, the day after his twentieth
birthday, at Magdalen College, having come with considerable
distinction as a classicist from Trinity College, Dublin. He would
spend four years at Oxford before moving to London during the
winter of 1878–79. The university in which Wilde spent those
years was in the main a place of easy charm and pleasant excitement, where the graceful play of ideas most often kept at bay the
sometimes violent differences of opinion that engaged the larger
world beyond its gates. To be sure, Oxford was alive to many of

the issues that were of urgent public concern; but what Wilde referred to as the "Oxford temper" was essentially an ability to evade commitment, to turn contemporary issues into historical curiosities and urgent concerns into material for future considerations and to leave the present to the delights of fancy. Yet although the university wore a mantle of disinterested nonchalance, at heart it was awake once more, after a comfortable snooze which had begun towards the end of the seventeenth century. For over a hundred years it had been often little more than a somewhat dreary retreat, where a few eminent scholars and men of letters hid—a place of "port and prejudice," Edward Gibbon called it. Any glimmers of light or sparks of excitement quickly flickered out; Methodism was given its name in Oxford, but found few inspirations for social work in a community whose energy was given over to petty squabbles and the building of Georgian monuments. The university closed its doors to nonconformists and opened them but seldom to new studies.

By the beginning of the nineteenth century, however, it began to revive, and within several decades the Anglo-Catholic counter-revolution which became known as the Oxford (also the Tractarian or High Church) Movement jolted it wide awake, with an appeal to an aesthetic ritualism and a questioning of the nature of secular and divine authority. The classicist J. W. Mackail, who eventually became Professor of Poetry at Oxford, and had known Wilde and his circle from the 1880s, gives a sense of the significance of this controversy that brought the university fully back to life:

> The movement itself, like the whole Romantic movement of which it was the spiritual and theological side, was partly reactionary and partly progressive. It went back to the Middle Ages and beyond them. It sought to undo all that had been done in the age of enlightenment. But it was also, like the young England movement that accompanied it in secular affairs, a serious attempt to rebuild an ordered structure of life. Both movements failed, because they did not take account of facts. But both had a vital principle within them, which produced very remarkable results, often at a distance of time and in unexpected quarters.[25]

It is important to understand how recently the university had become conscious of itself as a centre of controversial debate in

order to appreciate its sometimes quite adolescent spirit during
Wilde's time there, its mixture of frenetic excitement and its
comfortably drowsy pessimism. It is also important to recognize
the significant position that Oxford and Cambridge—but especially Oxford after the religious disputes for which it provided a
home—held in English intellectual affairs during the decades leading up to and in large measure including the 1870s. What was
thought and said and done at Oxford was attended to with a
keenness that only such an exclusive educational and profession-
ally vocational system could produce.

To many observers, especially during the decades following
the turbulent 1840s, what happened at Oxford became a measure of the possibility of building an "ordered structure of
life," informed by some civilizing "vital principle." The rites of
beauty and the rituals of truth, which the Oxford Movement
had tried to preserve in divine affairs, were also under siege in
the secular sphere. At Oxford beauty and truth were what people talked, worried and wondered about—not, perhaps, always
gracefully, but in a way that seemed to matter to those for
whom the idea of a civilized and cultured society was important.

The period of Tractarian controversy, a period which Tennyson
called "an awful moment of transition," was an unsettled time.
Throughout the 1840s there was a steady stream of propagandist
novels of social and spiritual concern, novels of a quite different
complexion than those which coincided with Wilde's Oxford
years (though the 1880s and 1890s saw a revival of the genre.) The
most notable were Disraeli's *Sibyl: or the Two Nations* (1845),
Mrs. Gaskell's *Mary Barton* (1848), Charles Kingsley's *Yeast*
(1848, subtitled *A Problem* in 1851), John Henry Newman's *Loss
and Gain* (1849) and J. A. Froude's *Nemesis of Faith* (1849). Not
everyone participated in the particular anguish of any one author,
of course; Carlyle described Froude's nonconformist novel (which
lost him his fellowship at Exeter College, Oxford) as "a wretched
mortal's vomiting up all his interior crudities, dubitations, and
spiritual, agonising bellyaches into the view of the public, and
howling tragically, 'See!' " Froude's implicit justification for sub-
mitting to public scrutiny the bellyaches of the age was contained
in a retrospective description of this time, ironically enough in his

book on *Carlyle's Life in London,* when he described the period
as

> an era of new ideas, of swift if silent spiritual revolution. . . . All
> were agreed to have done with compromise and conventionalities.
> . . . All around us, the intellectual lightships had broken from their
> moorings. . . . The present generation which has grown up in an
> open spiritual ocean and has learnt to swim for itself will never
> know what it was to find the lights all drifting, the compasses all
> awry, and nothing left to steer by but the stars.[26]

If there was a single event which could be said to have sent the
compass needle spinning, it was the defection of John Henry
Newman in 1845, when he joined the Catholic Church.

In the company that Oscar kept during the 1870s, the debates
(and the spiritual agonistics) that were precipitated by Newman's
action continued almost as though thirty years had passed unno-
ticed. The implications of his decision went far beyond the realms
which the spirit sanctified and had a profound effect on the character of secular and profane discussion down through the decades
of the nineteenth century.

> It is not easy for us to recapture the excitement or to feel the
> inherent importance of his secession. Disraeli a quarter of a century
> later called his loss a blow from which the Church was still reeling.
> To understand this one needs to enter into the general unquestion-
> ing assumption of all parties in England that Protestantism in some
> form or other was the best of all religions and that England was
> clearly the best of all countries. The loss of Newman struck a triple
> blow. It was a blow at the intellectual superiority of Protestantism,
> for no one could doubt that Newman's was one of the finest and
> most theologically instructed of contemporary minds. It was a blow
> at the moral superiority of Protestantism. . . . For Newman's selfless
> devotion to the cause of truth as he understood it did not admit
> of doubt. It was a blow at English insularity. It prepared the way
> for a new generation of intellectuals, whether Roman Catholic or
> High Anglican or agnostic, who were consciously European in their
> outlook. . . . A blow at insularity was thus a blow at what Arnold
> was later to call the philistinism of a great commercial country. The
> rapid growth of serious and discriminating interest in the arts
> bearing fruit eventually in such works as Pater's *The Renaissance*
> (1873) and J. A. Symonds's *History of the Italian Renaissance*
> (1875–86) can be traced in part to Newman's adhesion to a foreign
> ecclesiastical power.[27]

Long before Pater and Symonds wrote, Carlyle had turned to Germany (with its metaphysical profundities) and Arnold to France (with its centrally administered culture) for models of what England and things English lacked. Pater's study of the Renaissance provided an example of a critical analysis that was based on a strenuous imaginative effort to perceive a subject "relatively and under conditions," and to determine what was universal and what was unique about experiences which were celebrated at different times and in different places. The kinds of experience to which mankind gives imaginative assent became the centre of diverse attention. Not just aesthetic experiences came under scrutiny, for Newman among others had made it impossible to avoid considering religious experiences. Furthermore, Charles Darwin had reinforced an acceptance of any methodology that proceeded by means of analogy and logical inference. Looking at phenomena "relatively and under conditions" became quite the fashion.

Darwin's "humiliating discovery," as Carlyle called it, of the *Origin of Species by Means of Natural Selection, or the Preservation of Favoured Races in the Struggle for Life,* prompted a variety of related investigations. One of these was an application of the theory of evolution or development by natural selection to the history of cultures, which led to the publication in 1871 of E. B. Tylor's *Primitive Culture: Researches into the Development of Mythology, Philosophy, Religion, Language, Art and Custom.* Darwin himself moved into the field of cultural criticism in the same year with his volume on *The Descent of Man,* in which he concluded that

> the highest possible stage in moral culture is when we recognize that we ought to control our thoughts, and "not even in inmost thought to think again the sins that made the past so pleasant to us."[28]

The quotation from Tennyson's *Idylls of the King* reinforces the sternly orthodox nature of Darwin's conclusion; with religious doubts creating a very unsettled climate, the notion that culture and civilization involved what Freud would describe as the taming of the instinctual provided considerable comfort to those for whom the idea of order had epistemological as well as aesthetic implications.

There was a young student at Trinity College, Cambridge, of exactly Wilde's age and classical inclinations, who was profoundly influenced by Darwin's and Tylor's work and by the studies of William Robertson Smith, the editor of the great ninth edition of the *Encyclopaedia Britannica* and a noted exponent of the science of comparative religion. The student's name was James George Frazer, and in 1890, still "an obscure classical scholar who dabbled in anthropology," he published *The Golden Bough: A Study in Comparative Religion.* Frazer's methodology, as he described it in 1894 in a tribute to Smith, was in ways more significant than his discoveries, for it was premised upon a new attitude towards human experiences and commitments. It involved a study of

> the religions of the world not dogmatically but historically—in other words, not as systems of truth or falsehood to be demonstrated or refuted, but as phenomena of consciousness to be studied like any other aspect of human nature.[29]

The use of the "comparative method" was not entirely new, but it was brought to the fore in the 1860s and 1870s, and quickly became the orthodoxy. Montesquieu and Herder had applied the method in the eighteenth century, certainly, but it was the publication in 1861 of Sir Henry Maine's *Ancient Law: its Connection with the Early History of Society and its Relation to Modern Ideas* and J. F. McLennan's *Primitive Marriage* which gave significant impetus to this method. Maine's work in particular was of considerable importance to all of those who were interested in how individuals and societies regulate themselves through their arts and institutions. Wilde used Maine as a point of reference in many of his notes and annotations as he read and thought about such matters in the 1870s, and as late as 1894 "Maine, Mill and Hobbes" were lumped together by Oxford undergraduates to represent modern political philosophy, as against the wisdom of the ancients.

Comparative studies began to flourish during the 1870s, particularly under the inspiration of Friedrich Max Müller, Professor of Comparative Philology at Oxford while Wilde was there ("Oscar is now a scholar at Oxford and resides there in the very focus of intellect," his mother wrote. "Ruskin had him to breakfast and Max Müller loves him."). Müller's popular Hibbert lectures, delivered in 1878, on "The Origin and Growth of Religion as Illustrated by the Religions of India," along with his editions of translations of the great Eastern religious books, and his earlier studies on the "Science of Religion,"

> revealed to sceptic, scientist, and believer alike a vast wealth of sacred and moral wisdom previously little known in the West, at the very time when Christian thinkers were being forced to find new sanctions for their belief in the Christian revelation.[30]

It was Wilde's particular interest in the application of a comparative historical method in classical times that provided the subject for the essay which he wrote for the (unawarded) Chancellor's Prize in 1879, "The Rise of Historical Criticism." He obviously took the task seriously, and combined his knowledge of the classics and his deep interest in comparative and historical critical methodologies with his ambition to do something significant. After all, he might have reflected that J. A. Symonds's Chancellor's essay for 1863, on "The Renaissance," provided the basis for the formidable history that he was at that time working on, and the first volume of which had just appeared. Wilde appeared to have hoped (in his suicidal way) that his essay would win him a fellowship at Magdalen. It did not, which was probably for the best; though James Frazer's similar sort of exercise, a much more earnest and well-structured piece on "The Growth of Plato's Ideal Theory," gained him a long lifetime of affiliation with Trinity College, Cambridge.

There was one implication of Frazer's work that he himself later identified, but which was implicit in many of the psychological, sociological and anthropological, as well as in some economic, studies that appeared during this period. This was the sense, as Frazer described it, that

> the ground beneath our feet is thus, as it were, honeycombed by unseen forces. We appear to be standing on a volcano which may at any moment break out in smoke and fire to spread ruin and devastation among the gardens and palaces of ancient culture wrought so laboriously by the hands of many generations. After looking on the ruined Greek temples of Paestum and contrasting

them with the squalor and savagery of Italian peasantry, Renan said
"I trembled for civilization, seeing it so limited, built on so weak
a foundation, resting on so few individuals even in the country
where it is dominant."[31]

It is little wonder that many people of the time were disturbed
by such unsettling propositions, and by the enthusiasm with which
they were embraced by those who, some thought, should know
better. W. H. Mallock, a nephew of J. A. Froude and an Oxford
student who graduated the year that Oscar arrived, was deeply
perplexed by the "moral and intellectual condition to which [his]
Oxford experiences had by that time raised or reduced [him]." He
decided to write a book in which he would discuss current attitudes towards "the national aim of life, and the manner in which
a definite supernatural faith was essential, extraneous, or positively
prejudicial" to it. The result was *The New Republic: or Culture,
Faith, and Philosophy in an English Country House.*[32] It was an
amusing parody, with the novels of Thomas Love Peacock and the
Satyricon of Petronius Arbiter as models, of the opinions and
mannerisms of such notable figures as Matthew Arnold, John
Ruskin, Walter Pater and Benjamin Jowett. Mallock's sense of
the mood which prevailed at Oxford—and which, he feared,
was infecting the nation—found its perfect expression in the
epigram from the *Greek Anthology* that he provided for his
novel:

> All is laughter, all is dust, all is nothingness;
> For all things that are arise out of the unreasonable.

There was enough truth in his satire to strike the fancy of many
readers, and especially of those who were at the university in 1876
when the novel first appeared in shortened serial form in the
illustrated London magazine *Belgravia*. The "new republic" that
Mallock's country-house weekenders conjured up did not supply
a model for any ordered structure of life, of course, but the utopian
speculations upon which his satire depended pointed to a significant and widely expressed concern of the period. The human spirit
required certain things for its nourishment; the question, simply
put, was whether life and society could—and if so, whether they

would—supply these things. Some, such as William Morris (under the strong influence of Ruskin), saw hope for the creation of a fabric of alternative (socialist) values in places such as Oxford, where the destructive forces of fragmenting individualism and cynical commercialism might be held at bay until the new order prevailed. (Presumably, Morris would have joined the fierce opposition given by the university to the coming of the railway to town in 1844. The argument—and it would later appeal to dialectical materialists as well as to utopian socialists—was that technological changes create intellectual and spiritual, as well as economic and political, influences.) Others, following the lead of Matthew Arnold, envisaged Oxford as a haven for the "alien remnants" who would lead the dull majority towards the sweetness and light of a truly civilized society, by cultivating the qualities necessary for the full development of the self.[33]

The point is not that the means appeared antithetical, but that the end was the same—the creation of an environment in which the human spirit would be nourished and would become an autonomous force capable of sustaining as well as adorning the culture which it would bring alive. Only in such an environment would the human spirit discover meaning and purpose and become the "vital principle" upon which an ordered structure of life would depend.

With such an emphasis on environments and creatively ordered structures, it was inevitable that there would be something like agreement on a further principle: that it is the *form*—the style or manner—of experiences which can alone compel our assent, since we can only know things by the form in which they appear to us. There is, at the core of such an agreement, a sceptical philosophy going back to David Hume and recognizing truth only as a function of the force of subjectively perceived impressions. The age in which Wilde lived was ripe for this kind of impressionism, in which form provided both the primary appeal and the ultimate justification. Wilde's own career as a public figure began with his role as the apostle of aestheticism, a rather vague but quite entertaining creed which acknowledged and celebrated the primacy of form in the arts, and in the art of life. The rituals and revelations that religion offered—the forms that Newman called "the food of faith"—were, by this time, becoming less compelling; in their place, Wilde and his circle offered the rituals of secular worship and eventually the revelations of profane ecstasies. And not Wilde alone, nor aestheticism and decadence alone, followed this line, for there is every reason to see in the stoic activism of the likes of Rudyard Kipling and W. E. Henley (or the imperial determination of Cecil Rhodes, who was at Oxford during Wilde's time) a similar adherence to the forms and rituals of no less contrived pursuits, indulged on the playing fields of Eton or the dry plains of Africa. Nothing that Wilde could do would match the affectations in Sir Henry ("Play up! play up! and play the game!") Newbolt's perception of Francis Drake:

> Drake nor devil nor Spaniard feared,
> Their cities he put to the sack;
> He singed his Catholic Majesty's beard,
> And harried his ships to wrack.
> He was playing at Plymouth a game of bowls
> When the great Armada came,
> But he said, "They must wait their turn, good souls,"
> And he stopped, and finished the game.[34]

Finishing the game in the face of such peremptory demands requires a kind of self-confidence, poise and sense of the importance of maintaining a calm and consistent attitude that brings the stern disengagement of stoicism and the refined egotism of epicureanism together. Wilde tended to specialize in egotism, though a stoical disengagement certainly plays a central role in his ideas on the function of art; but stoicism in one or other of its flexible and indeed rather epicurean forms tended to have a more orthodox following among those who worried about the state of affairs in the nation or in its various enterprises. Epictetus, the stoic whose philosophy consisted basically of advice to find happiness within oneself, was for example celebrated by that "muscular Christian" Charles Kingsley for the intensity of his faith and the consistency of his "unconquerably constant" striving; and Arnold admitted to his friend A. H. Clough that the example of Epictetus "props . . . in these bad days, my mind." If one acknowledges that the form that action as well as contemplation takes is what principally matters, that our belief is compelled as much by style as by subject, that the structure of an experience is of more importance than its consequences (if only because we have some control over the one, but very little over the other), then the circle is completed, and the heros of Walter Pater's epicurean vision join hands with Kipling's stoical "soldiers of the Queen," whose pleasure it is to perform their duty with grisly aplomb:

> When you're wounded and left on Afghanistan's plains,
> And the women come out to cut up what remains,
> Jest roll to your rifle and blow out your brains
>   An' go to your Gawd like a soldier.[35]

A sense of duty was, in fact, the common denominator of the various sacred or profane enthusiasms of the period, and sustained the evangelical commitment that informed so many of its preoccupations. For the aesthetes, it was a peremptory and absolute duty to embrace that which was beautiful in the midst of sordid and mean surroundings, the aesthetic equivalent of the pillaging Afghan women. That is to say, to use Wilde's formula, it was an absolute duty to encourage crafts which united form and function and arts which combined perfection and personality. For the decadent, it was a duty in a crass utilitarian age to "bewilder the bourgeois," as Théophile Gautier had suggested, with unsettling inversions and perversities (though Arthur Symons later suggested, shrewdly, that the desire to bewilder the middle class was itself middle class). In any sphere of human activity, it was believed, an ordered structure of ritual obligations could sustain the spirit, provided the spirit recognized its own autonomy.

If there was one thing upon which people of very different persuasions and inclinations could agree, it was that the spirit needed some nourishing in those years. The artist no less than anyone else lives in a world, and at least initially that world as it is rather more than as he would make it determines his sense of reality and his sense of himself, while the transaction that he effects between these two senses determines the nature of his art, and the satisfactions that may console his spirit. The art of this period reflected the unstable currency which was available for this transaction, the very impure language of the tribe that was in current circulation.

It was not just that it was difficult, in an age in which the nature of self-consciousness was in dispute, to arrive at an adequate sense of self, though it surely was all but impossible to achieve anything like a clear definition. Rather more than this, however, there was a profoundly disturbing suspicion that, even more than when Wordsworth first expressed the predicament in his preface to the second edition (1800) of the *Lyrical Ballads,*

> a multitude of causes, unknown to former times, are now acting with a combined force to blunt the discriminating powers of the mind, and, unfitting it for all voluntary exertion, to reduce it to a state of almost savage torpor. The most effective of these causes are the great national events which are daily taking place, and the increasing accumulation of men in cities.

The deadening of the sensibilities that Wordsworth warned of had been aggravated by increased industrialization and urbanization. In addition, there was a strong feeling that the commercialism and economic individualism of the time were working against the development of the finer instincts, and that all that was left was a situation such as that in Balzac's Paris, where

> no sentiment can stand the stream of outside events, no passion can survive the flow. There, love is nothing more than desire. Hatred is only a whim. And there is no kin but the thousand franc note.[36]

None of Wilde's contemporaries was entirely ignorant of, or undisturbed by, such a lamentable condition. Once again, David Hume's model of the development of refined and moral taste or sensibility was brought to bear on the situation, along with the behaviourist notion which came down from the eighteenth-century theorists of the picturesque that sordid, mean and ugly surroundings generate sordid, mean and ugly people, while beautiful, calm and ordered surroundings instil those qualities in the minds of those who are daily exposed to them. Wilde's suggestion that architecture provides the basis for urban morality is based on this idea, as is much that he proposed in his one major essay which deals with social conditions, "The Soul of Man Under Socialism" (which appeared in the *Fortnightly Review* in 1891). Matthew Arnold arguing that art, as a "criticism of life," could be a morally powerful and unifying force in life; John Ruskin speaking of the redemptive power of art; Nietzsche proposing that culture is "the unity of artistic style, in every expression of the life of a people" —all were supporting a similar conception of the relationship of the aesthetic and the social sensibilities. Following this line, and in particular following Nietzsche, Alfred Orage wrote somewhat later (in the magazine that he and Holbrook Jackson founded, *The New Age*), that "the literature we despise is associated with the economics which we hate"—which was, for that group, liberal economic individualism—while "the literature we love is associated with the form of society we would assist in creating." Leaving aside its tedious polemic, what this assumes is that the arts have a mission; furthermore, if it is claimed that the arts embody and educate or draw out the aesthetic values and spiritual coherences upon which truly creative cultures and societies depend, then both the successes *and* the failures of societies and cultures may at least in part be ascribed to the success or failure of works of art to inform their audience. That is to say, just as the superior qualities of a work of art may be related to the superior qualities of a society, so the purported decadence of a work of art might be held to reflect and indeed perhaps to encourage, if not create, the decadence of society.

Even the most strident advocates in the nineteenth century of an insulated aristocracy of artistic temperaments were involved in a kind of evangelism (though this did change with the fierce insularity of artists such as Ezra Pound and Wyndham Lewis in the twentieth century). The program involved, roughly speaking, the turning of the artist's "sacred property" into a public commodity, the universalizing of the impulses that many were saying comprised the whole man—the artistic, sexual and religious or mystical impulses. Of course, there were standards. In 1881, the Oxford Union debated the resolution "that this House approves the efforts being made to bring Art and Literature within reach of the masses of Englishmen, but condemns the ridiculous class known as aesthetes". It was confirmed by a convincing division of 83–54.

It was perhaps natural that different individuals would discover different shortcomings in the world that they saw around them, and would champion the cause of proselytizing certain aspects of experience. One of the most notorious was Wilde's own "danger-ous" celebration of homosexual love, or what was euphemistically called "the love that dares not speak its name," in his own flagrant public posture as well as in articles such as "The Portrait of Mr. W. H." and novels such as *The Picture of Dorian Gray*. This pose had a definite evangelical aspect to it, as his opponents quickly recognized, though they seldom recognized any creative ways in which it might be consistent with his earlier attachment to the cause of aestheticism, the development of an acute sense of beauty. *Punch* suggested, while Wilde was in Holloway Prison in 1895 awaiting trial, that

> Art [has] a mission that may not be named,
> With "scarlet sins" to enervate the age.[37]

Missions need missionaries, and the more charismatic the better since, as Oscar once pointed out to his horrified wife Constance, their alternative function is as "the divinely provided food for destitute and under-fed cannibals." It was Paul Bourget, the French critic and novelist with a passionate interest in psychology, who first (in an essay on Baudelaire written in 1881) identified decadence in the arts with decadence in social structure, and thereby supplied an identification which was cannon fodder for the unfriendly. But Bourget's even more dubious though in some ways traditionally romantic contribution was his assertion that there may be a relationship between the decadence of a work of art and the decadence of its creator, or (more picturesquely) be-tween the decadence of a mission and the decadence of its mis-sionaries. As the century drew to a close and the concern over what Wordsworth called the "almost savage torpor" of the mind reached a height, the most celebrated denunciation of the times took the form of blaming the state of social and cultural affairs on current fashions in the arts, and these in turn on the degeneracy of the artists. The English translation of Max Nordau's *Entartung* (1892–93) appeared early in 1895 under the title *Degeneration;* it was exceptionally popular, in part because Wilde's trials had drawn public attention to the subject of decadent art and its decadent purveyors; but it is important to realize that a tradition of critical thought had prepared the way for Nordau to fulminate so devastatingly and be accepted as something other than the fanatic reactionary that he was.[38]

Arnold, his interminable lamentation intertwined with his formula of art as a criticism of life, certainly contributed in an important (albeit unintended) way to this critical tradition. He also provides an example of how astonishingly benumbed and desperate a relatively refined sensibility could become in the face of the anarchy and barbarism that Arnold no less—indeed rather more—than Wordsworth saw around him. In the opening essay ("The Function of Criticism at the Present Time") in his first series of *Essays in Criticism* (1865), he lamented the plight of a girl named Wragg who left the workhouse in Nottingham with her illegitimate child and was arrested on a charge of murder after the infant had been found strangled. Here is Arnold's response:

> *Wragg!* If we are to talk of ideal perfection, of "the best in the whole world," has anyone reflected what a touch of grossness in our race, what an original shortcoming in the more delicate spiritual perceptions, is shown by the natural growth amongst us of such hideous names—Higginbottom, Stiggins, Bugg! In Ionia and Attica they were luckier in this respect . . . by the Ilissus there was no Wragg, poor thing.[39]

Wilde played at this kind of response, especially during his years as high priest of the Aesthetes, but in general throughout his career. In "Pen, Pencil and Poison" (1889), Thomas Griffiths Wainewright's answer to a reproach for his murder of his sister-in-law, Helen Abercrombie, was, "Yes, it was a dreadful thing to do, but she had very thick ankles." In his "Phrases and Philosophies for the Use of the Young" (1894), Wilde proposed that "if the poor only had profiles there would be no difficulty in solving the problem of poverty."

There is, to a certain extent, simply the kind of deliberate confusion of categories upon which certain types of humour depend in these examples from Wilde. But behind that confusion there is a deeper motive, a gesture of psychological significance. Arnold provides the clearest case, for his grotesquely precious lament was both a defence against and a product of an environment that was sordid, mean, and dehumanizing. The economic structure was in part to blame, as novelists from Defoe to Dickens, and most splendidly Balzac, had realized. The social system, and most particularly the urban social context, provided a focus for this insight that would preoccupy European literature from Baudelaire to Eliot, as artists as critics of life described the estrangement of the individual from the sources as well as the consequences of individual emotions and thoughts—the estrangement from the inner self as well as from other selves—that such an environment can create . . . as in Tennyson's bleak vision where "ghastly thro' the drizzling rain/On the bald street breaks the blank day."

There is, indeed, much that is familiar in the perceptions of another and most formidable "critic of life" of this period. While Arnold was writing and publishing poems such as "Sohrab and Rustum" and "The Scholar Gypsy," three of Karl Marx's children died in London because his family could not afford food or medicine. The family had to borrow money to buy a coffin for one of the children. Marx's great work on *Capital* was not well known in his lifetime, nor indeed for some time after, in England, though the 1880s saw considerable interest in his theory of surplus value. He sent Darwin a copy, and in 1880 asked permission (and was politely refused on religious grounds) to dedicate a future volume to him, but Darwin's copy was uncut at his death. Marx and his comrade Friedrich Engels liked to compare their work with Darwin's, and Engels said in his funeral oration for Marx that "as Darwin discovered the law of evolution in organic nature, so Marx discovered the law of evolution in human history." Certainly Marx wrote for, and within, the critical traditions and intellectual structures of his time. And ideas that he espoused were certainly in the air. Marx and Morris provide reading for the heroine of *Marcella* (1894), a popular novel written by Mrs. Humphrey Ward, the butt of many of Wilde's critical jokes; and Stewart Headlam, who was so generous of his hospitality and his money to Wilde during his trials, was an early supporter of such contemporary analogues to Marx's work as Henry George's very popular *Progress and Poverty* (1881) and Henry Hyndman's more derivative *England for All* (1881). The formation of various socialist organizations, such as Hyndman's Democratic (later Social Democratic) Federation and the Fabian Society in the early 1880s gave focus to discussion on such matters, and Wilde was reasonably familiar with the complex personal and doctrinal inter-relationships that characterized the socialist cause. He was aware of the newest notions, and knew individual members of various socialist and workers' groups, including some of those involved in the organizing of the unemployed from 1884–87, and apologists such as Rev. Philip H. Wickstead and G. B. Shaw, who had taken part in a curious periodical exchange in 1885 on the merits of Marx's economic theory. Much of this was of minimal (or cerebral) interest, but the mass rallies and labour unions that became increasingly evident were powerful indicators of the changes that were surely coming. It was with the creation in 1893 by J. Keir Hardie of the Independent Labour Party that the reform agitation of the previous decades was brought together and addressed on a practical (though not always entirely socialist) level.

It is worth recalling the world that Engels and Marx described, for it clearly still captured the appalled imaginations of Arnold in the 1860s and Wilde in the 1880s and '90s—a world, as Wilde put it, of

> people living in fetid dens and fetid rags, and bringing up unhealthy, hunger-pinched children in the midst of impossible and absolutely repulsive surroundings.[40]

Had Wilde's fascination with the dark passages of life extended from the psychological to the social, he might have come up with descriptions not unlike the vision of horror that Engels gives:

> She lay dead beside her son upon a heap of feathers which were scattered over her almost naked body, there being neither sheet nor coverlet. The feathers stuck so fast over the whole body that the physicians could not examine the corpse until it was cleaned, and then found it starved and scarred from the bites of vermin. Part of the floor of the room was torn up, and the hole used by the family as a privy.

But this, for all its wretchedness, is but a decoration of the central thesis that was ubiquitous in the nineteenth century, and that provided the basis for responses as different as the rejection of bourgeois values and the embrace of utopian impossibilities. Engels gives its character when he recounts how he

once went into Manchester with such a bourgeois, and spoke to
him of the bad, unwholesome method of building, the frightful
condition of the working-people's quarters, and asserted that I had
never seen so ill-built a city. The man listened quietly to the end,
and said at the corner where we parted: "And yet there is a great
deal of money made here; good morning, sir."[41]

It was the ruthless intellectual and moral reductionism that
money prompted which most distressed nineteenth-century critics, for it was a reductionism which changed matters of quality,
individuality and opportunity into those of quantity, conformity,
and compulsion. Furthermore, it divorced material from spiritual
considerations and practice from principle, and in so doing it split
the consciousness and rendered anything like a unified self or a
unified society impossible. It was, like the structures of art, a form
of currency, but it was a currency that took no account of human
sensibilities or divine inspirations. And yet it had, as Marx recognized, a seductive sort of "divine power," for

> our power is as great as the power of money. The properties of
> money are my own properties and faculties. What I *am* and *can
> do* is, therefore, not at all determined by my individuality. . . .
> What I as a *man* am unable to do, and thus what all my individual
> faculties are unable to do, is made possible for me by *money*.
> Money, therefore, turns each of these faculties into something
> which it is not, into its *opposite*.[42]

Marx went further, to describe money as an instrument for the
exercise of that most divisive of capacities, the power to control
others. From this, Marxists developed the concept of "reifica-
tion," or the externalization and objectification of what might
otherwise be internal and subjective impulses or phenomena, with
the resulting fragmentation of the sensibility of the whole man.

Marx's perception was echoed by many socialists of the time;
and, as one might expect, most extravagantly by Shaw (in his
Preface to *Major Barbara*, for example). The point that was fairly
universally accepted was that individual self-consciousness and
self-respect could hardly flourish if their very existence depended
upon structures and relationships which were not organically continuous with their sustaining energies, as the structures and relationships of capitalist society appeared not to be. When Wilde

argued in "The Soul of Man Under Socialism" that socialism might be conceived as a higher form of individualism, he was taking part in the shift (that characterized the 1870s and 1880s) to perceiving the opposite of socialism as capitalism rather than individualism. His argument was in part ironic, but it nevertheless seriously advocated that a restoration of "society to its proper condition of a thoroughly healthy organism" might proceed by "converting private property into public wealth, and substituting co-operation for competition."[43] The context which he discovers in contemporary society, and especially in contemporary urban society, is one which frustrates this process by dividing material and spiritual aspirations as surely as the evil Christian orthodoxy that William Blake had denounced divided body and soul: "those who see any difference have neither," announced Wilde.[44] What the wisest of the "Victorian sages," those self-appointed proprietors of cultural values, realized was that virtually any reordering of society in which one participates should involve a commitment and fusion of material and spiritual impulses. The revolutions of the eighteenth century did so, or at least appeared to have done so. What the nineteenth century substituted was a splendid variety of havens for the beleaguered and divided self, and which included socialism and imperialism, mysticism and activism, the aesthete and the superman. Supporting all these havens was a simple principle: the unification of the self and the realization of the personality is the aim of cultural development, and this development is a creative accomplishment whose validity depends upon our understanding of the nature of cultural coherence.

There was an almost childlike fascination with the idea of culture in the nineteenth century. The word comes down from the Latin *cultura,* and cultivation of the soil is its most apparent derivation. As any reader of nineteenth-century literature or social history is well aware, cultivation of the soil became a metaphor for man's ordering of the natural world, and the particular order that was achieved by a given group of people was recognized as emblematic of a cultural identity, especially insofar as it was the product of a certain measure of artifice. In saying this, one must recognize that discussions about culture turned into something like a free-for-all during the second half of the century, and that (as Frederic Harrison put it in 1875) "the very silliest cant of the day is the cant about culture." Comte and Marx and many others were, to be sure, attempting to develop laws which related history to movements in thought and the patterns that the imagination develops, but there was nothing systematic about the general study of cultural structures. Nevertheless, there were typical attitudes, and when John Addington Symonds reflected on the "meaning and uses" of culture in an essay in his collection *In the Key of Blue* (1893) he came up with a fairly typical response:

> Judged by the etymology of the word, culture is not a natural gift. It implies tillage of the soil, artificial improvement of qualities supplied by nature. It is clearly, then, something acquired, as the lovelinesses of garden rose are developed from the briar, or the "savage-tasted drupe" becomes "the suave plum" by cultivation.[45]

What this model of cultural development created was a division between those who longed for the primitive, Edenic simplicities of an unimproved and natural state and those who were anxious to improve the natural through the ingenuities of imaginative artifice and the cultivation of hot-house cultural gardens of rare and exotic magnificence. The first group celebrated its participation in natural relationships and expressive gestures and included utopian dreamers and nostalgic medievalists, along with propagandists of action and adventure. The second group emphasized the "fictive" in all human endeavours and the way in which the artificial or the unnatural demonstrates a superiority over the limitations of the merely natural or the naturally haphazard; it included, among others, the aesthetes and the decadents of the period.

In fact, the natural and the unnatural were not so clearly opposite, since one of the primary justifications for satisfying a desire for "decadent" indulgences and the products of artifice was that these desires were themselves natural and were rooted in psychological and emotional needs that were both powerful and universal. This, indeed, was the basis of the appeal for the celebration and satisfaction of these impulses in art, which (in Wilde's words) "springs from and is only revealed to" personality. Those who advocated an art of pure and simple charm or primitive energy were convinced that it would satisfy equally unrequited impulses. Both advocates believed that their art provided a defence against the deadening or fragmenting impact of contemporary society. Both identified in the art of the other a threat to the psychic and social, as well as aesthetic, values which they promoted.

CHAPTER THREE

THE MOTIVE FOR ART

The obscure moon lighting an obscure world
Of things that would never be quite expressed,
Where you yourself were never quite yourself
And did not want nor have to be,

Desiring the exhilarations of changes:
The motive for metaphor, shrinking from
The weight of primary noon,
The A B C of being,

The ruddy temper, the hammer
Of red and blue, the hard sound—
Steel against intimation—the sharp flash,
The vital, arrogant, fatal, dominant X.

WALLACE STEVENS,
"THE MOTIVE FOR METAPHOR"

Wearing a green carnation was an obvious demonstration of one's superiority to the limitations of the merely natural as, in a way, was pederasty. The cultivation of refined aesthetic tastes and the indulgence in decadent obsessions were part of a movement of which Wilde was a leader, a movement that proclaimed individuality and self-consciousness as both the cause and effect of art. Within this orthodoxy, individualism was a defence against dissolution—of the self into society, of the part into the whole. The artistic orthodoxies of the time could also be fitted into this model, with symbolism being perceived as an affirmation of the unique value of certain significant individual parts which become representative of the whole, and impressionism as an affirmation of the importance of the subjective individual (and therefore in a sense partial) response as a valid interpretation of the whole.

It was during the 1830s that the rituals of this sort of self-defence began to be systematically worked out. The best defence, as an old tradition has it, is not a good offense but a pair of good legs to run away on, and certainly an early defence that grew out of the romantic paradigm of the artist as outsider advocated a retreat to a place in which the self and its sanctities would be inviolable. The idea of the poet contemplating the mysteries of the cosmos, alone at night in his lonely study, goes back to Milton's "Il Penseroso" and beyond, but the more specific image of the poet in his ivory tower comes from a poem written in 1837 by Charles Augustin Sainte-Beuve, in which Alfred de Vigny is described as

> plus secret
> Comme en sa tour d'ivoire, avant midi, rentrait.[1]

This kind of vision of the artist, secluded from the world in a place of refinement and beauty, became something of a commonplace in the decades following, in part as a reaction to the extreme politicizing of literature during this period. When Walter Pater described art as "a sort of cloistered refuge from a certain vulgarity in the actual world," he was proclaiming his faith and affirming his allegiance to a tradition which by the 1870s was well established.

This tradition had two aspects, that of the artist as a solitary, with obligations only to himself and to his vision, and that of art as purified of all vulgar contamination, with obligations only to its own principles or abstract ideals. There was a sense in which the artist had to deserve his role, and the art its function, and as a result certain types of art and certain kinds of artists tended to be admitted within the fold. It helped, for example, if the artist had suffered, or if the art was vilified by the popular critics. "There will always be solitude," claimed Villiers de l'Isle-Adam, "for those who are worthy of it." Being worthy, or at least appearing worthy, was a vocation in itself.

Worthiness in this context, like righteousness in another, was to some extent looked upon as a gift of grace. But there were certain preparations that were all but obligatory, and the most celebrated of these were the adoption of a pose of worldly weariness or luxurious idleness ("as for living—our servants will do that for us" suggested Yeats, quoting Villiers's Axël), an attachment to the products of artifice, and a contemplation of all of Beauty's forms. It was Gautier who began to chant this liturgy, and Baudelaire who gave it a diabolic form. In his Preface to *Mademoiselle de Maupin* (1835), Gautier wrote

> there is nothing really beautiful save what is of no possible use. Everything useful is ugly, for it expresses a need, and man's needs are low and disgusting, like his own poor, wretched nature. The most useful place in a house is the water-closet.... Though I am not a dilettante, I prefer the sound of a poor fiddle and tambourines to that of the Speaker's bell. I would sell my breeches for a ring, and my bread for jam. The occupation which best befits civilized man seems to me to be idleness or analytically smoking a pipe or a cigar.

Speaking to an age of earnest social reformers and diligent social scientists, he added that

> I am aware that there are people who prefer mills to churches, and the bread of the body to the bread of the soul. I have nothing to say to such people. They deserve to be economists in this world and in the next likewise.[2]

Wilde turned this wonderfully arrogant effrontery into a theory of art; and that was in many ways his chief accomplishment. He recognized clearly what Gautier saw dimly: an art that premises itself upon a denial of certain aspects of what we crudely call life must continually set up life as a straw man in order to deny it with aplomb and effect. It was one of Gautier's countrymen who would take this dialectic another paradoxical step and provide the twentieth century with its most celebrated denial of "the most useful place in a house,"[3] when Marcel Duchamp submitted a urinal (entitled "Fountain") to the 1917 exhibition of the Society of

Independent Artists in New York. Duchamp then moved his career to what he called "meta-irony," or the irony of indifference, but his presentation of the urinal as a work of art was informed by the same irony that Wilde perceived—that art both depends upon and denies life, just as a metaphor both depends upon and denies the logic that would call it nonsense.

Rejecting bourgeois utilitarian values, the values of material or necessary exchange, Gautier substituted a hermetic concept of usefulness which depends for its definition upon the aesthetic sense and which is enclosed by the prerogatives of the immaterial and the unnecessary. Out of this substitution comes both the idea of "art for art's sake" and, no less important, the idea of the artist as a personality dedicated to being, as Baudelaire put it, "a great man and saint for his own sake." The narcissism of the second, no less than the self-sufficiency of the first, is a pose as well as an ethic; perhaps it is most helpful to see both, in the way Wilde modified the "art for art's sake" slogan, as "not meant to express the final cause of art but [as] merely a formula of creation." The self-idolatry of Baudelaire's dandy is basically the refined egotism of romantic poetics, without which the artist can accomplish neither self-discovery nor self-destruction. In a fuller description, we hear that the dandy

> lives and sleeps in front of a mirror. He is a man of leisure and general education. He is rich and loves work. He works in a disinterested manner. He does nothing useful. He is either a poet or a warrior. He is solitary.

Implicit in this description are the heroic character, the contrived and the indulgent susceptibilities, the "equivocal mixture of asceticism and petty meticulosity" of the dandy. Charles du Bos, a French writer of André Gide's generation whose heroes were Giorgione, Keats and Pater and whose indulgence was Baudelaire, spoke of the dandy "feeling himself living only at the summit," seeking sublimity "without interruption," immobilized by constant introspection. The heroic qualities of this pose are matched only by its affectations, and by its occasional paralyzing melancholy. The pose involves "a spiritual aspiration which is sometimes reduced to a maniacal ritual, without control, but equally without recourse, a divided look which does not leave itself."[4]

There was another version of the dandy which was consistent with Baudelaire's ideal but was less heroic, more indulgent. Disraeli, a practitioner as well as a preacher, opens *Sibyl* with an example:

> "Nothing does me any good," said Alfred throwing away his almost untasted peach. "I should be quite content if something could do me harm."

For the Alfred Mountchesneys of Disraeli's only partly fictional world, "all that remained was to mourn, amid the ruins of their reminiscences, over the extinction of excitement."[5] Mountchesney himself lives, to use Samuel Johnson's phrase, "in the neighbourhood of dilapidated edifices," the structures of his aristocratic heritage. The Monchenseys of T. S. Eliot's *The Family Reunion*, though they changed the spelling slightly, are his descendants, as they watch the dilapidation of the suitably named family seat, Wishwood.

The literature of the century that passed between Disraeli and Eliot was preoccupied with the theme of decay. Pessimism, exemplified in the bleak vision of Thomas Hardy, was an attempt psychologically to control decay. Dandyism, or what Wilde called "the assertion of the absolute modernity of Beauty," was an attempt to forestall decay, a natural process, by proclaiming the virtues of the unnatural and the artificial. These virtues were often asserted by means of affectations of a languid and delicate sort, through new modes of dress and adornment, arcane habits of speech (one parody of Wilde was entitled "My Aesthetic Love or Utterly Utter Consummate Too Too"), an excessive attention to detail ("really well-made buttonholes," for example). "Bunthorne's Song" from Patience was only one of a number of satires of these affectations:

> Then a sentimental passion of a vegetable fashion
>   must excite your languid spleen,
> An attachment à la Plato for a bashful young potato,
>   or a not-too-French French bean!
> Though the Philistine may jostle, you may rank as an
>   apostle in the high aesthetic band,

If you walk down Piccadilly with a poppy or a lily
in your medieval hand.

But the affectations that were put on display had a more serious
motive than entertainment or publicity, though both of these were
always a part of the picture, from Baudelaire and Balzac to Whistler and Wilde.

Drawing on the aesthetics of Charles Baudelaire and the example of Charles du Bos, the sociologist Georg Simmel elaborated
the most fully developed theory of the flagrant and nervous individualism which he thought he had discovered behind the art
and life of the time. It was, Simmel suggested, a response to a
primarily urban environment which would destroy all but the most
frenetic or desperate individualism. Simmel himself, as if to exemplify his argument, collected lace because it represented what he
referred to as "the highest spiritualization of the material." It was
clear that what Max Nordau called "the rank growth of small
towns" conspired against the spirit of man; and the strategies that
were employed to sustain this spirit were intended to provide
protection against or an alternative to the ruthless materialism
which assaulted the individual. "The first duty in life is to be as
artificial as possible," offered Wilde in his "Phrases and Philosophies for the Use of the Young." "What the second duty is no
one has yet discovered." Hence the delicious languor and exotic
ennui that became such a fashionable pose in the 1890s.

Being as artificial as possible, or "assuming a pose" as Wilde
(who was an expert in the art of recycling) substituted elsewhere,
therefore has a purpose—somewhat ironically, of course, since it
was presented as an alternative to a utilitarian ethic. This purpose
is to protect the inner self, and the purity of spontaneous and
sincere impulses, by creating a facade of the most obvious and
insincere contrivance. The fascination with masks which occupied
the early twentieth century is a development from this style; it is
also related to the suspicion, that grew out of the deep distrust of
language which had begun with the Romantic poets, that truth
can be rendered only in gesture, a form of pre-articulate thought.
There is a clear line from Wilde, asserting "the truth of masks,"
to Hugo von Hofmannsthal, forty years later, outlining the plan
of a comedy in which a notorious liar decides to become a dancer

"because he adores the truth, and dancing is the only profession in which there is *nothing but* truth."[6] The late nineteenth century contemplated dance as embodying an intuition of unity, a fusion of matter and spirit, a glimpse of the kind of Dionysian ecstasy and pre-conscious primitivism that was an aspect of the imaginative aspiration of the period. As such, dance offered one link between aestheticism and decadence.

But there were other, more obvious, connections between these two phases in nineteenth-century art. The most important were the recognition that the affectations of aestheticism, and therefore of the dandy, involved a kind of heroic effrontery, a transgression of the limits of sober good taste; and, related to this, emphasis on a cultivated style and on the kind of exaggeration of taste and sensibility that aestheticism demanded. Baudelaire praised "l'hé-roisme de la vie moderne" by praising the artifice that refused to surrender itself to the natural or the simple; and he compared two women

> the one, a rustic matron, repugnant with health and virtue, bearing herself in a dull manner, indebted only to a simple nature; the other, one of those beauties who dominate and oppress the memory, uniting in her charm . . . all the eloquence of the dressing room . . . there would be no doubt about my choice.[7]

Such elegance, such attention to "preparing a face to meet the faces that you meet," was an essential aspect of the response of many of the most celebrated figures of the age, from the bizarre affectations of Aubrey Beardsley to the more humorous ones of Max Beerbohm. It was even said that Walter Pater's mustache should be added to the list of props. Baudelaire's famous "Eloge du maquillage," or tribute to cosmetics, consisted of a declaration that the heroic qualities of the age—beauty and goodness—could be achieved only by calculation and artifice. Max Beerbohm's satirical "Defence of Cosmetics" (originally entitled "The Philosophy of Rouge" and later changed to "The Pervasion of Rouge"), which appeared in *The Yellow Book* in 1894, suggested that

> only in an elaborate era can man by the tangled accrescency of his own pleasures and emotions reach that refinement which is his highest excellence, and by making himself, so to say, independent of Nature, come nearest to God.[8]

Beerbohm's satirical style is itself something of a "tangled accrescency," and the essay as a whole is diffuse, but it is on the mark in emphasizing indulgence and luxury as necessary conditions for the kind of game that he describes.

Baudelaire described the aesthetic sense which the art of his ambition required as one which could only be fully satisfied by "luxe, calme et volupté." There is some history to this idea of art, for it goes directly back to Virgil, superficially at least the poet of continuities and idyllic retreats. One of the key words of Virgil's poetry was *otium,* or leisure; he espoused idleness and leisure as conditions of aesthetic appreciation and he celebrated the blessed indolence of Elysium in a manner that defied even the more incorrigible adherents to an ethic of diligence and efficiency. Furthermore, he indulged his enthusiasms in poetry characterized by art and artifice, rather than by inspiration, achieving beauty and sublimity by means of what Dante praised as "lo bello stile."[9]

The kind of poetry that Virgil wrote, the kind that exemplifies the tradition of Western aesthetic culture for which he and the Alexandrian poets provided a model, is distinguished not so much by the romantic virtues of intensity or energy but by a classical perfection. The aesthetic appreciation of the qualities of such poetry requires an acceptance of the idea that formal perfection is a value in itself; that forms have an imaginative independence and exist in themselves as well as having a reference to reality and referring to that which they may represent; that form has an almost spiritual priority over content, or an almost spiritual capacity to transform. The grace for which the artist prayed referred to style—a cultured style—which was held to be of supreme importance. One of the slogans of this aesthetic attitude was that "une belle forme est une belle idée"; and it is probable that the commonly accepted view that, in Shelley's words, "language rules with Daedal harmony a throng of thoughts . . . which else senseless and shapeless were" predisposed the age to accept the priority of form over content. (The philology and anthropology of the day encouraged this, with the development of such formulae as the dubious "law of recapitulation," which was compressed into the slogan that "ontogeny recapitulates phylogeny", and which resulted in some very questionable psychological and psychogenetic speculation. Furthermore, its derivation from the assumption of *Natur-philosophie* that there is a parallel between the development of the individual and the evolution of the race reinforced the arguments of those who talked about decadent art and the degeneration of society.)[10]

Gautier's poem "L'Art," which first appeared in 1857, made explicit his celebration of formal perfection, his Parnassian concern to achieve the precise effect.

> Oui, l'oeuvre sort plus belle
> D'une forme au travail
> > Rebelle,
> Vers, marbre, onyx, émail . . .
>
> Lutte, avec le carrare,
> Avec le paros dur
> > Et rare,
> Gardiens du contour pur . . .
>
> Les dieux eux-mêmes meurent.
> Mais les vers souverains
> > Dermeurent
> Plus forts que les airains.
>
> Sculpte, lime, ciselle;
> Que ton rêve flottant
> > Se scelle
> Dans le bloc résistant![11]

This advice was the basis of the aestheticism upon which virtually all nineteenth-century art relied. The logic was simple: art is a unique endeavour, quite independent of moral or utilitarian values and prerogatives; its specific appeal is to the artistic temperament, rather than to any other aspect of our experience; the artistic temperament is conditioned by and responds to the aesthetic sense, which is to say to a sense of beauty; beauty is communicated by form. The only further step that was taken, and that particularly endeared John Keats to the generations which followed, was to associate beauty and truth, by the Aristotelian strategy of identifying the true and the beautiful as the most persistent orders of the desirable, and applying a Humean psychology to determine the truth or falsity of an experience by the force with which it impresses the perceiver. Therefore, the kind of criticism which is capable of dealing with artistic phenomena conceived in this manner is a criticism which "deals with art not as expressive but as impressive purely." For such criticism can alone appreciate "Beauty [which] has as many meanings as man has moods. Beauty is the symbol of symbols. Beauty reveals everything, because it expresses nothing."

This presumes, as Wilde certainly did, that "the real artist is he who proceeds, not from feeling to form, but from form to thought and passion." Furthermore, it leads to a further and more radical reflection, that

> it is not merely in art that the body is the soul. In every sphere of life Form is the beginning of things. The rhythmic harmonious gestures of dancing convey, Plato tells us, both rhythm and harmony into the mind. Forms are the food of faith, cried Newman in one of those great moments of sincerity that make us admire and know the man. He was right, though he may not have known how terribly right he was. The Creeds are believed, not because they are rational, but because they are repeated. Yes: Form is everything. It is the secret of life. Find expression for a sorrow, and it will become dear to you. Find expression for a joy, and you intensify its ecstasy. Do you wish to love? Use Love's Litany, and the words will create the yearning from which the world fancies that they spring. . . . To return to the sphere of Art, it is Form that creates not merely the critical temperament, but also the aesthetic instinct, that unerring instinct that reveals to one all things under their conditions of beauty. Start with the worship of form, and there is no secret in art that will not be revealed to you.[12]

From this obsession with form as the instrument of both beauty and truth, it was natural to concentrate on style as much more than decoration, indeed as "a mode of perception, a total responsive gesture of the whole personality" to the creative need to order reality, to render it true and beautiful. It is here that the interrelationship of art and life which provoked the age appears most obviously, for a sense of style is not at all limited to artistic matters. In fact, the preoccupations of the dandy were a kind of secular version of the sacred pieties of the realm of art; it was as though the dandy were being "virtuous"—that is, being obsessed with form and style—so that he might be received into a heaven of aesthetic bliss. As Wilde advised in both unimportant and important matters, "style, not sincerity, is the essential." It is a good educational program: if one can learn to be generous or polite or brave or whatever in small things, one will naturally follow suit when a big moment arrives. Hence the interest by Wilde in an attention to style in the most minor circumstances. Ultimately, as Wilde was fond of asserting, even beauty and truth become matters of style, conveying one's last mood (since style should be the manifestation of one's inner feelings, just as the form conveys the content of a work of art).

The next step was to recognize the artifice of style, and hence of beauty and of truth. In the first place, there must be, as Pater was fond of emphasizing, a structured quality inherent in any fine style which reveals the presence of a shaping imagination, for "a true understanding of oneself is the first condition of genuine style." It is our recognition of this structured quality that validates the work of art or the life that we observe: there must be a "logic" in it, though it may be the "illogic" of mask or metaphor. Secondly, this validation, this acceptance, because it follows from our recognition of an informing imagination and not from any external standards which are applied to the perception, is exempt from the ethical criteria which the Philistines are always anxious to employ in responding to aesthetic experiences. It is to this theme that Wilde refers when, in his Preface to *The Picture of Dorian Gray*, he suggests that "the perfect use of an imperfect medium" constitutes the "morality" of art, and that "there is no such thing as a moral or an immoral book. Books are well written or badly written. That is all."

Now this sense of style, of something being well or badly done, of a shaping intelligence creating a form which appeals to our aesthetic sensibilities, is a cultivated taste. It must be, if one is going to rely on one's impressions as the basis of aesthetic judgment. But the cultivation of taste has a quality of indulgence and luxury, an independence of ethical or utilitarian priorities, which it is easy to call decadent. Furthermore, in its elements of artificiality the idea of a cultivated taste conflicts with the idea of natural response, and anything that conflicts with the natural must be to some degree unnatural. And so we have the idea of decadence flowing at least partly from an emphasis on style. An excessive

fondness for lilies and sunflowers was only the most innocuous
example of an inclination that might lead to a fondness for young
boys or drinking absinthe in the Paris cafés.

It was Gautier who started this line of logic, both by his pose
of disregard for the content of art and his exclusive attention to
the form, and by his fascination with jaded sensibilities, afflicted
with the "awful yawn" that Byron spoke of and desperate for new
experiences. These experiences must permit one to be both disengaged and yet caught up in a net of sensuous pleasures and pains.
They must, in other words, be informed by a certain kind of
sterility, in that they are ends in themselves. In an essay on Baudelaire written in 1868 Gautier described how

> the poet of the *Fleurs du Mal* loved what is improperly called the
> style of decadence, and which is nothing else but art arrived at that
> point of extreme maturity yielded by the slanting suns of aged
> civilizations: an ingenious complicated style, full of shades and of
> research, constantly pushing back the boundaries of speech, bor-
> rowing from all the technical vocabularies, taking colour from all
> palettes and notes from all keyboards, struggling to render what is
> most inexpressible in thought, what is vague and most elusive in
> the outlines of form, listening to translate the subtle confidence of
> neurosis, the dying confessions of passion grown depraved, and the
> strange hallucinations of the obsession which is turning to mad-
> ness. The style of decadence is the ultimate utterance of the Word,
> summoned to final expression and driven to its last hiding-place.
> One may recall in this connection the language of the later Roman
> Empire, already marbled with the greenness of decomposition,
> and, so to speak, gamy, and the complicated refinements of the
> Byzantine school, the last forms of Greek art falling into deliques-
> cence. Such indeed is the necessary and inevitable idiom of peoples
> and civilizations in which factitious life has replaced natural life,
> and developed unknown wants in men. It is, besides, no easy thing,
> this style disdained of pedants, for it expresses new ideas in new
> forms, and in words which have not yet been heard. Unlike the
> classic style it admits shadow. . . . One may well imagine that the
> fourteen hundred words of the Racinian vocabulary scarcely suffice
> the author who has undertaken the laborious task of rendering
> modern ideas and things in their infinite complexity and multiple
> colouration.[13]

Paul Bourget, whose particular interest in decadence was an aspect
of his interest in the development and decline of individuals and
societies, expanded Gautier's definition in more explicit terms.

A similar law governs the development and decadence of that other organism which we call language. A style of decadence is one in which the unity of the book is decomposed to give place to the independence of the page, in which the page is decomposed to give place to the independence of the phrase, and the phrase to give place to the independence of the word.[14]

The style which is called decadent, therefore, is primarily distinguished by its subordination of the whole for the benefit of its parts, and in this respect is distinct from a classical style in which the parts of the whole are secondary to the harmonies achieved by the entire structure. It is worth noting in passing that a major tenet of nineteenth-century symbolism—that a part may embody the whole and yet still remain a part of it—fits easily with this aspect of decadent art. Since organic or natural forms were perceived to conform to classical harmonies and symmetries (themselves the laws of nature "discovered" and bodied forth in art), or, more precisely, since the reverse was recognized, that classical art imitates natural forms, there was something subtly unnatural about the decadent style and the social and psychological relationships, indeed the entire culture, that it was supposed to reflect.

Ever since the middle of the nineteenth century, there had been growing a belief that each age and each culture exhibits *characteristic* forms of art because of broad social conditions and conditions of production, or the particular sort of communality and individuality that achieve definition at the time, or the instinctive identifications upon which the age relies. Classicists such as Mahaffy suggested that an analysis of the "genesis of national taste" might flow from a consideration of the integrity of Greek art and life. Sociologists such as Georg Simmel gave analytic status to an aspect of this idea by accepting an independent life, or aesthetic autonomy, for all cultural phenomena, arguing that this is the only way in which one can achieve any sense of the form and function of a culture. Nietzsche, following a similar logic, affirmed that the world can only be understood as an imaginative creation. These, and innumerable other quite similar propositions, bore perhaps little more than heavy-handed witness to the importance of the structures and patterns of experience that were increasingly recognized during this period. Nonetheless, they identify one meaning of such phrases as Arnold's, that art is a "criticism of life," or such paradoxes as Wilde's, that art "is not symbolic of any age. It is the ages that are her symbols." And, at least in the latter half of the nineteenth century, the characteristic forms of expression which can be identified clearly display a division between two havens of the imagination: the idyllic pastoral retreat and the hot-house garden of rare delights. Both of these, however, exhibited characteristics which were identified with forms of decadence, the one an indolent indulgence and the other an indulgent exoticism. The styles in which these pursuits were presented reflected their origin; they were above and before everything else, the product of the imagination, their abstract quality bearing witness to the truth which they conveyed, and their artificiality matched only by their beauty.

Whatever beauty might be perceived in such styles, and whatever beauty might be championed by the new apostles of beauty and of decadence, was therefore dependent at least in part on its artificiality. Whether it was Baudelaire arguing for the beauty of the artificial or Wilde maintaining the artificiality of beauty, the equation was established. The line is direct to W. B. Yeats on the one hand, who "once out of nature . . . shall never take/[His] bodily form from any natural thing"; and to Wallace Stevens on the other, whose singer "sang beyond the genius of the sea . . . the single artificer of the world/In which she sang."15

The equation linking beauty and artificiality is, as Wilde was shrewd enough to see, a version of Keats' equation of beauty and truth, for truth is presented in the artist's fictions, by means of his style. Beauty, also, needed some redefinition at times, for it was not conventional beauty which was referred to any more than it was conventional truth. Indeed, if not the ugly then certainly the grotesque was proposed by Victor Hugo as central to modern art, in the same way that Wilde would propose the centrality of lies or Wallace Stevens advocate supreme fictions. The most notorious proponent of the grotesque in the late nineteenth century was the brilliant, mercurial artist Aubrey Beardsley, who remarked that "of course I have one aim—the grotesque. If I am not grotesque I am nothing."16

The ironies and ambiguities surrounding the idea of beauty were complex and unsettling. Yeats commented later, with reference to Beardsley's work, that there was almost never any representation of desire. . . . In 1895 or 1896, I was in despair at the new breath of comedy that had begun to wither the beauty [in his work] that I loved, just when that beauty seemed to have united itself to mystery. I said to him once, "You have never done anything to equal your Salomé with the head of John the Baptist." I think, that for the moment he was sincere when he replied, "Yes, yes; but beauty is so difficult." It was for the moment only, for as the popular rage increased, he became more and more violent in his satire, or created out of a spirit of mockery a form of beauty where his powerful logical intellect eliminated every outline that suggested meditation or even satisfied passion.[17]

Ezra Pound, the twentieth century's most eloquent analyst of the ugliness of beauty, recognized some of the ironies in the (Aristotelian) association of beauty and desire.

> La beauté, "Beauty is difficult, Yeats" said Aubrey
> Beardsley
>   when Yeats asked why he drew horrors
>   or at least not Burne-Jones
>   and Beardsley knew he was dying and had to
>   make his hit quickly
>
> hence no more B-J in his product
>
> So very difficult, Yeats, beauty so difficult.
>
> "I am the torch" wrote Arthur "she saith" . . .[18]

"Arthur" was Symons, whose poem "Modern Beauty" (1899) provides a nicely ironic statement of the theme.

> I am the torch, she saith, and what to me
> If the moth die of me? I am the flame
> Of Beauty, and I burn that all may see
> Beauty, and I have neither joy nor shame,
> But live with that clear life of perfect fire
> Which is to men the death of their desire . .
> I live, and am immortal; in mine eyes
> The sorrow of the world, and on my lips
> The joy of life, mingle to make me wise;
> Yet now the day is darkened with eclipse:
> Who is there lives for beauty? Still am I
> The torch, but where's the moth that still dares die?

Something profanely sacred had been embodied in the worship of beauty, of which Wilde had been an early apostle, something which Symons and Yeats held to with nostalgic longing, for the worship of beauty had seemed to possess, for Wilde's generation and for a time, a moral and spiritual function, in a sense replacing the moral and spiritual centre that Newman's departure had left all but empty. The exquisite agony of Christ was echoed in the elaborate anguish of art; the consolation of the redemption in the satisfaction of the aesthetic experience; the truth of the resurrection in the sudden rightness of the artist's insight; the comforts of communion in shared moments; the mediation of the saints in the celebrations of the critics; the soul at peace in the realized and unified personality.

But the beauty that was worshipped was anything but pure and simple, as the service came more to resemble some kind of black mass; it was Arthur Symons who attempted one of the earliest definitions in England of the new directions in art that were associated with new aesthetic religions that artists such as Baudelaire and Wilde proposed. In an article entitled "The Decadent Movement in Literature" (published in 1893 in *Harper's New Monthly Magazine*), Symons spoke of the "intense self-consciousness, restless curiosity in research, over subtilizing refinement upon refinement, spiritual and moral perversity" of decadent art, characterizing it as "a new and beautiful and interesting disease."[19] The decadent artist displayed what the poet Eugene Lee-Hamilton (speaking of Baudelaire) called "the gorgeous iridescence of decay," or what Pater (referring to Euphuism) called "the defects of the qualities of the work of art." It was natural to view decadent art in pathological terms, for it tended to display a fascination with decline and decay. And it was natural to embrace it, for in nineteenth-century European society in which utilitarianism, materialism and conventional rhetoric constituted health, one might as well be on the side of disease. (Furthermore, to those who took evolution seriously death and decay could paradoxically be sure signs of progress.) Symons, in fact, transferred his discussion of decadence into a later book, one of the most influential studies of late nineteenth-century French literature for many twentieth-century English-speaking writers, entitled *The Symbolist Movement in Literature* (1899). In it he portrayed symbolism as a defence against materialism, "offering us the only escape from our many imprisonments."[20]

Symons' initial article on decadence was put into final form to provide an answer to specific criticisms which had been directed at the work of a number of writers of Symons' circle. In particular, this circle included those who, beginning in 1891, met around the table at an eating house on Fleet Street called The Cheshire Cheese and who clubbed together (as the Rhymer's Club) for mutual comfort and a ritualistic sharing of common interests. The members and guests were various and included W. B. Yeats and Ernest Rhys (the co-founders), Lionel Johnson, Ernest Dowson, John Davidson, Richard Le Gallienne, Selwyn Image, Herbert Horne, John Gray, Edward Garnett and Symons himself. Wilde joined the group occasionally, usually when it met in a private house, where he shone brightest. Certainly his influence was in any event considerable; along with Symons and John Gray he provided a link with the new literary and artistic movements in France, the home of the decadent heart and anathema to the respectably philistine British public. When Beardsley and Henry Harland started a new quarterly in 1894, they called it *The Yellow Book* as a nod in the direction of the traditional cover of the supposedly wicked and decadent ordinary French novel of the time and *The Yellow Book* quickly became a synecdoche for the period itself.

The group that intermittently met at The Cheshire Cheese was a very mixed one, and their talents and inclinations were as diverse as their careers. Their point of contact was an interest in the contemporary arts, about which they held quite divergent views but which they all agreed were of central importance in determining the social and cultural environment of the time.[21] Of the group the one most inclined to diverge was the shrewd and handsome poet Richard Le Gallienne. In 1892 he published *English Poems*, in which he lamented the inclinations of poets such as Symons and prophets such as Wilde, at whose feet he had worshipped a few years before. Asking "shall we hear an English song again," he commented that

> . . . not of thee this new voice in our ears,
> Music of France, that once was of the spheres;
> And not of thee, these strange green flowers that spring
> From daisy roots and seem to bear a sting.[22]

The "strange green flowers" refer to Wilde, who had adopted the habit of wearing in his buttonhole a flower artificially coloured green. He later said that he "invented that magnificent flower"; whatever the case, it was also said to have been a kind of emblem sometimes worn by homosexuals in Paris. In 1894, Robert Hichens, who had met Wilde several times through their mutual friends E.F. ("Dodo") Benson, Reggie Turner and Lord Alfred Douglas, published a satirical novel, *The Green Carnation*, [23] with caricatures of Douglas and Wilde and an amusing reference to Wilde's mild hostility towards Beardsley and *The Yellow Book*, to which Wilde was never invited to contribute. (At the time of Wilde's conviction in 1895, Beardsley was tarred with the same brush and fired as Art Editor of *The Yellow Book* by its publisher, John Lane. When Beardsley later teamed up with Arthur Symons to edit *The Savoy* in 1896, he stipulated that Wilde was not to be published in the magazine. Their publisher was Leonard Smithers, who brought out Wilde's *Ballad of Reading Gaol* in 1898. It was a small world.) Esmé Amarinth, the aesthete in Hichens novel, decides at one point to

> "stay at home and read the last number of *The Yellow Disaster*. I want to see Mr. Aubrey Beardsley's idea of the Archbishop of Canterbury. He has drawn him sitting in a wheelbarrow in the gardens of Lambeth Palace, with underneath him the motto *J'y suis, J'y reste*. I believe he has on a black mask. Perhaps that is to conceal the likeness."
> "I have seen it," says Mrs. Windsor, "it is very clever. There are only three lines in the whole picture, two for the wheelbarrow and one for the Archbishop."
> "What exquisite simplicity!" Lord Reggie exclaims. [24]

This was entertaining enough, and very much in the spirit of the inevitable and seemingly ubiquitous cartoons and caricature pieces of the period. 1894 was a good year for parodies of Oscar. Hichens's novel led the pack, but there were also G.S. Street's clever *Autobiography of a Boy* (collected from the *National Observer*), and the short play *Aristophanes at Oxford*, by L.C.M.S. Amery, F.W. Hirst and H.A.A. Cruso.

Though somewhat earlier, Le Gallienne went rather further, and in a curious way touched on the ironic relationships that developed during the period between Wilde and many of his

sometime followers. Though Le Gallienne was himself attracted
to certain artificialities of the period—referring, for example, to
street lamps as "iron lilies"—he disliked the excesses that Wilde
in particular had come to represent and he was not shy in displaying his distaste in poems such as "The Décadent to His Soul":

> His face grew strangely sweet—
> As when a toad smiles.
> He dreamed of a new sin:
> An incest 'twixt the body and the soul.
> He drugged his soul, and in a house of sin
> She played all she remembers out of heaven
> For him to kiss and clip by.
> He took a little harlot in his hands,
> And she made all his veins like boiling oil,
> Then that grave organ made them cool again.
>
> Then from that day, he used his soul
> As bitters to the over dulcet sins,
> As olives to the fatness of the feast—
> She made those dear heart-breaking ecstasies
> Of minor chords amid the Phrygian flutes,
> She sauced his sins with splendid memories,
> Starry regrets and infinite hopes and fears;
> His holy youth and his first love
> Made pearly background to strange-coloured vice.[25]

It is not clear what notice Wilde took of this kind of denunciation by a disciple, though Theodore Wratislaw claimed that when
he mentioned the poem to him some months after it appeared,
Wilde expressed ignorance of its object being himself, and then
reflected in a Coleridgean fashion on the understandable ingrati-
tude of the grateful, on how love's excess often turns into words
of unmeant bitterness, and on the inclination of fine natures to
sordid acts.

In any case, Wilde's particular affectations came to represent
symbolic more than specific gestures, and just as Wilde represented in England the perversions that Le Gallienne deplored, so
there can be no doubt that the French writer Joris-Karl Huysmans
represented his seducer, according to the scheme that it was convenient for Le Gallienne to apply. (It is worth noting that after
Gautier's celebrated preface to the second edition of Baudelaire's
Les Fleurs du mal in 1868—widely read because Baudelaire was

widely read—the idea of being a decadent poet and a poet of a decadent age began to become fused.) Huysmans' novel, *À Rebours*, had been published in 1884 and immediately praised by a wide variety of writers and critics who, like Paul Valéry, welcomed it as their "Bible and bedside book." To Whistler it was marvellous; to Remy de Gourmont, memorable; to Guy de Maupassant, bewitching; to the psychological critic Paul Bourget it was a penetrating study of a neurotic intellect; to Edmond de Goncourt it brought a touch of fever to the brain; to George Moore it was like a dose of opium. Verlaine liked the parts about himself and Mallarmé liked it all. And Wilde had the hero of his own novel, Dorian Gray, turn the pages of this "poisonous book" while

> in exquisite raiment, and to the delicate sound of flutes, the sins of the world were passing in dumb show before him. Things that he had dimly dreamed of were suddenly made real to him. Things of which he had never dreamed were gradually revealed . . .[26]

All of these things, the sins of the world, were experiences which justified themselves (by the grace that was attached to the decadent theology) because they were perceived as part of a process of more intense individual awareness and more acute self-consciousness. That they were also indulgent merely proved how completely the total self, the soul and body united, was in natural harmony with the inclinations and instincts that were developed by the imagination. But indulgent or not, it was Wilde's unsettling thesis, put forward by Gilbert in "The Critic as Artist," that

> what is termed Sin is an essential element of progress. By its curiosity Sin increases the experience of the race. Through its intensified assertion of individualism, it saves us from monotony of type. In its rejection of the current notions about morality, it is one with the higher ethics.[27]

The basis of such antinomian assertions was, as stated by Lord Henry Wotton to Dorian Gray, that "the aim of life is self-development. To realize one's nature perfectly—that is what each one of us is here for." It would be very wrong, however, to associate this advice exclusively with the pernicious Harry Wotton. The confusion of secular with spiritual ecstasy and mission was a common trope at the time, especially since Pater. George Meredith, writing a couple of years before *Dorian Gray* was published, noted that "the way to spiritual life lies in the complete unfolding of the creature, not in the nipping of his passions. . . . To the flourishing of the spirit . . . through the healthy exercise of the senses. These are simple truisms."[28]

If the spirit and the sense are to be confused (or the distinctions between them obliterated) in this way, then aesthetic forms provide one manner in which a fusion may be achieved. When Swinburne praised Gautier's *Mademoiselle de Maupin* in a sonnet of his own, he was raising to a second power the paradoxical belief central to the decadent consciousness: aspects of life can be most intensely experienced in the artifices created by the imagination.

> This is the golden book of spirit and sense,
>> The holy writ of beauty; he that wrought
>> Made it with dreams and faultless words and thought
> That seeks and finds and loses in the dense
> Dim aim of life that beauty's excellence
>> Wherewith love makes one hour of life distraught
>> And all hours after follow and find not aught.
> Here is that height of all love's eminence
> Where man may breathe but for a breathing-space
>> And feel his soul burn as an altar-fire
>> To the unknown God of unachieved desire.[29]

"Unachieved desire" had been, since Blake counselled the repressed to "sooner murder an infant in its grave than nurse unacted desires," an evil in itself. Wotton's terrible advice to Dorian gives such counsel a picturesque and typically decadent form.

> The bravest man amongst us is afraid of himself. The mutilation of the savage has its tragic survival in the self-denial that mars our lives. We are punished for our refusals. Every impulse that we strive to strangle broods in the mind, and poisons us. The body sins once, and has done with its sin, for action is a mode of purification. Nothing remains then but the recollection of a pleasure, or the luxury of a regret. The only way to get rid of temptation is to yield to it. Resist it, and your soul grows sick with longing for the things it has forbidden to itself, with desire for what its monstrous laws have made monstrous and unlawful.[30]

Although decadent literature tended to be read as emphasizing desires of a sensual nature, however much they might be transformed or perverted in the mind, it was recognized by the more perceptive readers that behind the sensual anguish there was most often a deep spiritual agony. For example, Léon Bloy and Jules Barbey d'Aurevilly (himself a notable dandy in his time, and a model for Des Esseintes) discovered in Huysman's *À Rebours* an acute sense of spiritual affliction, a demonstration that "man's pleasures [are] finite, his needs infinite." In an article entitled "Les Répresailles du Sphinx" which appeared in *Le Chat Noir* (June, 1884), Bloy presented his convincing response.

> There is not a single page in this book where the reader can enjoy a breathing-space and relax in some semblance of security; the author allows him no respite. In this kaleidoscopic review of all that can possibly interest the modern mind, there is nothing that is not flouted, stigmatized, vilified, and anathematized by this misanthrope who refuses to regard the ignoble creatures of our time as the fulfilment of human destiny, and who clamours distractedly for a God. With the exception of Pascal, no one has ever uttered such penetrating lamentations . . .[31]

This perception was echoed by Hugo von Hofmannsthal when, in an essay on Wilde which he called "Sebastian Melmoth" (1905), he suggested that

> his aestheticism had a convulsive quality. The jewels among which he professed voluptuously to delve were like death-dimmed eyes, petrified because they could not bear the sight of life. Incessantly he felt the threat of life directed towards him. He was forever surrounded by a tragic air of horror. He kept challenging life unceasingly. He insulted reality. And he sensed life lying in wait in order to spring upon him out of the darkness.[32]

Wallace Stevens, somewhat later, wrote of a violence within protecting the self from a violence without, and the writers and artists of Wilde's generation would have understood the notion well. Furthermore, it is a familiar geneology that links Don Juan to the dandy and the decadent, and even to the Gidean Prometheus, the existentialist heroes of J.-P. Sartre and the *mauvais garçons* of Jean Genet.[33] As most of the English writers of the nineteenth century show, not only the fatal man but the "femme fatale" appear in this gallery and provide a rich ambiguity that lies close to the heart of the imaginative sensitivities of the period.

Tracing a line from Don Juan to the dandy and the decadent

is suggestive, for it outlines the sense of desperation, the boredom, the almost suicidal dejection which was a common trait and which led to instinctive identifications with symbols of powerlessness, natural decay and sterility. "The most frequent words of the post-1830 vocabulary are already those of the decadence: *spleen, melancholie, lassitude, ennui.* "[34] Pater, in his essay on Coleridge, suggests that "by what he did, what he was, and what he failed to do, [he] represents that inexhaustible discontent, languor, and homesickness, the chords of which ring all through our modern literature." The decadent artists of the latter part of the century displayed a "fascination with all the symptoms of declining life"; Baudelaire clarified this psychological state for the poets of his time, and the *Symbolisme* of the late nineteenth century took up the theme—an obsessive attraction to decay, a compulsive attachment to that which is sterile, an acute sense of suffering.[35]

The sterility of androgyny was one of the images used to convey this; the "perfect knowledge" of Tiresias, who has "foresuffered all" and who does nothing, in T. S. Eliot's *Waste Land* is its ancient and modern counterpart. The ambiguity of the sexual roles and the lunar imagery in Wilde's version of the Salome legend, the perversions which are indulged or implied, the extreme narcissism of Salome herself (first emphasized by Mallarmé in *Hérodiade,* in which the "purity" of the language also reflects a detachment from the process of creating speech)[36]—all of these embody the decadent sensibility. It may also be admitted that "art for art's sake," with its insistence on artifice and on an hermetic, hieratic autonomy, indicated a sterility that was the product of a disengagement from life and from the natural.

In Baudelaire, and most obviously in *Les Fleurs du Mal,* we discover the complex association of the decadent consciousness with evil. Wilde's Dorian Gray, for example, "looked on evil simply as a mode through which he could realize his conception of the beautiful." On the one hand there is the pride of Baudelaire or Melville "in having produced a book which breathes only the terror and horror of evil"; on the other, the self-indulgent fascination with remorse, with the eternally hounding Furies. Coleridge provided the nineteenth century with the psychology of a personality instructed in good and disposed towards evil, in defiance of the will committing acts of self-destruction, always going à rebours (against the grain), conscious of a terrible struggle but incapable of resolving it. Baudelaire provided the nineteenth century with the aesthetics of this condition, with the ability to appreciate its beauty and sublimity. In an essay entitled "The Cultured Faun" (1891), Lionel Johnson remarked on the "double 'passions' of decadent artists, the sentiment of repentant yearning and the sentiment of rebellious sin." There is not a little of the "divided self" or split personality in decadent art. In some ways, whatever tension it has is owing to this aspect.[37]

The counterpart to the celebration of evil was the celebration of death as what Freud called "the goal of all life," and of the Freudian struggle between Eros (or the life-instinct) and death. As Barbey d'Aurevilly put the challenge to Huysmans, after writing À Rebours there is left only a choice between "the muzzle of a pistol and the foot of the Cross." Wilde's version of this alternative was between the sphinx and the crucifix, or between the boy Antinous and the Christ child.

This fascination with death was the extreme of an obsession with decay and degeneration that gave to the artists of this period a reputation for morbidity. Wilde, among others, defended himself and his company against this charge by arguing that morbidity is the artist's subject and not his state of mind—one would not call Shakespeare mad because he wrote King Lear. Even more significantly, he suggested that the morbid and the sorrowful are as central to human experience as the lighthearted and the joyous, possibly much more central, and therefore belong at the centre of the arts. In this view, he was following in the footsteps of Walter Pater and extolling what Johnson called "exquisite appreciation of pain, exquisite thrills of anguish, exquisite adoration of suffering." "People sometimes say," remarked Wilde, "that fiction is getting too morbid. As far as psychology is concerned, it has never been morbid enough."

There was, however, no shortage of apparently morbid poetry, for a pose of languid despair or anxious lassitude was very much the fashion in the late 1880s and the '90s. Paul Verlaine was praised for introducing "a new shade of woe" into literature; the bitter tones of Giacomo Leopardi were in everyone's ears; and

Wilde's poem on *The Sphinx* was decorated with the figure of
Melancholia on the frontispiece. Edward Dowson and Lionel
Johnson both indulged, with Johnson adding a typically decadent
touch in writing of "The Dark Angel," and of how "all the things
of beauty burn/With flames of evil ecstasy." Dowson's melancholy is more familiar, and it was quite typical in its controlled
desolation. In despair, *de profundis, in extremis,* there was some
salvation, at the very least from a dull sameness.

> Strange grows the river on the sunless evenings!
> The river comforts me, grown spectral, vague and dumb:
> Long was the day; at last the consoling shadows come:
> *Sufficient for the day are the day's evil things!*
>
> Labour and longing and despair the long day brings;
> Patient till evening men watch the sun go west;
> Deferred, expected night at last brings sleep and rest:
> *Sufficient for the day are the day's evil things!*[38]

The entire decadent movement, and its ancestors and children
such as aestheticism and symbolism, were to some extent the
manifestation of a kind of alienation that afflicted all those who
were fully aware—as artists were—of their surroundings; they
each represented in different ways the artist's disaffection and
discord with his social environment. The rejection of bourgeois
standards in favour of the autonomy of the arts, which all espoused, was accompanied by a developing unease that culminated
in the profound (though also, to be sure, quite fashionable) disillu-
sionment of the nineties because, to take one model, having rejected the smugly Philistine middle class, most artists found it
difficult to identify with the new class, the proletariat. One answer
was a commitment to socialist values and ideals; critics have been
slow to recognize this prescription, passing by its complex expression in Browning's *Sordello,* in the utopian fiction, the socialist
argument, the evolutionary assumptions, and the spiritual enthusiasms of the time. Relating realism in literature to commercialism in society, as many did so vociferously in the early years
of the twentieth century, was the kind of crude response that
characterized much Marxist criticism (though Marx himself wrote
of the true artist as a type of man whose work is a pleasure in

itself); but it is closely related to much more satisfying distinctions, such as Wilde proposed, between the "imaginative reality" of Balzac and the "unimaginative realism" of Zola, the latter constituting "the true decadence . . . from which we are now suffering."

There was some inclination during this period to see cultural development and any kind of over-refinement (such as that represented by Zola's "realism") as inevitably decadent. Those who were particularly interested in individual psychology related such a process to the degeneracy of states of unusual distinction, and most obviously to types of genius. It began to be accepted that the over-subtilizing of the intelligence which seemed to correspond to the over-development of social and psychological inclinations resulted in an atrophy of the will, an inability to make and act upon choices. There was support for the view that this was the product of a metropolitan environment, which created a situation in which frantic and desperate gestures, unrelated to any continuum of knowledge and power, were the only and last refuge, for knowledge and power had become separated in the schizophrenic consciousness that was a product of urban society. "Sterile introspection, infinite delay" provide the model, and life becomes, in Strindberg's words, "like the tuning of an orchestra—which never begins to play."

The "problem of the will," as Bourget called it, had a broadly European fascination during the 1880s and 1890s. It was widely recognized that a unified personality, what Pater called "a complete though harmonious development of man's entire organism," was the ideal, and that the emergence of a part of the whole as a controlling force in the personality was characteristic of a decadent condition. This is not, of course, to say that it was therefore not admired; men and women of genius who developed an aspect of their personalities at the expense of others had a heroic quality, and the various psychological strategies of retreat—into Arcadia or Eden, the delights which Pan offered or those of the hot-house gardens of rank growth and poisonous flowers and exotic fragrances—were recognized as necessary defences against imaginative obliteration. Nonetheless, the complete realization and balanced satisfaction of man's complex needs and desires was accepted as the ultimate goal, and the struggle towards this occupied the attention of social scientists and theologians as much as critics, aestheticians and architects.

It is here that we arrive at the vortex of the spinning worlds of art and life. The kind of integration of the personality that the artists of this time envisaged needed models. Some, such as those supplied by Pater's numerous heroic "portraits," were instigated by the imagination; most were supplied by reality, transformed by the imagination.[39] Romantic literature had thought of the drama as a form which supplied a typology of experience, but it took several generations to produce great drama. Yet it was the drama that Wilde characterized as his most personal form of expression, and when von Hofmannsthal wrote about personality "becoming a positive value as soon as it embraces more than the merely individual and circumstantial," he referred to the theatre as the most likely setting for this to occur. This tradition of belief reaches its peak in the period from Richard Wagner to Oscar Schlemmer, when a "total" aesthetic experience which combined both a sense of determining personality and a conviction of objective impersonality became the ambition. Only on stage, or behind a mask, would truth be conveyed; the theatre, alone among the arts, demonstrated the essence of a complete aesthetic experience, for it had "the illusion of truth for method, the illusion of beauty for its result."[40]

By the end of the century drama had taken on a life and character of its own; it provided a special kind of fascination for Wilde in that it represented an exquisite confusion of life and art and embodied the paradox that the more art disengages us from life the more we are able to become involved in the great dramatic forms such as tragedy and comedy, and through them become more a part of life, escaping from it in aesthetic awareness only to return to it more comprehensively through the aesthetic experience. It is precisely because Hecuba means nothing to us, he suggested, that we can sympathize with her tragedy.

As one perverse example, Dorian Gray's worship of Sybil Vane, the actress in a third-rate theatre, is a worship of artifice; to Basil's comment that "Love is a more wonderful thing than Art," Lord Henry retorts that "they are both simply forms of imitation." It is Sybil who provides the novel with one of its central themes: the confusion between the imagined and the real, between surface and symbol, between affected and genuine emotion.[41] At the same time she is a type, both mortal and "all the great heroines of the world in one. She is more than an individual." The universality or symbolic character of figures in drama was an important element to Wilde's contemporaries, for they sought such an element in all phenomena. Symons, writing about Henrik Ibsen, suggested that great drama is distinct in that it deals with the relationship of man's soul to the universe and that its characters are the "ultimate types of energy." The uniqueness of art consists in its union of energy and structure, its presentation of a "patterned energy"; life and nature, on the other hand, tend to be rather disorganized, indeed at times positively messy. The dandy, in his guise as the aesthete or the decadent, attempts to provide life with a contrived structure, a specific form. Yet the emphasis on form which was characteristic of the age of Wilde existed in the presence of life and nature, took its cue from them in fact, though one of the dimmest areas in the criticism of nineteenth-century art is that which should deal with the relationship between imagined and real perceptions in the art of this period, and with the ways in which each informed the other.

There is, first of all, a paradox to which Keats drew attention, that the true appreciation of beauty and truth is an intense appreciation, even though it may be created by apparently trivial forms. Wilde took this paradox to its conclusion by having had Henry argue that "the only thing more superficial than Beauty is Thought." What artists such as Keats and critics such as Wilde came to realize was that intensity is an aesthetic function, conveyed by the forms of beauty and truth; and further, that these forms are available in life as well as in art, if only they can be properly—which is to say, imaginatively—perceived. Pater's counsel to "be present always at the focus where the greatest number of forces unite in their purest energy" is a counsel to apprehend experience with the imagination. The harmonious relationships of classical art were slipped into the fold by being perceived as the embodiment of compelling spiritual forces, but Pater's counsel is nonetheless an intrinsically romantic one, paradoxically celebrating art's function as what D. G. Rossetti called a "moment's monument/ Memorial from the Soul's eternity/ To one dead deathless hour." We tend to expect the romantic poet to exaggerate the divine inspiration that creates art at the expense of the secular inspiration that sustains life; in fact at the heart of romantic poetry there is a compulsion to bring art and life back together —the true focus of the typical romantic poem is not the prophet raging in the wilderness, but his re-entry in the future into the city or community that has heard his words and ordered itself accordingly.

There is a useful distinction between *allegoria* and *figura*, first proposed by Erich Auerbach, which supplies some theoretical support to this scheme.

> If you are writing an *allegoria*, you invent a set of persons and a story to represent a preformulated abstract meaning. For example, you might wish to celebrate the triumph of thrift over extravagance and carry out your design by describing a fight in which a poorly clad knight (called Thrift) succeeds in unhorsing a richly clad knight (called Extravagance). That is *allegoria*. *Figura*, on the other hand, is in the literary sphere a rarer and more interesting phenomenon. The writer of a *figural* poem does not frame a fictitious series of persons to convey the Significance; instead he encounters, in real life, a person or thing which is felt to be quite objectively significant, and this the poet need only describe, literally. Thus, whereas in *allegorial* poetry the overt story is fictitious though the Significance may be seriously asserted, in *figural* poetry both the representing figure and the thing figured are felt to be equally real. *Allegoria* can readily be seen as complex narrative metaphor, and the metaphor is the work of the poet as *fictor*, feigner. The *figural* poet, on the other hand, finds his metaphors walking about the real world, the streets of Florence or the Cumbrian fells, and so has no need to invent metaphorical structures of his own.[42]

The distinction was used by Auerbach to emphasize the uniqueness of Dante as a great figural poet, and there is much to support an argument that Wordsworth's poetry provides the most significant example of the figural mode in English. Without venturing into a long discussion of Wordsworth's poetry and influence, I would suggest that the manner in which significance is conveyed in Wordsworth's poetry is a presentiment of a major change in the way in which aesthetic significance is perceived by artists and critics by the end of the nineteenth century. When Walter Pater wrote about Wordsworth in *Appreciations,* he defined the nature of this change.

> To treat life in the spirit of art, is to make life a thing in which means and ends are identified: to encourage such treatment, the true moral significance of art and poetry. Wordsworth, and other poets who have been like him in ancient or more recent times, are the masters, the experts, in this art of impassioned contemplation. Their work is, not to teach lessons, or enforce rules, or even to stimulate us to noble ends; but to withdraw the thoughts for a little while from the mere machinery of life, to fix them, with appropriate emotions, on the spectacle of those great facts in man's existence which no machinery affects, "on the great and universal passions of men, the most general and interesting of their occupations, and the entire world of nature,"—on "the operations of the elements and the appearances of the visible universe, on storm and sunshine, on the revolutions of the seasons, on cold and heat, on loss of friends and kindred, on injuries and resentments, on gratitude and hope, on fear and sorrow." To witness this spectacle with appropriate emotions is the aim of all culture; and of these emotions poetry like Wordsworth's is a great nourisher and stimulant. He sees nature full of sentiment and excitement; he sees men and women as parts of nature, passionate, excited, in strange grouping and connexion with the grandeur and beauty of the natural world: —images, in his own words, "of man suffering, amid awful forms and powers."[43]

Pater's advocacy of a style called Euphuistic (in *Marius the Epicurean*), a style disengaged from moral obligations, is paradoxically an advocacy of the aesthetics of Wordsworth as well as of Gautier and Baudelaire, for Pater saw in such a style the possibility of a transformation of "ennui," and "spleen" into "rêve" and "idéal," into the visionary dream of reality that characterizes Wordsworth's "spots of time", his moments of acute awareness, the "single exquisite instants" that painting and sculpture capture, and poets such as Keats celebrate. This transformation proceeds from aesthetic impulses, but its motivation is also to obliterate the distinction between art and nature by uniting the kind of apprehension that one brings to both. This is only done, obviously, with the expectation that what is perceived will be significant, numinous, instinct with life and truth and beauty "quickened at single points," as Pater suggested. The symbolists carried the idea of this kind of apprehension, by means of which both art and life are perceived in their symbolic character, to the point where they affirmed the symbolic nature of all art and of all aspects of life which are imaginatively apprehended, or, to use the appropriate theological analogy, all aspects of life which are "revealed," by all apprehension which is "visionary." As Wilde recognized, this does not necessarily include only the serious aspects; the comic side, the side which the comedy of manners has traditionally taken as its province, is most effectively perceived and displayed in an aesthetic form, and involves the use of symbolic gestures.

W. B. Yeats noted that

> William Blake was the first writer of modern times to preach the indissoluble marriage of all great art with symbol. There had been allegorists and teachers of allegory in plenty, but the symbolic imagination, or, as Blake preferred to call it, "vision," is not allegory, being "a representation of what actually exists really and unchangeably." A symbol is indeed the only possible expression of some invisible essence, a transparent lamp about a spiritual flame; while allegory is one of many possible representations of an embodied thing or familiar principle, and belongs to fancy, and not to the imagination: the one is a revelation, the other an amusement.[44]

William Blake's annoyance with allegory derives, I think, from his instinctive sense that it involves the unnecessary intervention of metaphorical expression, whereas the metaphor should be inherent in the subject matter itself, and the style by means of which this subject is expressed should be as luminous, as crystal-like, as possible.

No poet, least of all Blake or Wordsworth, does without metaphor. The point that distinguishes romantic poets such as Blake, Wordsworth, Shelley and Keats is their assumption that reality is metaphorical, that life and its experiences are most properly, perhaps can only be, perceived in aesthetic terms. This attitude informed much nineteenth-century speculation and led to the confusion of art and life that characterized the age in which Wilde lived. Interpretations of social customs, individual inclinations, religious impulses, aesthetic tastes, as well as mythological systems,

tended to be similar insofar as they recognized the symbolic significance in such activities which gave them their appeal. This significance may, perhaps, be ethical; but the symbolic structure by
means of which the experience is realized is aesthetic. Therefore,
the only certain way of interpreting such phenomena is aesthetic
rather than ethical: the religion of Christianity is perceived as the
picturesquely conceived life of Jesus; the obsessions of sinful souls
are presented as the perversions of ordering or disordering (which
is to say in either case aesthetic) impulses.

In other words, life is perceived as art, or at least in aesthetic
terms; this is the simple premise underlying the antics and the art
of the aesthetes and decadents and it derives directly from the
romantic poets, and specifically from Blake, Wordsworth and
Keats. The matter of significance becomes an aesthetic judgment,
as both art and life become at once surface and symbol, like
Wordsworth's Leech Gatherer who "signifies" resolution and independence. The questions we ask of life, like the questions
Wordsworth asks the old man—How is it you live, and what is it
you do?—are excruciatingly irrelevant, like the bourgeois or utilitarian expectations that were addressed to art later in the nineteenth century. The questions that are not asked are answered
perfectly. Furthermore, the concept of rational or ethical motive
is seriously undercut by Wordsworth, as in "Anecdote for Fa-
thers" the young boy supplies an image, an aesthetic motive or
motif, as the "reason why" he prefers one place to another; the
poem was once subtitled "showing how the art of lying may be
taught." In this period in general, the importance of motive as an
ethical function in life and art is diminished, and replaced with
an aesthetic function. The motive is, to find expression; the motif
is the form or controlling function of that expression. The motif
of a work of art does not do anything, it *is* something; and in being
something, it creates a tense correspondence between the material
world—the world of reality—to which it belongs and which it
images, and the spiritual world—the world of the imagination—
in which the sources from which it draws power and life reside.[45]
It is to these sources that the poet would repair; any indication of
spiritual power or intense life is valuable in itself, and is indicated
by a corresponding power or intensity which the poet experiences.

The moment of such experience becomes valuable for its own sake, as does its structure, which is "available" only to the aesthetic sense, the sense of form.

The "luminous stasis of esthetic pleasure" in which Stephen Dedalus perceived the esthetic image and apprehended the beautiful (In James Joyce's *Portrait of the Artist as a Young Man*) is equivalent to the scientist's "understanding" of the phenomenon which he observes; both are determined by structures which the imagination recognizes and to which it responds. Both also operate within closed systems, as late nineteenth-century scientific theory was beginning to recognize; as Pater put it, "to the modern spirit nothing is, or can be rightly known, except relatively and under conditions." It was against the application of inappropriate conditions and the denial of relative perceptions that Baudelaire railed so righteously when he insisted that moral philosophy and moral propaganda, for example, cannot supply conditions for the creation or the criticism of art, since aesthetic conditions, like biological conditions or theological conditions or social conditions, constitute a closed system, just like arithmetic. And to speak of the moral implications of a work of art is like speaking of the area of the number seven or the divinity of poverty. It is the implicit recognition of this that Wilde admired so highly in the work of

> Darwin and Renan, the one the critic of the Book of Nature, the other the critic of the books of God. Not to recognize this is to miss the meaning of one of the most important eras in the progress of the world. . . . The Critical Spirit and the World Spirit are one.[46]

Thomas Mann, in a notable essay on Nietzsche, displayed a series of aphorisms and remarks by Wilde which sounded unsettlingly like Nietzsche in order to argue that Nietzsche was basically an aesthete. It will not wash, of course, for Nietzsche's primary concern was with ethics, not aesthetics. But it is especially illuminating of Wilde, for in an unintentional way it draws attention to Wilde's firm conviction that life and art are both structures of experience; that art is the expression of life, though not its routine imitator; that the energies of life and those of art are indeed continuous and in spirit identical, and it is the spirit to which the highest realms of both appeal; that the tensions of life (joy and sorrow, fact and fancy) correspond with those of art (ecstasy and melancholy, reality and imagination), and only the individual who is sensitive to those tensions and to the processes through which they are sustained and resolved can fully appreciate either.

CHAPTER FOUR

WHATSOEVER THINGS ARE COMELY

Two things were absolutely necessary for Wilde, contact with comely things, as Pater says, and social position.

ROBERT ROSS, IN A LETTER TO
ADELA SCHUSTER (1900)

The Scylla and Charybdis of nineteenth-century art and critical appreciation were, to use a distinction suggested by John Addington Symonds, "excessive intellectuality and excessive sensuousness." Symonds, like so many of his contemporaries, was coming to terms with Pater's celebrated definition of music as "the typical, or ideally consummate art, the object of the great *Anders-streben* of all art, of all that is artistic or partakes of artistic qualities."[1] Pater had proposed music as a prototype for the highest kind of art, in which form and content "inhere in and completely saturate each other." It was, within the same arbitrary dichotomy, assumed that the intellect tends to attach itself to content and the senses to form, and critics such as Symonds advised against excessive attachments of either sort. This same dichotomy, in fact, was used not only to focus on the prerogatives of form and content, but also to distinguish between the different appeals of impressionism and symbolism.

There is as much room for disagreement as for agreement on

the characteristics of these two artistic movements; Arthur Symons, when he tried to define the significant features of the decadent consciousness that followed from the hot-house aestheticism of the 1880s, described it as flitting between symbolism and impressionism. There was certainly a fascination with the nature of symbolic expression during these years, just as there was particular critical attention paid to the subtleties of aesthetic impressions. Uniting both was a belief that art is exempt from the limitations which apply to ordinary methods of communication, and from moral or utilitarian obligations.

Obviously, however, there were more specific distinctions, the most common of which was that impressionism has an almost anti-intellectual appeal. As Wilde noted, "the primary aesthetic impression of a work of art borrows nothing from recognition or resemblance. They belong to a later and less perfect stage of apprehension." It was not so much that impressionism denied the intellect—though Roger Fry, for example, would say of Cézanne that he was "too much of an intellectual to remain satisfied with pure Impressionism"—but that it required a suspension of interpretive impulses; the ideal condition was to be, like Marius the Epicurean, "absolutely virgin towards the experiences" that provided the subject matter of works of art. John Ruskin identified one aspect of this when he pleaded for a "recovery of what may be called the 'innocence of the eye' . . . a perception of flat stains of colours, merely as such . . . without consciousness of what they signify."[2] The example that he gave was sunlighted grass, which he suggested should be painted not green but yellow, the colour it appears. "Paint not the thing itself, but the effect that it produces," advised Mallarmé, and suggested to his friend Edouard Manet that the word *comme* should be struck out of his vocabulary—and Mallarmé was anything but a thoroughgoing impressionist. Claude Monet, who needed no advice, painted Rouen Cathedral under various lights from morning to evening, in colours from yellow to pink. The impressionist artist turned away from the referential aspect of form and colour and emphasized instead their existential qualities; what this often meant was that the appearance and the reality did not coincide. The impressionist answer to any objection on that score was that it is the appearance which alone gives the impression, which the artist communicates and which in turn presents to anyone who looks at the work a more real because more immediate and more realized reality than any which he might otherwise discover or invent. Impressionism, in other words, creates both the reality and the conditions for its apprehension—the appropriate mood. This, and the fact that it demands no "interpretation" outside of the "impressive" aesthetic experience, links it to decorative art; the work of art conjures up states of mind and sensation, rather than creating patterns of "meaning." Indeed there is, from the intellectual point of view, an indulgent sensuousness, what Wallace Stevens called an "essential gaudiness," about impressionist art; Yvor Winters once referred to Stevens's poetic development in his first and extremely impressionistic volume of poetry as a "hedonist's progress."

The subjectivism of the impressionist aesthetic was in contrast with the objectivity that symbolism claimed for the aesthetic experience, out of a somewhat confused acceptance of the notion that art deals with ideas, not things; more specifically, it was affirmed that art might embody a Platonic idea, a universal essence of which it represents a form, and that it is this idea which true art exists to convey. The particular is symbolic of the universal, went the argument, and it is the particular (word, colour, shape) which art presents to our perception. It is not difficult to see both why the impressionists tended to reject what they conceived as the intellectualism of the symbolists, and why it was easy to associate impressionism with a concern for form, and symbolism with a belief in the primacy of content. There is, however, a considerable community of interest which binds them, for the impressionist and symbolist critic would each claim, though perhaps in slightly different ways, that his most important (and initial) contact with a work of art is essentially irrational, and that the true critic is uncommitted to conventional verities, is "unfair, insincere and not rational," as Wilde put it. Language purified of its mere utilitarian functions, and forms that "tease us out of thought as doth eternity" (by implying truths which are of infinite application though embodied in the finite and essentially abstract shape of beauty) provide a common vehicle; and both impressionism and symbolism look to music as the ideal, for considerably different reasons. Both depend upon the enchantment and power of paradox; both contradict normal expectations and identifications; and both look to beauty as the instrument of truth and the ideal of art.

Pater's celebration of music was therefore of more than passing interest, for it provided a focus for ideas about art that were still very much in a state of flux. His argument was compelling:

> *All art constantly aspires towards the condition of music.* For while in all other works of art it is possible to distinguish the matter from the form, and the understanding can always make this distinction, yet it is the constant effort of art to obliterate it. That the mere matter of a poem, for instance, its subject, its given incidents or situation; that the mere matter of a picture, the actual circumstances of an event, the actual topography of a landscape, should be nothing without the form, the spirit, of the handling; that this form, this mode of handling, should become an end in itself, should penetrate every part of the matter:—this is what all art constantly strives after, and achieves in different degrees.[3]

Pater's quintessential example of an artist for whom this model applies is Giorgione, and his discussion of the painter (which first appeared in the *Fortnightly Review* in 1877) reveals further implications in Pater's ideal. In the first place, in Pater's view, Giorgione disappears, as it were, into the style of his work as his personality merges with his art in the kind of transparency that Pater called "diaphanous." Furthermore, Giorgione's style becomes symbolic of the imaginative environment in which he creates; and Giorgione himself is perceived as an "impersonation of Venice." It is this possibility, and the ideal and abstract character of such art, which would be used to relate architecture and music by many writers of the period, from Taine to Schopenhauer.

There were objections to Pater's proposal, to be sure. Symonds, for one, argued that it merely reflected "a way of expressing [a] sense of something subjective in the styles of artists or of epochs, not of something in the arts themselves"; and he disputed Pater's contention that art "is always striving to be independent of the mere intelligence, to become a matter of pure perception." But most artists shared Pater's instinct about the art that they were trying to create and that might embody the spirit of the age in its abstract and ideal forms. Such an art, in Pater's words, must "address not pure sense, still less the pure intellect, but the 'imaginative reason' through the senses"; and the work of art must therefore, as Wallace Stevens affirmed, "resist the intelligence/Almost successfully," and "address itself," in Wilde's words, "not to the faculty of recognition nor to the faculty of reason, but to the aesthetic sense alone." This elusive and somewhat ambiguous character is precisely what the highest forms of art attain, it was agreed, and these forms thereby become capable of rendering the equally elusive and ambiguous ideals which the artist perceives, and which themselves reflect or embody transcendent and eternal truths which the spirit alone can apprehend, and can apprehend only in the forms of beauty. To ensure that this transaction between spiritual truth and material beauty is uncontaminated by allegiances to, say, religious orthodoxy or social decorum, the work of art must insist upon its own currency, newly minted if need be, and trust that the genuine artistic temperament, to which alone it appeals, will recognize the true coin and reject the false. What distinguishes music from the other, and representational, arts, is that its true currency will not pass outside the single transaction between itself and the artistic sensibility of its audience. But any true work of art, whether representational or not, is an aesthetic form and, to the extent that it has no reference beyond itself, is hermetic, self-contained, self-sufficient. This is the characteristic of art that Wilde is trying to illuminate when he presents this paradoxical exchange in "The Decay of Lying":

> CYRIL: Surely you would acknowledge that Art expresses the temper of its age, the spirit of its time, the moral and social conditions that surround it, and under whose influence it is produced.

> VIVIAN: Certainly not! Art never expresses anything but itself. This is the principle of my new aesthetics; and it is this, more than that vital connection between form and substance, on which Mr. Pater dwells, that makes music the type of all the arts.[4]

That is, art primarily creates an aesthetic response, not an historical or ethical or sociological one, and the more purely artistic the work, the more purely aesthetic the response—a tautology which defines both fine art and its finer appreciation. The purest such response is, according to this view, created by music.

The impression of beauty and the revelation of truth could be discovered by particular critics in particular works of art; this was the critic's primary task. But there was a larger ambition that was a part of this aesthetic attitude, an ambition to show whether and how an age or a culture might manifest beauty and truth and demonstrate an aesthetic coherence. Pater and Symonds, though holding different views on many subjects, were of one mind in their belief that the Renaissance displayed such coherence. In 1873 Pater's *Studies in the History of the Renaissance* propounded the view that

> the Renaissance is the name of a many-sided but yet united movement, in which the love of the things of the intellect and the imagination for their own sake, the desire for a more liberal and comely way of conceiving life, make themselves felt, urging those who experience this desire to search out first one and then another means of intellectual or imaginative enjoyment, and directing them not only to the discovery of old and forgotten sources of this enjoyment, but to the divination of fresh sources thereof—new experiences, new subjects of poetry, new forms of art.

In addition, it was perceived as a period during which

> all breathes of that unity of culture in which "whatsoever things are comely" are reconciled for the elevation and adorning of our spirits. And just in proportion as those who took part in the Renaissance become centrally representative of it, just so much the more is this condition realised in them.[5]

The relationship of cultural values to more specifically religious values during the Renaissance was, as Pater recognized, quite complex, but the wonderful thing was that despite conflicts

> the human mind w[o]n for itself a new kingdom of feeling and sensation and thought, not opposed to but only beyond and independent of the spiritual system then actually realised.

This was a central insight, for the geographers of this new kingdom were the critics and artists of Pater's day, though until his day they hardly recognized their profession, or indeed their subject matter. When T. S. Eliot sneered at Arnold and Pater and at the notion of "aesthetic religion," he displayed a fairly typical refusal to admit the existence of this kingdom, which, as Ishmael (in Melville's *Moby Dick*) noted about Queequeg's home, "was not on a map, [but] true places never are."

But geographers of places that are not on maps have their problems, and the problems of proving the existence of such realms of the imagination preoccupied the aesthetic and cultural geographers of the late nineteenth century. There were two general structures of proof: one was to accept that the reality of the kingdom is conveyed by the impression we have of its ideal forms; the other was to assume that the ideal of the kingdom is available in our perception of its real and symbolic artifacts. The first solution is that of the impressionist, the second that of the symbolist. In fact, these two critical attitudes were less easily distinguished than I have implied, but their tendencies towards various versions of realism and idealism were fairly apparent.

Matthew Arnold had thrown down the gauntlet with his assertion that the aim of all true criticism is "to see the object as in itself it really is"; Pater (in his "Preface" to *The Renaissance*) modified this to assert that "in aesthetic criticism the first step toward seeing one's object as it really is, is to know one's own impression as it really is, to discriminate it, to realize it distinctly." Thereby he laid the foundations for an aesthetic approach in which impressionistic and symbolic prerogatives flow into one another. For those such as Pater who took up Arnold's challenge, the validity of a critical aesthetic response depended not so much on objective reality as on subjective perception. The romantic emphasis upon processes of self-consciousness, of the ways in which the shades of the prison house of consciousness begin to close around us until we become aware of our separateness, had pervaded the thinking of most late nineteenth-century philosophers and critics, as well as historians and social scientists, and they all tended to base their explanations on the view that one's only contact with that which is external to the self is provided by and limited to one's impressions of it, which then confirm or transform one's idea of reality. (It must be kept in mind that these kinds of arguments were being put forth and received by people who were committed to abolishing trite distinctions between mind and matter.)

There were several corollaries to this essentially impressionistic assumption. The first was that the art form most capable of rendering precise impressions will be the art which is most capable of putting us "in touch with", and of thereby giving us "confidence" in our idea of reality. Unfortunately, the nature of reality was still very much in dispute, so that there was a difference of opinion as to whether representational or non-representational art best conveyed its nature, or gave the best idea of it.

It was of course representational art that primarily got tagged realistic; it is well to remember that such realism was itself basically impressionistic, and realism and impressionism were often associated in the polemic of the time. Indeed, the impressionist painters acknowledged the priority of literary impressionism, and various of them received inspiration from realistic writers as different as Zola and Proust. Wilde's *Ballad of Reading Gaol,* and its various forerunners such as Thomas Hood's *Dream of Eugene Aram, The Murderer* fit into this category, at the extreme of which there was a call for an almost clinical naturalism, devoid of emotional decoration, and with a style which reflected the often sordid or tedious reality that was to be communicated.

There was a curious association of ideas that brought together under the banner of impressionism art that proceeded from quite different motivations. Just as a sterile clinical naturalism was one pole to which realism was attracted, so an equally stern emphasis on precise craftsmanship and imagistic purity focussed the formal realism of artists such as Gautier and the de Goncourts, and it was a common trope at the time that technical innovation preceded artistic inspiration. Both approaches emphasized a purity of style and both of course had rather different perceptions of reality; but it was nonetheless towards an aesthetic objectivity that both aspired. The difference was that, to use distinctions which Wilde employed, the latter combined perfection and personality, while the former did not, and was therefore "unimaginative" (as he characterized Zola's work). Wallace Stevens used to say simply that impressionists were "poetic Realists", which was to say that they presented a more real (because imaginatively informed) reality than that which nature offered. This element of personality, from which true art springs and to which it is addressed in Wilde's opinion, was not always perceived as a subjective intrusion of emotional content into the work—Gautier, for one, eschewed that kind of subjectivism. Furthermore, both kinds of impressionistic realism worked towards the creation of an effective impression of reality by means of formal devices and in a way that might even approach the non-representational. For non-representational art had the distinct advantage that the impressions it created were not confused by imitative distractions that often develop a false illusion of contact with reality. Gautier's impressionist poem "Symphonie en blanc majeur," in its deliberate frustration of conventional responses, was an early and influential example of the kind of confusion or correspondence of the senses that Baudelaire later celebrated, and of the analogies with the aesthetic principles of mucic upon which so much of this kind of art depended for its aesthetic validity. Wilde's own "Impressions" are in a line from this, and Paul Verlaine's "Art Poétique" gave this aesthetic a form which endeared it to the symbolists as well.

> De la musique avant toute chose,
> Et pour cela préfère l'Impair
> Plus vague et plus soluble dans l'air,
> Sans rien en lui qui pèse ou qui pose.
>
> Il faut aussi que tu n'ailles point
> Choisir tes mots sans quelque méprise:
> Rien ne plus cher que la chanson grise
> Où l'Indécis au Précis se joint . . .
>
> Car nous voulons la Nuance encor,
> Pas la Couleur, rien que la nuance!
> Oh, la nuance seule fiance
> Le rêve au rêve et la flûte au cor![6]

There is one other poet whose work was admired in the context that Verlaine advocated, and that was Edgar Allan Poe. In particular, poets from Baudelaire to Mallarmé were delighted to set forth Poe's account of the genesis of his poem "The Raven" as an example of the conscious "finding" of an appropriate form that was a part of the aesthetic that these poets embraced, and that highlighted the paradoxical relationship between beauty, artificiality and reality upon which this aesthetic attitude depended. (Ironically, it was Verlaine who was least inclined to accept Poe's somewhat contrived theory.) The theory against which Poe's "explanation" was used was the romantic notion of the poet creating in a frenzy of inspiration, his will suspended and his conscious mind outside the circle of creativity. There was, needless to say, some need for a fairly tactful use of Poe's theory since, whatever its polemical uses, it contradicted the idea of the artist "proceeding from form to function." But Poe's celebration of beauty as "the exclusive province of poetry" and his affirmation that "the goal of poetry is its own principle and must have nothing in view but itself" were too useful to ignore.[7]

Poe's emphasis on beauty as the province of art provided one condition; and the inclination of the realists and many of the impressionists to insist on the truth of their creations emphasized another. Together, they give focus to the problem which bothered almost everyone in the nineteenth century, the problem of how art communicates a sense of its beauty and its truth, or of what it would become fashionable in some quarters to call its "authenticity." The two most obvious ways were by convincing its audience of either the sincerity of its motivation or the exactness of its observations. A common categorization—it muddied the waters terribly but it must be addressed—put art into two types corresponding roughly to the two ways in which art "proves" itself: Romanticism and Realism. (This variation on the antique formula which opposed romanticism and classicism was necessary because a classical impulse could be recognized by the versatile critics of the nineteenth century behind all art.) Wilde used these categories in a superficial way to make fun of the inability of the barbaric nineteenth century to appreciate any art, whatever its motivations.

> The nineteenth century dislike of Realism is the rage of Caliban seeing his own face in a glass.

> The nineteenth century dislike of Romanticism is the rage of Caliban not seeing his own face in a glass.[8]

There was a more serious kind of discrimination that was possible, however, in which Realism tended to make its way by emphasizing its role as the purveyor of truth, while Romanticism attached itself to beauty. Artists of Wilde's time liked to diminish the distinction between beauty and truth and to view them as corresponding to different stages or functions in the perception of an aesthetic object, just as they liked to diminish the distinction between mind and matter, body and soul. Since the "aesthetic sense" was quite literally a "sense of beauty," it was with this idea that discussion of the topic usually began and always ended. Ironically, this predilection for identifying beauty and truth as aspects of an aesthetic experience tended to result in a proliferation (rather than in any consolidation) of artistic categories, each rigidly and earnestly defended. The reasons for this were partly social, but they also reflected different perceptions of the absolute or relative character of beauty and truth.

Since the middle of the eighteenth century it had been obvious, at least in England, that an easy definition of beauty was impossible; anyone who had followed the deliberations of Edmund Burke, Joshua Reynolds and Erasmus Darwin, not to mention the cogitations of the major Romantic poets, would have been quite convinced of that. Although the object of aesthetic contemplation did not, for the Romantics, specifically include the ugly, it certainly comprehended the awful splendours and terrifying attractions of evil and dabbled in the grotesque. Several generations of Gothic fiction and Byronic heroism developed this tendency, until by the second half of the nineteenth century ugliness formally entered the scene as a subject of art (and became, as Wilde said, a "commonplace of the schools"), largely owing to the enthusiasms of the Realists.[9] The result was a major redefinition of the adjective "aesthetic"; no longer was it in any limited way a "sense of beauty," but rather, since "the artist is the creator of beautiful things" by definition, an aesthetic response became understood as a response to or an impression of those qualities which the artist's creation expresses. And beauty and truth would inhere in these qualities, again as it were by definition.

The conventional response to claims of this kind of redefinition (of beauty which includes ugliness, for example, or truth which includes falsehood) is to reflect that such definitions always need to be clarified by context anyway, and that what we have is not a redefinition but a recognition that what is beautiful or true in one context of reality may be perceived as ugly or false in another. Yet this assumes that the qualities perceived by the imagination

have no absolute validity, and what united such apparently opposite artistic movements as aestheticism and naturalism was their
strenuous denial that art is subject in any way to the definitions
which reality provides. Beauty and truth, the argument went on,
do not exist primarily because of a context, but because of an
aesthetic apprehension; their imaginative autonomy is absolute, as
must be the autonomy of the work of art by which they are
communicated. There may be, indeed will always be, an imaginative context within which beauty and truth may be realized in a
work of art, but this context has nothing to do with the conventional distinctions which social conditions or fashions define. The
artistic temperament will, if freed from restrictions and habits
which convention imposes, respond to the aesthetic qualities
within a work of art and recognize the beauty and the truth which
they embody and by which they are informed. As George San-
tayana explained in his very Aristotelian essay on *The Sense of
Beauty* (1896), beauty is "pleasure objectified"; and truth is, as
Wilde assured his readers, a matter of feeling rather than fact: "in
matters of religion, [truth] is simply the opinion that has survived.
In matters of science, it is the ultimate sensation. In matters of
art, it is one's last mood."[10]

If this scheme is accepted, as it was by Wilde and his friends,
then the emphasis shifts from the categories of experiences to
their intensity, the energy and sense of life which they convey, the
appeal which they possess for the active imagination. In other
words, the work of art must compel; the ultimate compulsion is
provided by the ecstatic moment, Wordsworth's "spot of time"
or Eliot's "still point."[11] Short of that, the test is whether the work
of art impresses itself upon us, whether it appeals to our aesthetic
sense and our artistic temperament, whether it finds an answering
counterpart in our own soul. One of the more subversive aspects
of this aesthetic attitude is that it is at least superficially easy to
legitimize subject matter that is perverse or positively evil on the
argument that it appeals to the dark passages of the psyche, and
therefore fulfils the kind of "aim of life" that Lord Henry Wotton
talks about, "to realize one's nature perfectly." Such perfect realization is possible only in art, and its achievement characterizes
such art as beautiful and true. It is this kind of implication that

Walter Pater's "Conclusion" to his *Studies in the History of the Renaissance* appeared to hold, with its advice to

> be present always at the focus where the greatest number of vital forces unite in their purest energy. To burn always with this hard, gemlike flame, to maintain this ecstasy, is success in life.

And to create the conditions for such ecstasy is success in art. Pater's nervousness about this admonition persuaded him to delete the conclusion in the second edition of *The Renaissance;* it was returned to the third edition.[12]

It was not that art might choose as its subject something that was immoral or vicious. That was routinely answered by critics such as Hippolyte Taine (in the preface to his *Histoire de la literature anglaise* [1864]) with his argument that vice and virtue are elements of reality, just like vitriol and sugar; Wilde completed the argument by asserting that "the moral life of man forms part of the subject matter of the artist," and that "vice and virtue are to the artist materials for an art." He added, however, that "thought and language are to the artist instruments of an art." Furthermore, it is a sense of form—conveyed by harmonies, rituals, moods—that is central to the social and ethical as well as aesthetic consciousness. Ruskin was one of the more outspoken proponents of this idea, with his affirmation that taste is essentially a moral quality. The implications and the refutations of this belief were numerous, but the most significant focussed on the implication that moral forces and aesthetic energies might be interdependent. Those who supported this Hellenic concept also advanced the notion that the abstract and ideal forms in which art is conveyed correspond to the abstract and ideal truths which mankind has imaginatively and emotionally embraced, and suggested that the forms and ideals of arts must provide access to that which is universal and eternal in human existence. When Schopenhauer proposed that music is the only art which can express transcendent ideas or universal archetypes directly, a proposition that the legions of Wagner enthusiasts popularized and the platoons of symbolists adopted, he was proposing a typology of art which assumed certain things about what it is that art does.[13] And when Wilde added that "the spirit of an age may be best expressed in the abstract ideal arts, for the spirit itself is abstract and ideal," and that "the more abstract, the more ideal an art is, the more it reveals to us the temper of its age," he was saying (as Shelley had before him) a great deal about the subject matter of art, which he further developed by suggesting that "if we wish to understand a nation by means of its art, let us look at its architecture or its music."

If one is an impressionist one implicitly assumes that art has an aesthetic appeal or impresses itself upon us because of our educated sensitivity to the forms in which it appears, and that this process is the only one which authentically communicates to the single self, is the only language which man understands, and therefore provides one's only key to the mysteries of cultural and social phenomena. The more abstract and ideal the presentation, the more "beautiful" it is, the more purified and undefiled will be the perception of that which the work of art signifies, its truth— and this beauty in a very real way depends upon this truth. To the symbolist, the truth which a work of art conveys certifies, as it were, its beauty, its coherence and aesthetic significance, just as this truth depends upon the beautiful forms in which it obtains. The "intuition of union with the world" that art is said to provide, the tangible equivalent or correlative of a spiritual truth which it expresses, give a sacramental significance to the aesthetic experience that is not at all unlike the sacramental significance of the Eucharist to the Christian. It is no less dependent upon the belief that the bread and the wine, or the symbol in the work of art, really is the body and the blood of Christ, or really is the material and lasting *realization* of intense and spiritual experiences in as well as out of time. The notion that earthly phenomena correspond to spiritual realities, which was commonly celebrated during this period, attached itself to the household of symbolist art. Moreover, Heraclitus's enigmatic conjunction of above and below, surface and symbol, made it impossible (at least for the many who knew Heraclitus) to ignore the profound assumptions upon which such art depended, and which in turn it sustained.

The dual obligation of the work of art is, in these terms, almost excessively paradoxical; that is, a work of art has both existential and intentional significance. It is *or* means only; it means *and* is also; it both *is* and *means* something. This something may or may not be the same; crudely speaking, the impressionists would say that it is, while the symbolists would say that it is not. This kind of distinction on its own, however, helps no one except the unfriendly reviewer, for the nature of paradox is so intimately related to the nature of meaning and being that about all that it is safe to say is that the paradox of impressionist art is inseparable from the paradoxical quality of our recognition of beauty or of being in a work; and that the paradox of symbolist art is a part of the paradoxical assent that we give to truth or meaning in art. One critic of poetic language has recently spoken of "poetic form" as "the stasis achieved in the poem between all the interests it activates";[14] impressionism and symbolism each predicate a particular kind of stasis, and our response to a particular artistic form will be different according to whether the interests that are activated in our imagination follow impressionistic or symbolic tenets. Ultimately, however, the stasis that is achieved will be rather like a hovering between opposing inclinations: between art and nature, meaning and being, the imaginative and the real, the spiritual and the material, sense and nonsense, cause and effect.

It was Walter Pater who gave the most explicit formulation to the kind of aesthetic response which, whatever its categorical allegiance, was necessary in principle in order fully to appreciate the complexities that art was thought capable of embodying and fully to take advantage of the imaginative rewards which it offered in order, if you wish, to "hover" successfully. In 1866, Pater published his first essay (on Coleridge), in which he argued that

> modern thought is distinguished from ancient by its cultivation of the "relative" spirit in place of the "absolute." Ancient philosophy sought to arrest every object in an eternal outline, to fix thought in a necessary formula, and the varieties of life in a classification by "kinds", or *genera*. To the modern spirit nothing is, or can be rightly known, except relatively and under conditions. The philosophical conception of the relative has been developed in modern times through the influence of the sciences of observation. Those sciences reveal types of life evanescing into each other by inexpressible refinements of change.[15]

The psychology of perception, appreciation and understanding upon which this kind of knowing depended became accepted by Pater's generation, with the reservation that the aesthetic sense retained its ideally autonomous character. With reference to art however, it was recognized that the fullest critical response depended upon a complex kind of awareness, and upon the completest possible understanding of the past as well as the future of one's present aesthetic instincts and disposition. As a consequence it was affirmed that critical appreciations must begin with an approach which combined impressionistic and historical criteria. The "conditions" in which nineteenth-century criticism was especially interested had been suggested by Arnold's mentor Sainte-Beuve and by Taine, and had been reinforced by the studies in the history of civilization undertaken by H.T. Buckle and W.E.H. Lecky (to whom Wilde paid considerable if discriminating attention); these conditions included race, milieu or environment, and the historical "moment" or point at which cultural, social and psychological factors intersected. These conditions modified what Wilde called the "humiliating confession [that] we are all of us made out of the same stuff," and gave variety and richness to "that dreadful universal thing called human nature." They also provided the subject matter of the new studies in psychology, philology, anthropology, economics and sociology, which in turn generated new attitudes towards both the form and the content of human experience by insisting on its conditional and conditioned nature. But the main point was not so much that experience was relative and conditioned, but that it could be understood by an act of the imagination. There is more than a hint of a structuralist approach in Wilde's assertion that "Criticism will annihilate race-prejudice, by insisting upon the unity of the human mind in the variety of its forms." Furthermore, the crucial notion that scientific commentary is descriptive rather than prescriptive (though it was clearly recognized that science was essentially predictive) was carried over into the social sciences and into artistic criticism and provided another link between such apparently opposite attitudes as naturalism and aestheticism. On this basis, Wilde as well as Taine rejected any attempt to ascribe a moral content to works of art or a moral intent to the author, proposing instead that morality, like manners, was a name given to individual and social forms of behaviour which it is the artist's function to describe, and that the artist does not have a prescriptive role. The artist may, however, say that if a situation or process continues, then certain consequences will undoubtedly come to pass; but his statement must be based on patterns of experience which have been transformed by the imagination both out of time and into the accepted understanding of the human condition. The predictive analogy with science holds here, as the nineteenth century clearly understood; but the poetic function was as old as alchemy, and was called prophecy.

What becomes obvious is that a particular critical attitude developed during the middle of the nineteenth century and, at least in art criticism, it had both classical and romantic sources. The emphasis was neither on the critic (or the artist as critic of life), as in a more purely romantic methodology, nor on his subject, as in a classical scheme, but on the critic or artist's relationship with his subject matter. This relationship displayed, as Noel Annan has said, "both a method and a disposition of mind." The disposition of mind was one which identified ignorance, false premises and inappropriate expectations as constituting the chief impediments to intellectual and imaginative development, and which advocated the most complete openness and receptivity to all that impinged upon the creative critical consciousness. The method was one in which strict (and so often archaic) classification was denounced as an unnecessary and pernicious limitation; absolute external criteria of any kind were rejected as contemptibly parochial, and empirical and relativistic approaches were proposed instead; teleological biases were condemned as unwarranted interference with free speculation and with the application of inductive reasoning. Instead, an exquisite susceptibility to observed phenomena, a powerful inclination to relate experiences of different sorts under "types" of explanations, and a replacement of purposive with mechanistic (or organic) explanations informed what was viewed as the new approach. In aesthetic terms, this led to a contemplation of the form or pattern which a work of art displays and an initial disengagement from its intentions or implications. What this disengagement then allowed was a purely imaginative sympathy with the subject, no matter how removed from one's experience, no matter how morbid or ecstatic; for the imagination, it was proposed, is first engaged (and, as it were, purified) by the form or style and, through the energies and tensions displayed in the form, is introduced to the content or subject in a way that prohibits any mistaken identification with reality, and yet convinces one that it is real.[16]

Wilde was intrigued by this kind of critical process and praised for their application of it "a great man of science, like Darwin . . . a fine critical spirit, like M. Renan, a supreme artist, like Flaubert." He consistently praised Balzac's "imaginative reality," whose characters "defy scepticism," and wrote of "the most perfect art [as] that which most fully mirrors man in all his infinite variety." This infinite variety is what art reveals to us, if we are critically disposed to accept its revelations. And this critical disposition will recognize the perfection and the personality inherent in a great work of art, and by means of this recognition will enable us "to realize, not merely our own lives, but the collective life of the race, and so to make ourselves absolutely modern, in the true meaning of the word modernity."[17]

All of this puts the lie to any overly simplistic classification of Wilde's critical position, or that of aesthetes and decadents, impressionists and symbolists, as a group. Thus, to take Flaubert for a moment, his naturalism obviously was in Wilde's opinion consistent with the aestheticism that the advocates of "art for art's sake" espoused. What made it consistent was the intrinsically imaginative nature of its methodology, its display of essentially the right sort of critical intelligence, and its concern for the imaginative values inherent in style and form. It is often forgotten, in the enthusiasm over Wilde's entertainingly inverted description of the critic as artist, that he also celebrated the artist as critic; he played about with Matthew Arnold's notion that art is a criticism of life, but he also carried Arnold's insight into new areas and developed it in new ways. The "development of the critical spirit" was, in short, the ambition of the leading figures in all areas of intelligent discussion. The artist was a critic because, in Wilde's opinion, "all fine imaginative work is self-conscious and deliberate . . . and self-consciousness and the critical spirit are one." Indeed,

the critic occupies the same relation to the work of art that he criticizes as the artist does to the visible world of form and colour, or the unseen world of passion and of thought. He does not even require for the perfection of his art the finest materials. Anything will serve his purpose. . . . Out of the sordid and sentimental amours of the silly wife of a small country doctor in the squalid village of Yonville-l'Abbaye, near Rouen, Gustave Flaubert was able to create a classic, and make a masterpiece of style.[18]

There is something salutary in this reminder that life—vice, virtue and all of that—indeed provides the subject matter of works of art. Wilde's hero Balzac had once stated his desire to "express his century"; and Wilde reflected that the *Comédie Humaine*

is really the greatest monument that literature has produced in our century, and M. Taine hardly exaggerates when he says that, after Shakespeare, Balzac is our most important magazine of documents on human nature.

What Taine had said, as he tried to develop a sociology of literature, was that a work of art is a document because it is a monument, by which he meant that it provides an imaginative synthesis of the cultural values of the time. If one accepts that a work of art is capable of this kind of synthesis, then one is accepting that

culture *itself* is a work of art whose motif and formal construction are capable of being "voiced" or "reflected" through some particular aesthetic object. In other words, while some ideologies demand of history that it flow in certain "teleological" rhythms, others ask of social systems that they be aesthetically impressive. And it is not difficult to see why the second of those views should be so appealing to . . . men unwilling to separate the sociological from the "poetic" understanding of history, uninterested in its prosaic aspects, and moved only by elegant generalities, conventionally noble enterprises, the spectacle of great events, and the "soul" and "ideals" of peoples and nations.[19]

This appeal was both exceptionally elusive and entirely central in nineteenth-century critical thought, though it was often lost in the polemic supporting art for art's sake. The idea of culture represents the ultimate confusion of life and art.

It is, in short, utter folly to expect that neat distinctions between art and life, and the way in which they mirror or reject each other or in which we apprehend either, can be assumed. As George Saintsbury reflected some years after Wilde died,

when we praised [Baudelaire and Flaubert] and others, when we
rejoiced in them because they had followed art for art's sake, it was
also . . . because they had followed life's sake *as well.* In fact you
cannot do the first without doing the second, though you certainly
may do the second without doing the first.

Form *without* matter, art *without* life, are inconceivable. . . . But
unless you train yourself to value the art and the form and the
literature apart from, though by no means to the neglect of, the
matter and the life, you are likely to fall, as a delightful phrase of
the Articles has it, into "wretchedness of the most unclean [criti-
cal] living."[20]

The best way of avoiding unclean critical living was to accept that
art is primarily impressive and that the "first step" in any critical
apprehension is the "realiz[ing] of one's own impressions." The
next step, at least along the particular road that was travelled by
many in the nineteenth century, was to realize the significance of
one's impressions in the context of one's consciousness that experience was relative and might even be less than certainly real.
Whatever value or significance might be assigned to various kinds
of experiences would therefore depend less on objective criteria
than on a subjective interpretation of the imaginative context and
therefore of the nature of such experiences.

The concepts which symbolism embodied developed out of this
kind of subjective relativism and posited a correspondence between two orders of existence: between real or material
phenomena and spiritual or imaginative significance; or between
chaotic sense-data and its orderly interpretation. Heraclitus, with
his puzzling epigrams about the way up and the way down being
one and the same, or about the Logos having both a subjective and
an objective identity, provided the most celebrated examples of
the paradoxes that inhere in this kind of relativism.[21] The new
interest in and understanding of psychological processes that engaged the attention of Wilde's contemporaries provided an obvious context within which such aspects of life could be considered.
In this respect, the profusion of societies for the investigation of
extra-ordinary psychic phenomena was quite consistent with the
general direction of critical interest.

Perceiving objects or events in the physical world was always
simple enough in an impressionistic way; perceiving them as sym-

bolic of natural processes or laws was facilitated when the idea of evolutionary change became identified with something like an all-pervading life force. Translating this into cerebral terms, so that mental facts or events were recognized as symbolic of psychological processes or spiritual laws, was quite easy and became very much the fashion, in part because of the practice of assuming some structural analogies between psychic and physical processes. Furthermore, the late nineteenth century witnessed an increased interest in the way in which *ideas* were conveyed, and consequently in the ways in which one might create an ideal order (or an ordered idea) out of the flux of experience with impressionist disregard of any "irritable reaching after fact and meaning"; or might abstract from reality its ideal character and embody this in some form of symbolic expression. The important thing was to insist upon the autonomous nature of the imaginative apprehension of the idea, and to subvert possible identifications with that which was trivially real. If one could achieve sufficient self-consciousness—what Coleridge called "a kind of being and a kind of knowing, and that too the highest and farthest that exists for us" —then this autonomy would be guaranteed by the very nature of artistic and critical apprehension.

> No artist recognizes any standard of beauty but that which is suggested by his own temperament. The artist seeks to realize, in a certain material, his immaterial idea of beauty, and thus to transform an idea into an ideal. That is the way an artist makes things. That is why an artist makes things.[22]

Therefore the true critic, though he may undoubtedly have inclinations, is neither exclusively an impressionist nor a symbolist, neither a romanticist nor a classicist, but simply a man with an artistic temperament, sensitive to all that art embodies, and with considerable knowledge, aware of the conditions of creative activity and the limitations as well as the possibilities of imaginative enterprise. This is Wilde's constant theme and his most important insight.

The function of the critic is to be sensitive to that which is aesthetically "impressive"—this may be a work of art, a culture, a life—and to move from his impression to a new work of his own, that need not necessarily bear any obvious resemblance to the thing it criticizes. The one characteristic of a beautiful form is that one can put into it whatever one wishes, and see in it whatever one chooses to see; and the Beauty, that gives to creation its universal and aesthetic element, makes the critic a creator in its turn . . .[23]

For the critic criticizes "Beauty itself, and fills with wonder a form which the artist may have left void, or not understood, or understood incompletely."

Criticism therefore, like art itself, is defined and confined only by the impression of beauty it creates and the truth it symbolically reveals. Both art and criticism, insofar as they communicate a sense of beauty, express nothing; and insofar as they communicate a sense of truth, they reveal everything. It should be added that there was something other than the apologetics of some "hairdresser's dummy of a stylist," as one critic called Théophile Gautier, in all of this. For the logic behind this perception of art and criticism was the logic that informed the critical method of the sciences and the study of mankind, a method that responded first to phenomena as impressive, for to acknowledge them as expressive meant that their interpretation was beyond the scheme of a critical attitude that admitted the validity of descriptive analyses only. That this description must proceed without obligations, as it were, to its subject was obvious, just as it was obvious that one tried to set one's Christian beliefs aside in writing a "Life of Jesus," or that one attempted to write a social or national history or a fictional *Comédie Humaine* that was other than an apology for one's class or country, or that one wrote about other cultures with the least possible ethnocentricity. It is easy to see how this position shifts easily into a critical relativism such as Pater espoused and into an emphasis on the development of a particularly sensitive historical consciousness, for the critic must to a certain extent get out of his own temporal and spatial condition as well as into that of another time and place.

Behind the Renaissance ideal or the medieval ideal or the post-industrial ideal—all of which had advocates during the last half of the nineteenth century—there was an irony that could not escape the attention of artists and critics who had been nourished on

Romantic art. Yearning after ideals, whether social, sexual or spiritual, was hardly unique to the nineteenth century, but it had become rather the fashion for various historical and cultural reasons during the last decades of the eighteenth century. The Promethean accents of the Romantic period are generally remembered, for Faust and the Byronic hero caught the popular fancy, and the psychological need for some sort of encyclopaedic assent was nothing less than an almost universal state of mind. For at least a century, from about 1760, English literature had been especially fascinated by the ideal of a purified human order, purified of its mortal clogs as well as of its moral limitations. Blake, Shelley, and Keats wrote differently of this dream, while Wordsworth and Coleridge spent their energy wondering whether indeed it was a dream. Each, however, recognized that while the final accomplishment might be "pinnacl'd dim in the intense inane," the struggle to achieve that goal was very much anchored in the intense here and now. Browning's Sordello provide the most anguished and ironic link with the later priests of this order and gave expression to a truth that had been implicit in the work of the earlier poets. This truth was, to use Demogorgon's scheme, "imageless," for it was simply the dark side of a bright hope which did have an image in the striving spirit of Prometheus or (for a later generation) Ulysses. The truth was not that it is foolish to extol certain ideals and to seek to attain them, but that it is an inescapably human folly to *see* them at all and to recognize their relationship to the self, for sooner or later one (such as Shelley's archetypal poet or Wordsworth's solitary) will

> see
> Too clearly, feel too vividly, and long
> To realize the vision, with intense
> And ever-constant yearning;—there—there lies
> The excess, by which the balance is destroyed . . .[24]

Such excess is folly, as Blake tells us, but it is also the only defence for the spirit, the only way of ensuring that the creative energy that is in us does not atrophy. The most celebrated proponents of this impetuous ardour in the late nineteenth century were Wilde and Nietzsche, though Pater's advice "to burn always with this hard, gemlike flame" provided an early statement. But ecstasy is not the same as excess—indeed, the moment of stasis or "hovering" which defines ecstasy is in a way antithetical to it—and the quest of the self for its own image which Shelley wrote about in *Alastor* provided an example of the kind of extravagant obsession which led not to a moment of ecstasy, of perfect balance and repose in the midst of intense forces, but to a waste of energy and ultimate self-destruction. Examples of other and equally ever-constant yearnings were common in the century. The argument was the same in all cases: the commitment to "realize the vision" (of Empire, a new Hedonism, a "moral aesthetic," a vigilant morality) was worth the price because the striving, the process, the quest was of value in itself. Some even wrote their novels or poems or plays or painted their pictures or played their music with this principle in mind; and some still do. There is considerable irony in the fact that this excess is, in its way, a function of the yearning for ideal forms of experience, of beauty and truth.

A further irony plagued the age and, under the aegis of Yeats, has had its influence on what is sometimes referred to as the "modern tradition." Once again Shelley had developed it and associated the irony with Prometheus as he is tormented with the thought that, as a result of "the clear knowledge [he] waken'dst for man,"

> Then was kindled within [man] a thirst which outran
> Those perishing waters; a thirst of fierce fever,
> Hope, love, doubt, desire, which consume him for ever.[25]

The lesson was, in less apocalyptic terms, that man's imagination was both creative and destructive and that these functions were inextricably linked and mutually dependent. The confession of Mrs. Arbuthnot, the *Woman of No Importance* in Wilde's play, that her love for her son Gerald is sustained and made powerful by her hatred for his natural father, George Harford, Lord Illingworth, is one example of this paradox, as is our sense that the good which Dorian Gray, or Lord Arthur Savile, accomplishes (in turning life into an experience of sensations and pleasures, or in coming to Sybil purged of all extraneous temptation) is sustained and given coherence by the evil which each does. There is a terrible truth in the refrain of *The Ballad of Reading Gaol*, that "each man kills the thing he loves" (as well-meaning Hamlet kills Ophelia). Yet who would forego love because of it?

This terrible truth was only one of a complex group of paradoxes that characterized the art and criticism of the period. If there is one single prerequisite for an understanding of the age of Wilde it is an acceptance of what Philip Wheelwright (referring to Heraclitus) has called "the ontological status of paradox—an acceptance, that is to say, of the view that paradox lies inextricably at the very heart of reality." Paradox (including the paradox at the heart of metaphor) is an extremely complex device, and its analysis is not helped by the presence of so many superficial paradoxes and epigrams which pass for serious paradoxical statements. Trivial or superficial paradoxes are those which can be "explained away" or "unsaid," or whose dramatic effect depends upon a grammatical restatement of some kind of acceptable similitude. G. K. Chesterton's "nothing is so miraculous as the commonplace" is of this sort, as are many of the witty aphorisms that Wilde was so adept at delivering, such as his claim that "it is only the superficial qualities that last. Man's deeper nature is soon found out." Such paradoxes entertain, but they do not disturb. The reason is adequate to cope with them, while our imagination simply allows us to appreciate their humour.

The paradoxes which more obviously characterize the complex and self-conscious age in which Wilde lived are those which do not depend upon a "removable confusion," but whose impenetrability is an inseparable part of the complexity or ambiguity of that which is being expressed. The obscurity of writers such as Robert Browning and the paradoxes inherent in the spiritual affirmations of John Henry Newman in some respects prepared the way for this fascination with the nature of paradox; and Wilde, with his defence of obscurity and his statement that "only the great masters of style ever succeed in being obscure," had declared his affiliations. But the use of paradox was related more to an attempt to illuminate relationships between art and life on the one hand and between self-consciousness and naive or imaginative identification on the other than it was to any attempt simply to present difficult truths in beautiful forms.

"A man is known by the dilemmas he keeps"; and so, we might add, is an age.[26] These dilemmas are expressed in terms of alternatives, of categories into which questions are fitted, of choices that are presented and in terms of which a discussion is structured. Bacon called them "Idols of the Theatre," which tend in the nature of things to become the "abstract and ideal" truths, including the aesthetic truths, which the particular age accepts. Therefore, aesthetic structures are not of themselves adequate to the task of resolving these dilemmas; on the other hand, aesthetic forms generally display their origins and implications in a shamelessly open way and thereby reveal the nature of the idolatry by which the age is enchained and by which its dilemmas are defined. It was for this reason that Wilde paid so much, and such perverse, attention to the critical issues upon which the aesthetic attitudes of the time depended; the most obvious examples were the dichotomies between form and content, the imaginative and the real, and the subject and object. Breaking down or confusing these distinctions proved a useful strategy and, while poetry has always had as one of its functions the baffling of the easy solutions proposed by logical language and categorical thought, Wilde added that function to criticism, which could also be employed to such didactic ends. Furthermore, he deliberately expanded the confusion of the obligations of the critic and the artist that Arnold had introduced and emphasized the continual flux rather than any momentary permanence in all human endeavours. He went far beyond any easy call for creative inconsistency and concentrated his attention on a more radical doubt that he felt it was the obligation of the artist to develop about the possibility of achieving any certain understanding of anything. Either intense and momentary perceptions or perceptions that are continually vulnerable, and continually expanding, are all that one can expect, and it is precisely such perceptions that metaphor and paradox encourage. The "wilful paradoxes" of Lord Henry prompt equally wilful metaphors to describe Dorian's feelings, and the "meanings" of both are equally evanescent, equally illuminating about the limitations of the dichotomies (between good and evil, soul and body, duty and desire, appearance and reality) upon which the verities of the age depended.

The "meanings" of significant (or what might be called "authentic") metaphor and paradox go far beyond any solution of the "riddle" that they present, though that is a very basic (and very ancient) aspect of their initial appeal. One analogy that may be useful is to compare the creative tensions of authentic metaphor and paradox with the creative tension that Lionel Trilling has described between the self and an "opposing self," or that Carl Jung outlined in his analysis of how the attitude and function types of the ego operate in the process of individuation—while remembering that the critic of the arts is in general more interested in something called the imagination than in something called the mind. By the recognition of and engagement with this fictive "opposing self," the individual psyche is able to realize its own involvement with life—or what Taine would have called the "moment"—as well as to become conscious of its own autonomy, and its own separateness.

As against this kind of creative tension, which has obvious Hegelian associations, many psychologists and critics of Wilde's day and later set the uncreative division of the self into two opposing categories. It was a division, it was generally agreed, which supplies no creative tension but only an exhausting opposition, and which has an analogy in the metaphor or paradox that degenerates into a questioning of meanings within strictly alternative categories, or in the atrophy of the will (in the face of paralyzing choices) that was the proprietary despair of the period. The opposing self can lead the psyche to an entirely new definition, a new consciousness of its situation; the divided self can only frustrate the incomplete ambitions of its separate aspects and arrive at a limited and partial awareness of its predicament. The fascination of the artists of the period with dual structures displays the ambiguity that this condition embodies.

There is, then, in the structure of the creative tension in which the late nineteenth and early twentieth centuries were especially interested a central and paradoxical kind of predicament, for it could not be denied that a tension was nonetheless a tension even if it was creative, and that a schizophrenic psychic condition was still a kind of curse, though perhaps also (as R.D. Laing might insist) a kind of blessing. This has a counterpart in a profound

metaphor which should illuminate the nature of the truth that
paradox in general displays, and which concerns the central problem of sin in a Christian world. T. S. Eliot gives a version of it in
"Little Gidding":

> Sin is Behovely, but
> All shall be well, and
> All manner of thing shall be well.[27]

Lady Julian, who lived as a recluse in a cell attached to the Church
of St. Julian in Norwich, and whose *Revelations* provided the text
that Eliot used, learned from her conversations with God "that sin
is no shame, but worship to man." It is not so far at all to Wilde,
claiming that sin is an essential element in the progress of the race.
The paradox of *felix culpa*, the fortunate fall, is so central to
Wilde's genius that we easily miss it. Jesus comes and dies not for
the righteous, but for the sinner, to call him to repentance—not by
any means an unflattering reward for sinning. If Adam had not
sinned there would be no need for Christ's atonement. Are we to be
grateful to Adam? The paradox is shudderingly complete, cannot
be unsaid, will not dissolve into redefinition. This is its major key; in
a minor key, it takes the form of an acceptance that out of sorrow
will come joy; indeed, only out of "the sorrow that endureth for
ever" comes "the pleasure that abideth for a moment." If, as Wilde
suggests, "the meaning of joy in art" is "making sorrow musical,"
then do we wish sorrow and suffering, a share of infinity and a part
of knowledge, a perpetually anguished psychic tension, on the
artist? Do we wish the artist metaphorically to lose his life—or his
sanity—in order to find it? Ecstasy and suffering are intimately
related, as St. Teresa and Crashaw and Bernini knew so well.

> O how oft shalt thou complain
> Of a sweet and subtle pain!
> Of intolerable joys!
> Of a death, in which who dies
> Loves his death, and dies again.
> And would for ever so be slain!
> And lives, and dies; and knows not why
> To live, but that he thus may never leave to die.[28]

There is much that looks forward to Keats in this perception of
Crashaw's; it was this aspect of Keats that especially fascinated

Wilde. It was Hugo von Hofmannsthal who elaborated more completely the implications of this kind of paradox with respect to Wilde's life and career, as well as to aesthetic comprehension as a spiritual exercise.

> We must not degrade life by tearing character and fate asunder and separating [Wilde's] misfortune from his fortune. We must not pigeonhole everything. Everything is everywhere. There are tragic elements in superficial things and trivial in the tragic. There is something suffocatingly sinister in what we call pleasure. There is something lyrical about the dress of a whore and something commonplace about the emotions of a lyrical poet. Everything dwells simultaneously in man. He is full of poisons that rage against one another. There are certain islands whose savage inhabitants pierce the bodies of their dead relatives with poisoned arrows, to make sure that they are dead. This is an ingenious way of expressing metaphorically a profound thought and of paying homage to the profundity of Nature without much ado. For in truth the slowly killing poisons and the elixir of gently smouldering bliss all lie side by side in our living body. No one thing can be excluded, none considered too insignificant to become a very great power. Seen from the viewpoint of life, there is not one thing extraneous to the Whole. Everything is everywhere. Everything partakes of the dance of life.
>
> In the words of Jalal-ud-din Rumi, "He who knows the power of the dance of life fears not death. For he knows that love kills."[29]

Sufism, which flourished in the west during the late nineteenth century in the form elaborated by the thirteenth century Persian poet proposed that suffering was the essential condition for joyous union with the sources of power and love; suffering was an aspect of the mystic union of the human bridegroom with the Divine bride. The romantic poets, especially Wordsworth and Keats, had seen this, and Wilde (following Baudelaire, especially) transposed it into an aesthetic of exquisitely paradoxical charms.

There is something unnatural about all of this, something perverse, something that defies logic. Something *à rebours*. But then, there was something quite unnatural about the romantic infatuation with obsessive self-consciousness, which culminated in such images as the Wordsworthian solitary, the Shelleyan questor and the Byronic hero, and which included sorrow and suffering as an initiation into the "nature of infinity." With this intense self-consciousness comes intense isolation, as, in Pater's words,

we continue to dwell in thought on this world, not of objects in
the solidity with which language invests them, but of impressions,
unstable, flickering, inconsistent, which burn and are extinguished
with our consciousness of them . . . the whole scope of observation
is dwarfed to the narrow chamber of the individual mind. . . . Every
one of those impressions is the impression of the individual in his
isolation, each mind keeping as a solitary prisoner its own dream
of a world.[30]

Other than in death, one escape from this prison was paradoxically
inwards, the (in this case unsuccessful) quest of the poet of *Alastor*
for his own image, with as its grail a union of the poet with his
opposing self (another aspect or a projection, depending upon
one's psychology), and a consequent escape from the cocoon of
"spinning selfhood" that Blake had described so vividly.

If the quest of and for the self offered one escape from the
terrible isolation that Pater described, the questioning of and
for the self provided another, and one with a very long history.
Milton, calling on "the Cherub Contemplation" to the accompaniment of the violated and mute Philomel, provides the
most familiar example, as he asks that his

> Lamp at midnight hour,
> Be seen in some high lonely Towr,
> Where I may oft out-watch the *Bear*,
> With thrice great Hermes, or unsphear
> The spirit of Plato to unfold
> What Worlds, or what vast Regions hold
> The immortal mind that hath forsook
> Her mansion in this fleshly nook:
> And of those *Daemons* that are found
> In fire, air, flood, or under ground,
> Whose power hath a true consent
> With Planet, or with Element.[31]

Retiring to the "watch-tower" became a common enough Romantic ploy, but the questions that arose as the poet sat musing the
obscure were not always contemplated with equanimity, nor were
they always the same questions. Wordsworth's perplexity (despite
the fact that he occasionally shared a "maniac's anxiousness") was
predominantly wistful and elegiac, though he often became confused as to exactly where the question that perplexed him came

from. Coleridge, with that staggeringly naive honesty that charac-terized his mind, could only avoid the awful questions that he raised by leaving the room, as it were, to attend to the man from Porlock, either exiting with a rhetorical flourish or leaving his "speculation" unfinished, a perfect Pierrot of the mind. Keats was ready to ask and answer and had a set of wonderful images and dialectical skills at hand to deploy where he might; but he died before he had a full opportunity. Each poet, however much he left the stamp of his personality on his musings, also opened up the world of the "Daemons that are found . . . [and] whose power hath a true consent," and directed our gaze to the dark and deep truths that can be discovered there, if only the right questions can be asked. They left a legacy that deeply influenced the nineteenth century, and especially those of Wilde's circle. W. B. Yeats, born into the midst of this questioning and one of the most persistent questioners, settled for "mummy truths," the logical solution when the truths are not disclosed in images of routine availability.

> Whereat the living mock,
> Though not for sober ear,
> For maybe all that hear
> Should laugh and weep an hour upon the clock.
>
> Such thought—such thought have I that hold it tight
> Till meditation master all its parts,
> Nothing can stay my glance
> Until that glance run in the world's despite
> To where the damned have howled away their hearts,
> And where the blessed dance;
> Such thought, that in it bound
> I need no other thing,
> Wound in mind's wandering
> As mummies in the mummy-cloth are wound.[32]

Such meditation, following a well-trodden path, concentrates on the parts, the particulars, until eventually it is joined in the universal comprehension. This process has a direct analogy in a crucial, and final, aspect of nineteenth-century aesthetics, the way in which the particular instance (or ideal) that is the symbol coalesces with the universal idea that the symbol reveals and illuminates by the impression that it makes upon us. (The paradox in this is the implicit identification of the whole with the part, the infinite with the finite.) Romantic critics such as Coleridge and Goethe had defined symbols using the notions of the particular and the universal, and symbols were understood at the end of the nineteenth century as they had been defined at the beginning, as "consubstantial with the truths, of which they are the *conductors* ... an actual and essential part of that, the whole of which [they] represent."

> A symbol [which is always tautegorical] is characterized by a translucence of the Special in the Individual or of the General in the Special or of the Universal in the General. Above all by the translucence of the Eternal through and in the Temporal. It always partakes of the Reality which it renders intelligible; and while it enunciates the whole, abides itself as a living part of that Unity, of which it is the representative.[33]

What makes this somewhat numbing definition important is that, as one discovers with so many of Coleridge's definitions, it has application (as indeed it arose) in fields far from the purely literary. By the late nineteenth century, and in particular under the influence of Pater, an aesthetic philosophy was of little interest unless it could be transformed into a theory of cultural rebirth, and in particular into an image of the Renaissance. In this case, what was significant was the concept of a "radically implicit" universal which could not be abstracted from its particular context. Goethe, more than any other poet, made this kind of universality the governing condition of his poetry and held that the world is intrinsically symbolic, each

> quality, character, happening [being] at once concrete event [Phänomen] and archetype [Urphänomen] ... [which] exists only in and through the particular, and hence can be known only by opening our eyes and ears and hearts to the sensuous living world.

There is something very akin to the "figural" in Goethe's distinction between symbolism and allegory:

> It makes a great difference whether the poet starts with a universal idea and then looks for suitable particulars, or beholds the universal *in* the particular. The former method produces allegory, where the particular has status merely as an instance, an example of the universal. The latter, by contrast, is what reveals poetry in its true

nature: it speaks forth a particular without independently thinking
of or referring to a universal, but in grasping the particular in its
living character it implicitly apprehends the universal along with
it.[34]

This kind of distinction, furthermore, is reasonably analogous to
the distinction between (in the latter case) an artist who beholds
the subject in the form, and one who proceeds from a subject or
idea and then scouts about for a suitable form in which to display
it; and it was this distinction which was so important to nineteenth
century aesthetic and cultural theory. The natural and social
sciences, as well, attempted to operate after the latter fashion,
though what they apprehended was a law, a special sort of universal.

Coleridge devoted a considerable amount of his time and energy to the analysis of particulars and universals, and of the ways
in which symbols unite both in one entity. His descriptions of the
Bible and his descriptions of Shakespeare's work are, for example,
quite similar in praising "that union and interpenetration of the
universal and the particular, which must ever pervade all works of
decided genius and true science." For Coleridge, religion provided
the only form in which universal truths attained particular reality
(or beauty); and if "in its too exclusive devotion to the *specific* and
individual it neglects to interpose the contemplation of the *universal,* [it] changes its being into Superstition," and becomes

> more and more earthly and servile, as more and more estranged
> from the one in all, [and] goes wandering at length with its pack
> of amulets, bead-rolls, periapts, fetisches, and the like pedlary, on
> pilgrimmages to Loretto, Mecca, or the temple of Jaggernaut, arm
> in arm with sensuality on the one hand and self-torture on the
> other, followed by a motley group of friars, pardoners, faquirs,
> gamesters, flaggelants, mountebanks, and harlots.[35]

This kind of fate threatened cultures as well as religions; in the
scriptures of both, "Facts and Persons (or artifacts and institutions) must of necessity have a two-fold significance, a past and a
future, a temporary and a perpetual, a particular and a universal
application. They must be at once Portraits and Ideals."

Now Wilde, and of course Pater, proceeded from precisely
these assumptions. What is often lost sight of is the fascination

of this period with stages of imaginative as well as social development, and with the origin of imaginative structures and beliefs. Wilde was fond of reflecting that "all great ideas seem to be cradled at their birth . . . in theological form." Furthermore, he felt with Plutarch that "while science brings the supernatural down to the natural, yet ultimately all that is natural is really supernatural," and he quoted as unlikely confirmation the opinion of Herbert Spencer that "when the equation of life has been reduced to its lowest terms the symbols are symbols still." It is fairly easy to see that he would probably find little to fault in Coleridge's declaration that

> in all the ages and countries of civilization Religion has been the parent and fosterer of the Fine Arts, as of Poetry, Music, Painting &c. the common essence of which consists in a similar union of the Universal and the Individual. In this union, moreover, is contained the true sense of the Ideal. Under the old Law the altar, the curtains, the priestly vestments, and whatever else was to represent the BEAUTY OF HOLINESS, had an *ideal* character: and the Temple itself was a masterpiece of Ideal Beauty.[36]

Wilde lived in an age in which, despite many earnest attempts, traditional Christianity could no longer easily be reconciled with the classical tradition and aspects of the later humanistic revivals of it such as the Renaissance. This being so, it was all the more important that the new culture of the time, and its altars and curtains, documents and monuments, must embody the ideas and represent the ideals that this 'new republic' embraced. Moreover, *only* within this cultural coherence would there be produced those "masterpieces of Ideal Beauty" which would represent to the world the beauty not of holiness but of (Keatsian) truth.

This interest in ideal forms depended upon a particular kind of apprehension of reality and a certain philosophical disposition. By the end of the nineteenth century there was sufficient scepticism about the value of any orthodoxy, least of all a philosophical one, to mitigate overly doctrinaire approaches. Yet the value of critical judgment and the high store that was set by the finely developed critical spirit are too often forgotten in the enthusiasm for the artistic and cultural achievements of the age. The diversity and the energy that characterized both were the product of a critical awareness and an imaginative approach to one's subject. Though we may tend to emphasize the critical intelligence as it operated in scientific or philosophical areas, aesthetic criticism had since Johnson and Coleridge included within its province all that was increasingly seen to matter. "In aesthetic criticism attitude is everything," Wilde had asserted, adding that

> just as it is only in art-criticism, and through it, that we can apprehend the Platonic theory of ideas, so it is only in art-criticism, and through it, that we can realise Hegel's system of contraries. The truths of metaphysics are the truths of masks.[37]

Hegel's "system of contraries" was a system of progressive revelation of the truth (and the beauty) which inhered in the imaginative fusion of opposites, the opposites which defined human experience and perception. In perpetual flux there is coherence and order; the subjective and the objective depend upon each other for their definition; form and matter are separable yet inextricably and inexplicably linked in an indissoluble union; music combines unity and variety and, when we contemplate the ideal "music of the spheres," we possess the ultimate conception of a single harmonious order and the infinite variety of the cosmos—these are only some of the themes which a consideration of Hegel had brought to a focus. But this focus was sharpened by a contemporaneous adaptation of Hegelian dialectic to Platonic dialogue, and even to the Darwinian struggle for survival, especially when it was further suggested (by Benjamin Jowett among others) that "the struggle for existence is not confined to the animals, but appears in the kingdom of thought." In this kingdom, ideas eventually prevail, ideas informed and authenticated by the imaginative spirit of man, the same spirit that can hear the "music of the spheres," and that recognizes that the beauty of harmony and proportion corresponds to the truth of the purest instincts, the most moral impulses, of the self. It is this sort of conception that generates such opinions as Wilde's that "it is the spectator and not life that art really mirrors."

Ideally, then, art should mirror "the accumulated capital of the whole experience of humanity." This will only be possible, however, if the spectator is informed by a critical sensitivity to the forms in which that experience is communicated

> For he to whom the present is the only thing that is present, knows nothing of the age in which he lives. To realise the nineteenth century, one must realise every century that has preceded it and that has contributed to its making. To know anything about oneself one must know all about others. . . . Do you think that it is the imagination that enables us to live these countless lives? Yes: it is the imagination; and the imagination is the result of heredity. It is simply concentrated race-experience. . . . The culture that this transmission of racial experiences makes possible can be made perfect by the critical spirit alone, and indeed may be said to be one with it. For who is the true critic but he who bears within himself the dreams, and ideas, and feelings of myriad generations, and to whom no form of thought is alien, no emotional impulse obscure? . . . The contemplative life, the life that has for its aim not *doing* but *being*, and not *being* merely, but *becoming*—that is what the critical spirit can give us. The gods live thus: either brooding over their own perfection, as Aristotle tells us, or, as Epicurus fancied, watching with the calm eyes of the spectator the tragi-comedy of the world that they have made.[38]

CHAPTER FIVE

THE CRY OF MARSYAS

*I am sorry to leave with a cry of pain—a
song of Marsyas, not a song of Apollo; but
Life, that I have loved so much—too much
—has torn me like a tiger, so when you
come and see me, you will see the ruin and
wreck of what once was wonderful and brilliant, and terribly improbable.*

OSCAR WILDE

In a letter to Carlos Blacker written in March, 1898, Wilde
likened *The Ballad of Reading Gaol* to "a song of Marsyas, not
a song of Apollo," and in *De Profundis* he reflected that

> when Marsyas was "torn from the scabbard of his limbs". . . he had
> no more song, the Greeks said. Apollo had been victor. The lyre
> had vanquished the reed. But perhaps the Greeks were mistaken.
> I hear in much modern Art the cry of Marsyas. It is bitter in
> Baudelaire, sweet and plaintive in Lamartine, mystic in Verlaine.
> It is in the deferred resolutions of Chopin's music. It is in the
> discontent that haunts the recurrent faces of Burne-Jones's
> women. Even Matthew Arnold, whose song of Callicles tells of
> "the triumph of the sweet persuasive lyre," and the "famous final
> victory," in such a clear note of lyrical beauty—even he, in the
> troubled undertone of doubt and distress that haunts his verse, has
> not a little of it.[1]

Wilde had long displayed a fascination with the legend of foolish Marsyas who, as a master of the flute, challenged Apollo, the patron god of the lyre, and in defeat was flayed alive for his affront. The cry of Marsyas was a cry of almost comic despair, for Marsyas in defeat was a true grotesque; his skin, which was hung outside the cave from which the river Marsyas issued, was said to dance with joy at the sound of a flute. The most effective nineteenth-century generalization of the predicament of Marsyas was the figure of Pierrot, and Wilde's version of his own dilemma as he fought against madness in the company of his fellow prisoners was that "we are the zanies of sorrow. We are clowns whose hearts are broken. We are specially designed to appeal to the sense of humour."

But there was more than a sense of humour involved, though that was always central in Wilde's imaginative vision of reality. Marsyas was a Silenus or primitive woodland god of Phrygian origin who, because he played the flute, was associated with the worship of Dionysus and Cybele; in his contest with Apollo he often was known as Pan. English literature took seriously his story as a subject from the late sixteenth century, though Pan as a patron of ruminants figures in earlier post-classical literature. Geoffrey Whitney presented a *Choice of Emblems* in 1586, one of which was the "perverse judgment" of Midas, who in the contest between Apollo and Marsyas (or Pan) decided in favour of the flute. He was overruled by the Muses, and punished for his stupidity:

Presumptuous Pan, did strive Apollos skill to passe:
But Midas gave the palme to Pan: wherefore the eares of asse
Apollo gave the Judge: which doth all Judges teache
To judge with knowledge, and advise, in matters paste their reache.[2]

Wilde recognized in Pan an emblem of rich potential, especially when the opposition between Pagan and Christian values was only one of several polarities—between hedonistic and moralistic attitudes, for example, or between the world of romance and the world of science—that preoccupied the age, and within the structures of which Pan nicely ruled one half. He would know of the earliest literary cult of Pan in the pages of the *Greek Anthology*, which he often recommended, and his celebration of the Arcadian virtues of which Pan provided an image and which were possibly lost forever was at least in his early work quite conventional.

> The Gods are dead: no longer do we bring
>> To grey-eye Pallas crowns of olive-leaves!
>> Demeter's child no more hath tithe of sheaves,
> And in the noon the careless shepherds sing,
> For Pan is dead, and all the wantoning
>> By secret glade and devious haunt is o'er:
>> Young Hylas seeks the water-springs no more;
> Great Pan is dead, and Mary's son is King.
>
> And yet—perchance in this sea-tranced isle,
>> Chewing the bitter fruit of memory,
>> Some God lies hidden in the asphodel.
> Ah Love! if such there be, then it were well
>> For us to fly his anger: nay, but see,
>> The leaves are stirring: let us watch awhile.
>> (Santa Decca)

He played this tune many times; he sang to Theocritus, the "singer of Persephone," in a villanelle that was later included by Gleeson White in 1887 in a very influential collection of *Ballades and Rondeaus, Chants Royal, Sestinas, Villanelles, etc.*, which bore witness to the interest generated by Andrew Lang's *Lays and Lyrics of Old France* (1870). (The first poem in Gleeson White's collection was one entitled "Where are the Pipes of Pan.") Elsewhere, Wilde wrote of "Panthea" in quite recognizably Wordsworthian tones, predicting that "new splendour [shall] come unto the flower, new glory to the grass." Indeed, his image of the spirit that rolls through all things foreshadows remarkably the poetic instincts of *The Ballad of Reading Gaol:*

> for we are part
> Of every rock and bird and beast and hill,
> One with the things that prey on us, and one with
> what we kill.[3]

We have, then, two images: the first, of Pan (or Marsyas) challenging the authority of Apollo, taking up and transforming the possibilities of a new instrument, humiliated and rejected by orthodoxy, yet becoming symbolic of a kind of melancholy rebellion, a pure expression of the artistic impulse. The second image

is of Pan the goat-god, nourished by and nourishing pastoral retreats as well as the energies and intensities of primitive forces,
filled with ardour for the Arcadian nymph Syrinx, who was
changed into a reed when she came to a river (Ladon) in her flight
from his attentions. She was further transformed into "Pan's pipe"
when the god, who was, in Keats's words, "full of sweet desolation
—balmy pain," delighted in the exquisitely tender and mournful
sound that he produced on the reed.

It was Elizabeth Barrett Browning who gave the Victorian age
its more explicit and most capable literary statement of the theme
of "The Dead Pan" in her poem of 1844; its transformation by
Nietzsche into the claim that Dionysus is dead, or more precisely
that "Die Tragödie is tot!" is its best known cultural counterpart.
But it was in her long narrative poem *Aurora Leigh*, which Wilde
praised so highly, that a more Wildean note emerges:

> Good love, howe'er ill-placed,
> Is better for a man's soul in the end,
> Than if he loved ill what deserves love well.
> A pagan, kissing, for a step of Pan,
> The wild-goat's hoof-print on the loamy down,
> Exceeds our modern thinker who turns back
> The strata . . . granite, limestone, coal, and clay,
> Concluding coldly with, "Here's law! where's God?"[4]

It is a somewhat earnest hedonism, to be sure, but nonetheless
there are the seeds of that celebration of the union of desire and
satisfaction in art and life that Pater would crystallize and the next
generation extend.

Pan as a repudiator of authority provided another image that
linked his pastoral role more closely with his appearance as Marsyas. One of the numerous writers on the "nineties," Osbert
Burdett, recognized what he called "The Beardsley Period" as
representing "the return of Pan":

> Mr. Thomas Hardy has remarked that there is no better sign of the
> vitality of art than the delight of its master-spirits in grotesque.
> One reason why Beardsley was great was that he shared and
> indulged this impulse to the full. The true artistic criticism of
> Victorian art is that it lacked this playfulness, that it created a
> convention in which there was no room for the grotesque; the final

gaiety (even in Dickens) was beyond its power. It barely tolerated
Punch, until it had made him a pillar of respectable society. It is
the only recent age that attempted to ignore Pan and Punch and
Pierrot. The Beardsley period was the moment of their long-
delayed revenge.[5]

Even the comic opera of Gilbert and Sullivan caught the spirit;
in *Patience*, there is a call to

> Let the merry cymbals sound,
> Gaily pipe Pandean pleasure
> With a Daphnephoric bound
> Tread a gay but classic measure.

Somewhat earlier in the century, William Hazlitt had given a
more general assessment of English Romantic literature as

> Gothic and grotesque; unequal and irregular. . . . It aims at an
> excess of beauty or power. . . . Our understanding is not . . . smooth
> . . . but full of knotty points and jutting excrescences, rough,
> uneven, overgrown with brambles; and I like this aspect of mind
> . . . where nature keeps a good deal of the soil in her own hands.
> Perhaps the genius of our poetry has more of Pan than of Apollo;
> "but Pan is a God, Apollo is no more."[6]

The competition between the lyre and the flute again informs the
image, with the Parnassian laurel of Apollo and the artistic perfection and noble beauty of his music juxtaposed with the earthy
passion and melancholy ecstasy of Pan. Wilde's remark that "the
singer of life is not Apollo but Marsyas" is in this tradition, which
runs directly from Shelley (with his companion Hymns of Pan and
of Apollo) and Keats (who begins his poetic development in "the
realm of Flora and old Pan"). By the time it reaches Wilde, he
is able to make routine distinctions between "the strength of the
lyre [and] the sweetness of the pipe," and to speak of how pleasant
it is "sometimes to leave the summit of Parnassus to look at the
wild-flowers in the valley, and to turn from the lyre of Apollo to
listen to the reed of Pan." Yet it is with considerable emphasis that
he proposes that the age in which he writes may be symbolized
by, or be the symbol of, the cry of Marsyas and the piping of Pan,
and thereby embody the most creatively awkward of confusions
between life and art. There is a redefinition underway, quite
clearly; the most extreme example is in Nietzsche's identification

of Dionysus (in whose train Pan followed) as the god of music, of
enthusiasm and ecstasy and the truth about human existence—
that it is defined by sorrow and suffering. Apollonian versions of
experience, on the other hand, are imagistic reflections or imita-
tions (however perfect) rather than direct expressions (however
unpolished).[7] The Dionysian association was an obvious extension
of an identification of Dionysus with the dithyramb, a hymn
(celebrating his sufferings) sung at the festivals of his worship to
the accompaniment of a flute and a dance around the altar. There
is an apparent contradiction inherent in Wilde's celebration of the
cry of Marsyas, for in another scheme he did not much wish to
be the singer of life, but rather the singer of art. The key to the
puzzle is deceptively simple, as we shall see, and depends upon his
conviction that sorrow and fear are both the fundamental condition of life and the standard for—indeed provide the basis for the
celebration of joy in—all great art.

It was Coleridge who described the more unsettling aspects
of Pan in a way that was part of this reinterpretation of the
nature and function of art, as he spoke of

> the idea of the mysterious Pan, as representing intelligence
> blended with a darker power, deeper, mightier, and more uni-
> versal than the conscious intellect of man—than intelligence.[8]

This conception was pervasive in the latter part of the nineteenth century, and it is fairly easy to see why. It derives from
the Orphic version of the story of Pan, which emphasized his
universality; the Homeric version tended to concentrate on his
pastoral associations. While a somewhat sentimental pastoral
enthusiasm was certainly never far from the scene, the last
decades of the century witnessed a clear emphasis on urban
rather than rural verities, and in this scheme a more profound
and psychologically involved Pan was a considerably more compelling image. It was not such a long step, but nonetheless an
important one, to associating fear and terror with Pan as the
soul of all (and hence compounded of good and evil). Robert
Louis Stevenson spoke of the "wizard strains, divine yet bru-
tal" of Pan; and many poets—Swinburne foremost among
them—took Wordsworth's notion of beauty and fear fostering
the creative imagination and extended it to a gothic fusion of

ecstasy and terror in an intensity that could be called panic.

Perhaps the most basic dilemma, and certainly the one which was at least superficially apparent in the chorus that "Pan is dead," had to do not with art but with religion. If Pan was dead then Christ must be alive, went the logic. Of course, the Victorian age liked to have it both ways and would cry "Pan is still alive" almost as often as "Pan is dead," for there were dialectical oppositions in the psyche as well as in society that were generally recognized and could not easily be denied. (Wilde forced the issue somewhat in *The Sphinx* by stating that "only one God has ever died;" but the statement, like the poem itself, was left rather unresolved.) What was unique in Wilde's later work, and specifically in *De Profundis*, was his implicit suggestion that the birth and death of Christ prompted the rebirth of Pan, for all that is associated with Christ can also be associated with the strange, sorrowful, terrifying, joyous martyrdom of Pan. It was G. K. Chesterton, suitably enough in a book on *William Blake*, who made this association explicit, equating Pan with primitive Dionysian energy and with the wonder and mystery of the recesses of the forest or the mind. He suggested that not Christ but Roman rationalism killed Pan and that when Christ was born Pan "began to stir in his grave." Wilde associates the cry of Marsyas, the challenger of Apollo, with the artist's need to find expression, for

> expression is as necessary to me as leaf and blossom are to the black branches of the trees that show themselves above the prison wall and are so restless in the wind. Between my art and the world there is now a wide Gulf, but between Art and myself there is none. I hope at least that there is none.[9]

Furthermore, Wilde associates Christ—who, as he says, like "the lunatic, the lover and the poet" are "of imagination all compact" —with the same impulses.

> Wherever there is a romantic movement in Art, there somehow, and under some form, is Christ, or the soul of Christ. He is in *Romeo and Juliet*, in the *Winter's Tale*, in Provençal poetry, in "The Ancient Mariner," in "La Belle Dame sans Merci," and in Chatterton's "Ballad of Charity."
>
>   We owe to him the most diverse things and people. Hugo's *Les Misérables*, Baudelaire's *Fleurs du Mal*, the note of pity in Russian novels, the stained glass and tapestries and quattrocento work of

Burne-Jones and Morris, Verlaine and Verlaine's poems, belong to
him no less than the Tower of Giotto, Lancelot and Guinevere,
Tannhäuser, the troubled romantic marbles of Michael Angelo,
pointed architecture, and the love of children and flowers.[10]

Wilde's vision of Christ is complex, but through it runs a single
theme, of Christ as the image of the Man of Sorrows—"despised
and rejected of men . . . and acquainted with grief"—the supreme
poet, the perfect individualist, the triumphant expression of
"truth in art [which] is the unity of a thing with itself: the outward
rendered expressive of the inward: the soul made incarnate: the
body instinct with spirit." If there was one central insight upon
which Wilde based his mature reflections, it was that "sorrow,
being the supreme emotion of which man is capable, is at once
the type and test of all great art."

Wilde came to his own particular terms with art and life while
in cell C.3.3 Reading Gaol, and explicitly in his long and at times
understandably bitter *apologia* written to Lord Alfred Douglas
and later published (originally in an expurgated form) as *De Profundis*. It was a place and a time of anguish for Wilde, and that
fact undoubtedly coloured his reflections. But it was also a time
and a place that concentrated his mind wonderfully and provided
him with an occasion on which to celebrate the symbolic relationships between himself and the art and culture to which his life
belonged. In his earlier days, Wilde used to quote the remark of
Hegel's with which William Wallace had introduced his
Prolegomena, that "the condemnation which a great man lays
upon the world is to force it to explain him." Now he was forced
to explain himself; but that was agreeable as well, in a way, for he
had always thought of the confessional mode as central to much
of the best art and criticism. It was, perhaps, rather too easy for
Oscar to fancy himself as "despised and rejected of men, a man
of sorrows and acquainted with grief: and [men] hid as it were
[their] faces from him." It is not a congenial association: Oscar
Wilde—deploying wit and paradox to decorate a life of idleness
and pleasure—as the servant of Isaiah. Indeed, H. Montgomery
Hyde concludes his recent biography of Wilde with Bernard
Shaw's appeal to

please let us hear no more of the tragedy of Oscar Wilde. Oscar
was no tragedian. He was the superb comedian of his century, one
to whom misfortune, disgrace, imprisonment were external and
traumatic. His gaiety of soul was invulnerable.[11]

But Shaw, though he saw that "there was more laughter between
the lines of [De Profundis] than in a thousand farces by men of
no genius," also recognized that "Wilde, like Richard and Shakespeare," found in himself no pity for himself. And he cautioned
that "let those who may complain that [Wilde's testament] was
only on paper remember that only on paper has humanity yet
achieved glory, beauty, truth, knowledge, virtue and abiding
love."[12]

We can dismiss Wilde's retrospective reflections at our peril, for
to do so is to dismiss that which gives his "gaiety of soul" an
exquisite sense of being besieged by suffering and sadness. It is a
sense that is embodied in so many of the emblems of the period
for, like Ishmael in *Moby Dick*, Wilde suspected that

the sun hides not the ocean, which is the dark side of this earth,
and which is two thirds of this earth. So, therefore, that mortal
man who hath more of joy than sorrow in him, that mortal man
cannot be true—not true, or undeveloped. With books the same.
The truest of all men was the Man of Sorrows, and the truest of
all books is Solomon's, and Ecclesiastes is the fine hammered steel
of woe. "All is vanity." ALL. This wilful world hath not got hold
of unchristian Solomon's wisdom yet.[13]

Speaking *de profundis* or *in partibus,* Wilde often went further,
and affirmed Ishmael's contention that "there is a Cat-
skill eagle in some souls that can alike dive down into the blackest
gorges, and soar out of them again and become invisible in the
sunny spaces." He was fascinated by the blackest gorges quite as
much as by the sunny spaces, and whether speaking of crime as
the signature or vice as the passport or melancholy as the test of
freedom, he auditioned for the role of the forsaken with sceptical
enthusiasm. This role was in a play both sacred and profane, as
secular as a story from the Bible, as religious as a comedy of
manners. It provided a wonderful opportunity for the development of a sense of personality and individuality through the paradoxical mechanism that art has always employed, that it is only
when man wears a mask that he displays his true self, for art is "a

veil rather than a mirror." The belief that a "mortal man who hath more of joy than sorrow in him, that mortal man cannot be true —not true, or undeveloped" was more intimately related to a late nineteenth-century view of personality and of cultural identity than is usually recognized, or usually admitted. Partly, this belief was a legacy of the type of the Romantic hero that culminated, for Wilde, in the Wandering Jew figure in the disguise of Melmoth and for whom sorrow and suffering were

> permanent, obscure, and dark
> And share[d] the nature of Infinity.[14]

"The world," as Wilde knew, "will never weary of watching [the] troubled soul in its progress from darkness to darkness." Partly also, it was a belief that derived from the renewed interest (that we have already touched upon) in the incapacity and indeed irrelevance of the active will, an interest that certainly had Romantic links but which had been given its most impressive form in the hesitations of Hamlet, and would be given its most compelling analysis in Freud's studies of the "night-side of nature." Furthermore, the "scientific principle of Heredity" had, as Wilde remarked,

> shown us that we are never less free than when we try to act. It has hemmed us round with the nets of the hunter, and written upon the wall the prophecy of our doom. We may not watch it, for it is within us. We may not see it, save in a mirror that mirrors the soul. It is Nemesis without her mask. It is the last of the Fates, and the most terrible. It is the only one of the Gods whose real name we know.[15]

It was Ernest Renan, in his life of Jesus, who gave the age of Wilde its most vivid portrait of a personality in whom sorrow and suffering were central and in whom the will was perceived as an instrument of a higher power. Wilde's own perception of the life of Jesus was very much informed by Renan's critical study, and he added to Renan's picture a sense of life interpreted according to the canons of art and a sense of art as embodying the central values which life displays—a sense of wonder at the idea that Christ,

> with the artistic nature of one to whom Sorrow and Suffering were modes through which he could realise his conception of the Beauti-

ful, [feeling] that an idea is of no value till it becomes incarnate
and is made an image, makes of himself the image of the Man of
Sorrows, and as such has fascinated and dominated Art as no Greek
god ever succeeded in doing . . .
The two deep suggestive figures of Greek mythology were, for
religion, Demeter, an earth-goddess, not one of the Olympians,
and, for art, Dionysus, the son of a mortal woman to whom
the moment of his birth had proved the moment of her death
also.[16]

It was to Demeter and Dionysus that Pater, before Wilde, had
turned with reverence, seeing in these figures a type of grief and
sacrifice which was of pervasive aesthetic inspiration, and seeing
in their cyclical joy—the return of Persephone to Demeter in the
spring, and the awakening or unbinding of Dionysus to the fruit-
fulness and delirium of summer—an image of cultural as well as
artistic renewal. Pater's essays were of profound influence on
Wilde and many other writers of a later time; D. H. Lawrence's
essay "David" (1919), for example, is indebted to and in parts
almost a rewriting of Pater's "Study of Dionysus."

Pater's essay on Dionysus is subtitled "The Spiritual Form of
Fire and Dew," and is a richly varied description of the origin and
significance of Dionysus in Greek worship. He is fire-born, the son
of lightning, for his mortal mother Semele was destroyed by the
lightning of her lover Zeus, the father of Dionysus.

> In thinking of Dionysus as fire-born, the Greeks apprehend and
> embody the sentiment, the poetry, of all tender things which grow
> out of a hard soil, or in any sense blossom before the leaf, like the
> little mozereon-plant of English gardens, with its pale-purple,
> wine-scented flowers upon the leafless twigs in February, or like the
> almond-trees of Tuscany, or Aaron's rod that budded, or the staff
> in the hand of the Pope when Tannhäuser's repentance is ac-
> cepted.[17]

Dionysus's second birth is of the dew, which protects him as the
influence of the cooling clouds, the lower part or "thigh" of his
father the sky, protects the plant which Dionysus originally inhab-
ited in the primitive stages of his worship.

> The nursery, where Zeus places [Dionysus] to be brought up, is a
> cave in Mount Nysa, sought by a misdirected ingenuity in many
> lands, but really, like the place of the carrying away of Persephone,

a place of fantasy, the oozy place of springs in the hollow of the
hillside, nowhere and everywhere, where the vine was "invented."

Pater expands his discussion to include the multitude of concep-
tions of Dionysus that provided such a rich source of artistic
inspiration. He mentions, for example,

one element, which his connexion with the satyrs, Marsyas being
one of them, and with Pan, from whom the flute passed to all the
shepherds of Theocritus, alike illustrates, his interest, namely, in
one of the great species of music. . . . As Apollo inspires and rules
over all the music of strings, so Dionysus inspires and rules over all
the music of the reed, the water-plant, in which the ideas of water
and of vegetable life are brought close together, natural property,
therefore, of the spirit of life in the green sap. . . . The religion of
Dionysus was, for those who lived in it, a complete religion, a
complete sacred representation of the whole of life; and as, in his
relation to the vine, he fills for them the place of Demeter . . . so,
in this other phase of his being, in his relation to the reed, he fills
for them the place of Apollo; he is the inherent cause of music and
poetry; he inspires; he explains the phenomena of enthusiasm
. . . the secrets of possession by a higher and more energetic spirit
than one's own, the gift of self-revelation, of passing out of oneself
through words, tones, gestures.

Pater's description brings in further analogies to the particular
enthusiasms of Wilde's time. He recounts how "we may trace his
coming from Phrygia, the birthplace of the more mystical elements of Greek religion, over the mountains of Thrace . . . over
the hills of Parnassus . . . to Thebes . . . at last to Athens, at an
assignable date, under Peisistratus; out of the country, into the
town." And so Dionysus becomes urbane, and begins

to contribute through the arts to the adornment of life, yet perhaps
also in part to weaken it, relaxing ancient austerity. Gradually, his
rough country feasts will be outdone by the feasts of the town; and
as comedy arose out of those, so these will give rise to tragedy. For
his entrance upon this new stage of his career, his coming into the
town, is from the first tinged with melancholy, as if in entering the
town he had put off his country peace. The other Olympians are
above sorrow. Dionysus, like a strenuous mortal hero, like Hercules
or Perseus, has his alternations of joy and sorrow, of struggle and
hard-won triumph. It is out of the sorrows of Dionysus, then—of
Dionysus in winter—that all Greek tragedy grows.

The idea of a summer and a winter Dionysus was central to the tale and became in ways (suitable to their respective attachments to the grape and to the grain) identical with that of Demeter.

The association of Dionysus with Persephone, and with Demeter, belongs here; and, as Pater suggested, "no chapter in the history of human imagination is more curious than the myth of Demeter, and Kore or Persephone"; "one of the few myths," James Frazer remarked, "in which the sunshine and clarity of the Greek genius are crossed by the shadow and mystery of death." In the earliest phase of the myth, Demeter is the earth "in the fixed order of its annual changes, but also in all the accident and detail of the growth and decay of its children." The transition to a poetic interpretation was subtle and smooth; her daughter (by her brother Zeus) was Persephone, who as a maiden—her name in this role was often Kora—was taken off by Hades to the lower world with the consent of her father. Demeter searched for her daughter in vain and, in her grief, brought upon the earth a year of famine, until Zeus sent Hermes to persuade Hades to let Persephone return. This was allowed, but she had eaten part of a pomegranate that he had given her, signifying her marriage to him and her duty to spend two thirds of the year with her mother and the rest with her husband as the sinister goddess of death. The two images—of the goddess of summer and the goddess of death, Kora and Persephone—were joined in a complex stage of development of the myth, wherein death and resurrection are united in the same figure. Persephone is the daughter of the earth, to be sure, but

> the summer as bringing winter; the flowery splendour and consummated glory of the year, as thereafter immediately beginning to draw near to its end, as the first yellow leaf crosses it, in the first severer wind. . . . Her story is, indeed, but the story, in an intenser form, of Adonis, of Hyacinth, of Adrastus . . . of the English Sleeping Beauty. From being the goddess of summer and the flowers, she becomes the goddess of night and sleep and death, confuseable with Hecate, the goddess of midnight terrors.[18]

Dionysus too (whether sleeping or bound in winter, awake or released in summer) is twofold then—a *Döppelgänger;* like Persephone, he belongs to two worlds, and has much in common with her, and a full share of those dark possibilities which, even apart from the story of the rape, belong to her. He is a *Chthonian* god, and like all the children of the earth, has an element of sadness; like Hades himself, he is hollow and devouring, an eater of man's flesh—*sarcophagus*—the grave which consumed unaware the ivory-white shoulder of Pelops.

And you have no sooner caught a glimpse of this image, than a certain perceptible shadow comes creeping over the whole story; for, in effect, we have seen glimpses of the sorrowing Dionysus all along. Part of the interest of the Theban legend of his birth is that he comes of the marriage of a god with a mortal woman; and from the first, like merely mortal heroes, he falls within the sphere of human chances.

A further image of Dionysus is that of the hunter, storming on the hills in winter, bitter and terrible, his enemies torn to pieces by the sacred women (who eat, in mystical ceremony, raw flesh and drink the blood of the sacrificial victims at Halicarnassus), or by wild beasts, or by the fangs of cold. The ceremonies which were associated with Dionysus Zagreus became confused with the worship of Cybele (or Rhea) and Attis. To close the circle, we may recall that it is Marsyas who pipes to Cybele to console her for the death of Attis.

With Persephone, Dionysus personified the fears and the hopes of the mortal condition, embodied in the seasons of sorrow and joy. Dionysus, in a shadowy tradition, even becomes the son or brother of Persephone and has his place with her in the Eleusinian mysteries, as Iacchus. And Dionysus, like Persephone, comes to represent

a type of second birth . . . open[ing], in his series of annual changes, for minds on the look-out for it, the hope of a possible analogy, between the resurrection of nature, and something else, as yet unrealized, reserved for human souls; and the beautiful, weeping creature, vexed by the wind, suffering, torn to pieces, and rejuvescent again at last, like a tender shoot of living green out of the hardness and stony darkness of the earth, becomes an emblem or ideal of chastening and purification, and of final victory through suffering. It is the finer, mystical sentiment of the few, detached from the coarser and more material religion of the many, and accompanying it, through the course of its history, as its ethereal, less palpable, life-giving soul . . . with some unfixed, though real, place in the general scheme of Greek religion, this phase of the worship of Dionysus had its special development in the Orphic literature and mysteries.

It was this finer mystical sentiment to which Wilde always hoped that art would attach itself and with which he identified most completely in his later years. But it was never far from the centre of his thought.

> The Mystical in Art, the Mystical in Life, the Mystical in Nature —this is what I am looking for, and in the great symphonies of Music, in the initiation of Sorrow, in the depths of the sea I may find it. It is absolutely necessary for me to find it somewhere.[19]

In one of those wonderful touches that so often accompany Greek myth, it was the fair narcissus, the flower of death and sterile passion, that Persephone had just picked when she was carried away by Hades. What Pater especially wished to illustrate in his account of these figures was their embodiment of the central conditions of life and the most compelling conditions of art— conditions which are as paradoxical as the nature of Pan and as unavoidable as death. The evil aspect of nature was one perception, worshipped in part by the Greeks as Gaia, by the Phrygians as Cybele, by the Egyptians as Isis or Hathor, by the Babylonians as Ishtar, and described by Darwin in the 1840s as the "wilfully cruel" functioning of Dame Nature, "red in tooth and claw" as Tennyson suggested. "What a book a devil's chaplain might write on the clumsy, wasteful, blundering law, and horribly cruel works of nature," suggested Darwin later, in 1856, still compelled by a metaphor that the Greeks had transformed into myth. How much more a part of this paradoxical condition the human psyche might be was slowly being realized, as love and hate became recognized as offspring of the same instinct. Matthew Arnold, in his inaugural lecture (1857) as Professor of Poetry at Oxford, expressed his irritation at the Lucretian "depression and ennui" which characterized English poetry of his day. But other critics recognized it as a condition of life and art and, though they might not applaud its sentimental indulgence, still saw sorrow and suffering as defining the human condition and "making sorrow musical . . . the meaning of joy in art." Pater, and Wilde after him, knew that the truth about life which they could not avoid, and which gave imaginative coherence to art, had been given form by the Greeks and that this form was filled with wonderful possibilities. As Pater expressed it,

> the legend of Demeter and Persephone, perhaps the most popular of all Greek legends, is sufficient to show that the "worship of sorrow" was not without its function in Greek religion; their legend is a legend made by and for sorrowful, wistful, anxious people, while the most important artistic monuments of that legend sufficiently prove that the Romantic spirit was really at work in the minds of Greek artists, extracting by a kind of subtle alchemy, a beauty, not without the elements of tranquility, of dignity and order, out of a matter, at first sight painful and strange.

Painful and strange indeed was the story of Demeter and her daughter Persephone; it became profound when the dual nature of Persephone's significance—as the maiden of summer and vegetable life and the goddess of dreadful shadows and death—was linked with the character of Dionysus, who belonged to the world below as well as to the world above. In the fusion of these two aspects which the myths and the highest art accomplish, there emerges the possibility of which Pater was enamoured: of a hope for rebirth which is born out of death, a hope which (as Shelley realized in the unbinding of his bound god, Prometheus) "creates, from its own wreck, the thing it contemplates." This hope had cultural as well as individual and religious import, obviously; the concept of a renaissance was deeply ingrained in the consciousness of the age and came to the surface in the work of several generations of nineteenth-century writers, from Ruskin and Pater to Wilde and Shaw. When William Carlos Williams, the prophet of a later generation but the same tradition, announces in *Kora in Hell* (1920) that "out of bitterness itself the clear wine of the imagination will be pressed and the dance prosper thereby" we can recognize the Dionysiac rhythms upon which the (supreme) fiction of a new cultural coherence depends. But when he celebrates the dance, we are rather surprised at its frenzied ambiguity.

> THIS is the only up-cadence. This is where the secret rolls over and opens its eyes. Bitter words spoken to a child ripple in morning light! Boredom from a bedroom doorway thrills with anticipation!

The complaints of an old man dying piecemeal are starling chir-
rups. Coughs go singing on springtime paths across a field; corruption picks strawberries and slow warping of the mind, blacking the
deadly walls—counted and recounted—rolls in the grass and
shouts ecstatically. All is solved! The moaning and dull sobbing of
infants sets blood tingling and eyes ablaze to listen. Speed sings in
the heels at long nights tossing on coarse sheets with burning
sockets staring into the black. Dance! Sing! Coil and uncoil! Whip
yourselves about! Shout the deliverance![20]

The new integrations that are envisaged here had their counterpart in the integrations of contrary states which Dionysus and
Demeter and Persephone embodied, as well as in the psychological integrations of dissociated or divided sensibilities, and of opposing or second selves, which preoccupied the writers and artists
no less than the social scientists of the period.

It is the intensity and the tension of such a process of realization
that chiefly engages the imagination; ironically, it was a modified
and morbid version of the Narcissus legend, a form which was
imbued with the complexity of Dionysus and the ambiguity of
Persephone, that Wilde employed as the central motif in *The
Picture of Dorian Gray* to portray a realized disintegration, as
distinct from an imaginative integration.

Undoubtedly the vision that is supremely horrible for us all, perhaps in a broad sense the only vision that is horrible for any of us,
is that of Death. To say this is not to contradict that the evil second
self is always implicitly the Devil. Basically the Devil *is* Death; not
physical death but inward, spiritual deathfulness . . .
In *Dorian Gray* what we have . . . is the Narcissus legend reset in
the framework of Victorian England. . . . The youthful hero sees
his own image not in a mirrored reflection that his smallest touch
will destroy but in the apparently fixed and permanent form of a
picture. . . . This later Narcissus stares more deeply and sadly than
did the legendary one, and he does not become the victim of what
to the modern reader is a naive mistake. He does not fall in love
with "himself" (at this point the picture is nothing but a picture)
but with his own beauty, as it is revealed to him by Basil Hallward's
masterpiece. And at once this love brings him grief rather than joy,
for like Keats he knows that Beauty is accompanied by the hand-
maids Death and Decay, the processes of becoming ugly that are
inseparable from the process of becoming beautiful. He wishes that
in his case alone this inseparability might be broken, and trans-

ferred to the picture. Magically his wish is granted . . .
Thus far we have only a fairy tale; it is the psychological and moral
consequences of this miracle that constitute the real story.[21]

The inseparability of Beauty from Decay and Death, and of joy
from sorrow, is perhaps *the* major theme of the age of Oscar
Wilde; with it, and once again given compelling form by Pater,
there was the moral and spiritual as well as aesthetic ambiguity
associated with androgyny, the perfect fusion of opposites, the
perfect expression of beauty in decadence. One figure that Pater
chose to represent this paradox was the unworldly character—*sibi
unitus et simplificatus esse*—that he describes in his essay "Dia-
phaneitè" as representing a

> sort of entire transparency of nature that lets through uncon-
> sciously all that is really lifegiving in the established order of things;
> it detects without difficulty all sorts of affinities between its own
> elements and the nobler elements in that order. . . . [It] is revolu-
> tionist from the direct sense of personal worth, that pride of life,
> which to the Greek was a heavenly grace.

Art provides the opportunity for the individual to realize his identity, and to give form to his own sense of dignity and worth. But
what if the artist's conception of life and perception of himself is
essentially debased and fundamentally lacking in grace and hope?
Then, paradoxically, he cannot be a true decadent and artist, for
at the heart of darkness there must be light. It is in this perspective
that Baudelaire's anguished cry, which Wilde heard early and
remembered late, may be understood:

> O Seigneur, donnez-moi la force et le courage
> De contempler mon corps et ma coeur sans dégoût.

Whatever sentimentality may be apparent in Pater's description is quickly dispersed as he suggests that his "figure of the
capable imagination" displays a disturbing ambiguity,

> a moral sexlessness, a kind of impotence, an ineffectual wholeness
> of nature, yet with a divine beauty and significance of its own.
> Over and over again the world has been surprised by the hero-
> ism, the insight, the passion, of this clear crystal nature. Poetry and
> poetical history have dreamed of a crisis, where it must needs be
> that some human victim be sent down into the grave. These are
> they whom in its profound emotion humanity might choose to
> send. "What," says Carlyle, of Charlotte Corday, "what if she had

emerged from her secluded stillness, suddenly like a star; cruel-
lovely, with half-angelic, half-demonic splendour; to gleam for a
moment, and in a moment be extinguished; to be held in memory,
so bright complete was she, through long centuries!"[22]

Dionysiac sacrifice and suffering become conditions of change and
renewal and evolution of renaissance and rebirth. The finer spirit
is a refined spirit, purified in the fires of hell even as Kora is purified
each year and reintegrated even as the torn Dionysiac figure is in
one version of the myth reintegrated, with the return of the sun
under the aegis and in the person of Apollo, whose other names
—Phoebus and Lycius—make specific the traditional identification of Apollo as a god of light associated with brightness and
purity, the transparence of "a mind of taste lighted up by some
spiritual ray within." All of Pater's heros, from Denys L'Auxerrois
to Marius the Epicurean, display various versions of this opposition between dark and light, sorrow and joy, and various forms of
its Heraclitan transcendence.

There was another kind of opposition that fascinated the period, and that found a focus in the conception and image of
androgyny. The origins of this are obscure; religious sources supply
some patterns, especially the androgynyous Adam of occult and
mystical philosophy associated with such Judaeo-Christian traditions as the Kabbala, gnosticism, freemasonry, rosicrucianism and
the philosophy of Boehme, and Christ's androgyny has been a
staple of the mystical tradition from gnosticism and Boehme to
Blavatsky.[23] The image of the androgyne figures in the study of
alchemy, of which there was a revival in the 1870s and 1880s, and
C. G. Jung's *Psychology and Alchemy* describes the androgyne as
an archetype of the collective unconsciousness. Hovering in the
background is the pervasive myth of Narcissus, of powerful appeal
to Wilde and his cohorts.

When the nymph Echo pined away of unrequited love, she left
behind her more than a voice crying in the wilderness; she left both
a moral and a mystery. . . . But far more famous as an example of
this mystery is the sequel to Echo's story: that of the beautiful boy
who in his vanity broke her heart, and paid for his vanity with the
fact of his vanity, and in his enchantment with his own face faded

away in his turn, not into a voice but into a flower. The face that enchanted him, as either boy or flower, was of course his own; yet gazing up out of the fountain's surface into the down-gazing face above it, desired as object as the other as subject, it was *not* his own; indeed the separateness between these faces is no less important to the legend of Narcissus than is their sameness. What we are to deal with, then, is the mystery of a contradiction, of simultaneous distinction and identity, of an inescapable two that are at the same time an indisputable one.[24]

This "mystery of a contradiction" was imaged in the androgynous figure in various ways; most schematically, with two quite distinct implications. On the one hand there was the hermaphrodite as representing the perfect "union in love of a man and a woman; for by joining with woman man hopes to recover his former androgyny and immortality; in woman he hopes to find the divine virgin, his lost half, the divine image which has become effaced in him." This was Boehme's conception; behind it is the rise of the idea of androgyny as an image for ideal and absolute perfection, for the three cardinal virtues and their utopian realization, for a closing of the circle (sexual, psychological, social), for the transcendence of sin and the evil that comes of separateness, for a participation in the mysterious essential forces of life that alchemy strove to discover.[25]

The other set of implications was less positive and much more the obsession of the nineteenth century. Instead of an image of virtue it became a symbol of vice, particularly of that curiously and fastidiously cultivated mental erethism and cerebral lechery that characterized the age, as well as of "demonality, onanism, homosexuality, sadism and masochism." It is important to remember that this attitude derives quite directly from the hermetic conception that the votaries of "l'art pour l'art" embraced, and the rejection of reality and the moral and aesthetic standards which it represented. The withdrawal and disengagement that this enthusiasm supported provided conditions for luxuriating in the ambivalence and the ambiguity, the paradox and the perversity, and above all the unnaturalness and impossibility, that this enclosed (androgynous) world of artifice highlighted. The extension of the image of the androgyne during this phase constituted one of its most considerable achievements, culminating in its embodiment of the *vice suprême* which can be only indulged in and satisfied by art.

Gautier had helped to inaugurate the nineteenth-century version of the image with the perverse sexual confusions of *Mademoiselle de Maupin* and the unsettling charms of poems such as "Contralto" in *Emaux et camées,* in which the hermaphrodite is spoken of as

> Chimère ardente, effort suprême
> De l'art et de la volupté,
> Monstre charmant, comme je t'aime
> Avec ta multiple beauté.

The drawings of Burne-Jones and Simeon Solomon gave the image an ethereal quality; Solomon's drawings of "Antinous" and "Love dying from the breath of lust" were especially notorious in their way, and his "Bacchus" received much attention. The faces in Solomon's portrait, in Arthur Symons words, were

> without sex; they have brooded among ghosts of passions till they have become the ghosts of themselves; the energy of virtue or of sin has gone out of them, and they hang in space, dry, rattling the husks of desire.[26]

Gustave Moreau added to the gallery an image of a decidedly unsettling and more sinister hermaphrodite, who appears in both of his famous paintings of Salomé—the oil painting *Salomé* and the water-colour *L'Apparition.*

While certainly relying upon sexual ambivalence, the image derived much of its charm from, and joined with the implications of other images in, its development of more general ambivalences —between good and evil, in particular, as well as between the real and the ideal. The androgynous figure had associations both with virginity and lechery; both conditions were seen as the product of disengaged sensibilities, of divisions between the spirit and the flesh, and as emblematic of unnatural repression or desire. The androgyne was thereby linked with the femme fatale, "vierge et lubrique," as Huysmans said of Salomé; and the figure of the Sphinx became a powerful symbol of destructive forces, linked with Blake's murderous Female Will and representing everything from knowledge without power to sexual anxiety, until her worshippers became, as one wag remarked, positively "asphynx-iated."[27] Something of the flexibility of the androgynous image may be gathered by noting Arthur Symons' further comment on Simeon Solomon, that "the same face, varied a little in mood, scarcely in feature, serves for Christ and the two Marys, for Sleep and Lust." The ambiguities implicit in Leonardo's portrait of Saint John, at least in the general art literature of the late nineteenth century, provided for a fashionable confusion of good and evil, saint and sinner; it was a commonplace that owed much to Walter Pater, with his perception of

> the so-called "Saint John the Baptist" of the Louvre—one of the few naked figures Leonardo painted—whose delicate brown flesh and woman's hair no one would go out into the wilderness to seek, and whose treacherous smile would have us understand something far beyond the outward gesture or circumstance. But the long, reed-like cross in the hand, which suggests Saint John the Baptist, becomes faint in a copy at the Ambrosian Library, and disappears altogether in another, in the Palazzo Rosso at Genoa. Returning from the last to the original, we are no longer surprised by Saint John's strange likeness to the *Bacchus* which hangs near it, which set Théophile Gautier thinking of Heine's notion of decayed gods, who, to maintain themselves, after the fall of paganism, took employment in the new religion. We recognize one of those symbolic inventions in which the ostensible subject is used, not as matter for definite pictorial realization, but as the starting point of a train of sentiment, as subtle and vague as a piece of music. No one ever ruled over his subject more entirely than Leonardo, or bent it more dexterously to purely artistic ends. And so it comes to pass that though he handles sacred subjects continually, he is the most profane of painters.[28]

Pater had written earlier, in another part of the essay on "Aesthetic Poetry" from which the "Conclusion" to the *Renaissance* essays was taken, of the "decadence" of the medieval religious passion:

> Into this kingdom of reverie, and with it into a paradise of ambitious refinements, the earthly love enters, and becomes a prolonged somnambulism. Of religion it learns the art of directing towards an unseen object sentiments whose natural direction is towards objects of sense. Hence a love defined by the absence of the beloved, choosing to be without hope, protesting against all lower

uses of love, barren, extravagant, antinomian. It is the love which is incompatible with marriage, for the chevalier who never comes, of the serf for the *châtelaine*, of the rose for the nightingale, of Rudel for the Lady of Tripoli. Another element of extravagance came in with the feudal spirit. Provençal love is full of the very forms of vassalage. To be the servant of love, to have offended, to taste the subtle luxury of chastisement, of reconciliation—the religious spirit, too, knows that, and meets just there, as in Rousseau, the delicacies of earthly love. Here, under this strange complex of conditions, as in some medicated air, exotic flowers of sentiment expand, among people of a remote and unaccustomed beauty, somnambulistic, frail, androgynous, the light almost shining through them. Surely, such loves were too fragile and adventurous to last more than for a moment.[29]

The most common association of the androgynous figure was with virginity and was related to an obsession with sterility and the artificiality of the imagination; the dream, the ideal, the gesture become conditions of existence and create spells which must not be broken. The images of the virgin, the hermaphrodite, Narcissus, and art in the abstract, turn in upon themselves rather than out to the world. The movement from a cold and chaste and spiritual virginity to the hot and lustful passions of the flesh is a movement which for the androgyne—such as Mallarmé's Hérodiade—is self-enclosed and cyclical and returns to the narcissistic withdrawal which characterizes the image. Des Esseintes, the hero of Huysmans' *À Rebours,* identifies Mallarmé's Hérodiade with Moreau's Salomé by reading the one while he gazes on the other, and creates an atmosphere of sterile and artificial decadent desire; it represented a central feature of the image of the androgyne and conditioned the presentation of images such as that of Salomé.

> O miroir!
> Eau froide par l'ennui dans ton cadre gelée
> Que de fois et pendant les heures, désoleé
> Des songes et cherchant mes souvenirs qui sont
> Comme des feuilles sous ta glace au trou profond,
> Je m'apparus en toi comme une ombre lointaine,
> Mais, horreur! des soirs, dans ta sévère fontaine,
> J'ai de mon rêve épars connu la nudité![30]

It was, indeed, the figure of Salomé which provided one of the most unsettling images of the age—one which, though not always quite androgynous, drew upon many of the elements that gave the androgyne its compelling attraction. Versions of the Salomé legend were easily available, from the Bible and the histories of Flavius Josephus to the more colourful and detailed elaborations of Ernest Renan (in his *Vie de Jesus*) and Heinrich Heine (in a remarkable passage in *Atta Troll*). The third of Gustave Flaubert's celebrated *Trois Contes* brought an artistic historical authenticity to the subject, for his *Herodias* certainly served as something of a model for the later embellishments of the Salomé legend. It is not exactly clear whence Flaubert's immediate inspiration came, whether from his recent re-reading of the Bible, paintings of Moreau's that he had seen in 1876, or perhaps a scene depicting the banquet and execution scenes relating to the death of John the Baptist in Rouen Cathedral. Whatever the case, it is clear that much of the sense of time and place that informs Flaubert's story derives from the elaborate description of the Baptist incident given by Renan. It is notable, for example, that Flaubert's Baptist is much closer than tradition would lead him to Renan's picture of "un jeune ascète plein de fogue et de passion." Furthermore, Renan's account of the sectarian divisions within Judea, and to some extent between Roman and Judean cultures, made its way into Flaubert's novel, as it did into Wilde's play. The other notable version of the legend was presented by Mallarmé in his poem (originally conceived as a poetic tragedy) *Hérodiade*, which combined fascination with the subject with the poet's particular obsession with the nature of poetry as an hermetic and hieratic art in which the limitations of physical being are transcended in an experience of spiritual beauty, which is yet informed by physical passion and desire. Mallarmé was preoccupied with the possibilities of achieving (in poetry) a unity of soul and ideal (which is manifest in beauty), and with the way in which a work of art both accomplishes and mirrors this achievement. Hérodiade provided an apt emblem, for her beauty was canonical, and her virginity and narcissism symbolized the self-conscious autonomy that Mallarmé associated with art.

The other image which captured a sense of the autonomy and imaginative reality of art as well as of the pure desire and self-sufficiency that were associated with the image of the androgyne was the dance, what Frank Kermode has referred to as "the most primitive, non-discursive art . . . and intuitive truth . . . the emblem of the Romantic image. Dance belongs to a period before the self and the world were divided, and so achieves naturally that 'original unity' which modern poetry can produce only by a great and exhausting effort of fusion." Achieving something like this "original unity" was an aspiration that the androgynous figure also represented, embodying as did the dance an

> inner freedom from the practical desire,
> The release from action and suffering, release from the inner
> And the outer compulsion, yet surrounded
> By a grace of sense.[31]

In Paul Valéry's dialogue, *Dance and the Soul,* Socrates suggests that the dance of Athikte embodies "the instant between speech and silence," and continues to give a statement of an ideal of which androgyny was but one symbol:

> Without doubt the unique and perpetual object of the soul is that which does not exist: that which was and no longer is; that which will be and is not yet; that which is possible, and impossible—all that is the soul's concern—but, never, *never* that which is![32]

He who "knows the power of the dance," quoted Hofmannsthal (from the Persian) in his essay on Wilde, "knows that love kills." When Wilde sent Beardsley a copy of the Paris edition of *Salomé* in March of 1893, he inscribed it: "For Aubrey: for the only artist, who, besides myself, knows what the dance of the seven veils is, and can see that invisible dance." Salomé's dance in Wilde's play brings about the prophesied changes—the moon becomes red as blood, the stars fall like ripe figs, the sun becomes black like sack-cloth of hair, and the kings of the earth are afraid—and thereby purity, chastity, light and hope are fused with evil, lust, darkness and fear. The dance, like the androgyne, embodied a confusion which might be perceived as optimistic or pessimistic, healthy or diseased; the late nineteenth century perceived the image, almost without exception, as pessimistic and diseased.

There is no doubt about Wilde's conscious intermingling of these implications and images in the play: the moon is introduced like a dead woman, and yet as well like a dancing princess; Salomé greets the moon as cold and chaste, with a virgin's beauty. Both the moon and Salomé are likened to the narcissus and, as C. S. Nassar has argued in a particularly demonic reading of the play, Salomé is identified with the grim Cybele (in some places worshipped as the foster mother of Dionysus) whose apocalyptic worship provides a model for the frenzied dionysian scenes of death (of the young Syrian Narraboth, Iokanaan, Salomé herself) in the play. Iokanaan in turn is imaged in the same terms; he is "like a thin ivory statue . . . an image of silver. I am sure he is chaste, as the moon is. . . . His flesh must be very cold, cold as ivory." The changes in Salomé, her visible evil, are reflected in changes in the moon—"like a mad woman . . . seeking everywhere for lovers. She is naked too. She is quite naked."(Wilde once suggested that her clothing for the play should be a green colour, like that of some curious poisonous lizard.) The ambivalence of Salomé's attempted seduction of Iokanaan is an aspect of the ambivalence of purity and sterility, of love and lust. Salomé is attracted to the deathlike sterility that she perceives in Iokanaan, a sterility that becomes complete in death, when "neither the floods nor the great waters can quench" Salomé's passion for him. Iokanaan himself displays the desire and lust that the new religion which he announces has sublimated, and we cannot but think of those "decayed gods" of Heine, seeking employment in the new religion—the gods whom "the Romans have driven out," as the Cappadocian says: "There are some who say that they have hidden themselves in the mountains." Iokanaan's view is that "the centaurs have hidden themselves in the rivers, and the nymphs have left the rivers, and are lying beneath the leaves in the forests." The terrible ironies and the awful paradoxes which we have seen inherent in so many of the images and devices of the period are brought together here, in this vision of the light at the heart of darkness, as what we recognize as evil and vice appear only in the forms of beauty, itself paradoxically beyond good and evil, beyond virtue and vice.[33]

What is finally predominant, perhaps, is the intuition of autonomy that comes through, an autonomy that is, of course, the signature of the art itself as well as of the characters and their conditions. The inviolability of Salomé and the inviolability of Iokanaan are juxtaposed in the play; the unsettling truth is that it is disturbingly unclear which prevails.

When Gustave Moreau showed his *Salomé* and *L'Apparition* at the Spring Salon in Paris in 1876, these qualities became embodied in an immensely compelling plastic form. The contemplative withdrawal, the refuge in sphinx-like solitude, the confusion of evil and pride and beauty and horror—they are the qualities that Moreau captured and that provided Salomé a distinction as the embodiment of "fatality, Evil and Death incarnate in female beauty," a "femme fatale" whose "passion is a flame that sears without heat, a corruption cold as the snow, whose ceremonial of seduction bears almost the semblance of a consecrated rite." Wilde had referred to Salomé several years before he wrote his play as "la bella donna della mia mente", a line of Petrarch's which translates as "the fair lady of my dreams". Huysmans' Des Esseintes, who attempts to create for himself an artificial paradise of exotic richness and depraved inclinations, finds in Moreau's two paintings the object of his desires and the embodiment of his vertiginous fears, epitomized in the human terrors that accompanied the recognition of (and the subjugation of one's will to) the charms of the dancer, which are as "the charms of a great venereal flower, grown in a bed of sacrilege, reared in a hot-house of impiety."[34]

There is a fine irony in the androgynous John the Baptist and the androgynous Salomé coming together in this way, which perhaps says more about the nature of nineteenth-century artistic preoccupations than it does about the nature of androgyny. The tragic detachment from all that gives life stability, the isolation of the self from all that gives life meaning, the perverse fascination with all that makes life terrible, the fatalistic obsession with all that destroys life, all combine to make Oscar Wilde's Salomé a figure of hypnotic power and an image of compelling complexity.

Huysmans used the Salomé material in part as symbolic of luxury, "deified by paganism, which celebrated luxury under her several incarnations as Venus and Priapus"; later, luxury became a Christian sin, symbolized in the carnal dance of Hérodiade. This luxury was what Baudelaire required in art, that it be "luxe, calme et volupté." The calm, the only calm that the end of the century recognized, was the sickly calm of ennervating dissatisfaction or the awful calm of obsessive detachment; luxury gave to art its useless charm and beguiling fascination; and voluptuousness united the body with the soul in an agony of desire and passion, of which the passion of Christ was the most stirring example.

Barbey d'Aurevilly remarked, after reading *À Rebours*, that

> Baudelaire, the Satanic Baudelaire, who died a Christian, must surely be one of M. Huysmans' favourite authors, for one can feel his presence, like a glowing fire, behind the finest pages M. Huysmans has written. Well, one day, I defied Baudelaire to begin *Les Fleurs du mal* over again, or to go any further in his blasphemies. I might well offer the same challenge to the author of *À Rebours*, "After *Les Fleurs du mal,*" I told Baudelaire, "it only remains for you to choose between the muzzle of a pistol and the foot of the Cross." Baudelaire chose the foot of the Cross. But will the author of *À Rebours* make the same choice?[35]

A sense of this choice must have been behind Wilde's decision to take as his surname in exile after his release from prison the name Melmoth, the central figure of Maturin's strange Gothic novel. Melmoth was a figure to whom (as one of his companions remarked) "crime gave a kind of heroic immunity," the more heroic because the crime was the more terrible, was in fact a crime against God; he displayed the "simplicity of profound corruption." There was also in this choice an instinct that Wilde had been conscious of for some time—that the marriage of heaven and hell is a convincing metaphor for the mortal as well as the immortal condition; that love and hate are like warp and woof, and the fabric that is woven is the fabric of life; that beauty and goodness and truth are aspects of ugliness and evil and lying, and that the true artist is the one who recognizes all aspects. And finally, as Baudelaire knew, that there is something terrible about the laughter of the damned . . . and we are all damned.

> And thus the laughter of Melmoth, which is the highest expression of pride, is forever performing its function as it lacerates and scorches the lips of the laugher for whose sins there can be no remission.[36]

Baudelaire completed the scheme by proposing Satan as not only the perfect sinner but the perfect dandy, and dandyism as "a kind of religion" offering salvation for the decadent and ennervated spirit. Melmoth becomes one emblem of this condition—Melmoth, who is said to be a native of Ireland—a country that no one knows, and which the natives are particularly reluctant to dwell in from various causes—

and whose

> destiny forbid[s] alike curiosity or surprise. The world could show him no greater marvel than his own existence . . . he himself passed from region to region, mingling with, yet distinct from all his species, like a wearied and uninterested spectator rambling through the various seats of some vast theatre.[37]

His predicament is, in Baudelaire's perception, emblematic of the predicament of all who exercise their divine faculty of imagination, and in so doing sin against God:

> His frightful suffering lies in the disproportion between his wonderful faculties, acquired instantly by a satanic act, and the milieu where, like a creature of God, he is condemned to live.

He is, like the archetypal Romantic artist, an outcast, an outsider; like Pan, he is halfway between a god and a man, "weak / Before Gods, and to shepherds a fear, / A holiness, horn and heel," as George Meredith expressed it in his suggestive poem "The Day of the Daughter of Hades."

The most disturbing alienation to which the age gave an image was that of the superbly eponymous comedian Pierrot, that precarious outcast with "un coeur plein de dandysme / Lunaire," killing (like Hamlet) the thing he loves, and bearing "witness to the only style of heroism recognized by the *fin de siècle:* the heroism in this case of Sancho Panza twisted by the dreams of Don Quixote,"[38] or Marsyas by the dreams of gaining the laurels of Apollo.

The figure of Pierrot underlies much of the ambiguous response to the challenges of life and art that characterized the age in which Wilde lived, and that which he anticipated. From Baudelaire to Picasso, from Jules Laforgue and Paul Verlaine to T. S. Eliot and Hart Crane, from Aubrey Beardsley to Arnold Schönberg, the possibilities of pure or unadulterated folly were confused with the certainties of sorrow and suffering. The tale of Pierrot as a nineteenth-century phenomenon begins with his transformation from a figure out of Italian *commedia dell'arte* and late seventeenth and eighteenth century English theatrical entertainments into a pantomime figure if not created at least immortalized by a genius of a mimic by the name of Gaspard Deburau, who performed (along with some dogs, acrobats, and farcical clowns) for one Madame Sagi in the street *Théâtre des Funambules* during the late 1820s. Gaspard's son Charles carried on and extended the tradition (which included the appearance of Pierrot as hermaphrodite or devil), adding to his father's naive *grotesquerie* a neurotic touch, the perplexed and paranoid consciousness of the artist as an outcast and an alien. The figure quickly caught the attention of Victor Hugo, for example, who was no doubt fascinated by the grotesque qualities that were part of the creation, and by Gautier, who on his birthday in 1862 wrote and performed a sketch *Pierrot posthume*, with decor by Puvis de Chavannes. Jean Richepin put on a *Pierrot assassin* at the Trocadero with Sarah Bernhardt in the title role; Huysmans (and Leon Hénnique) wrote a *Pierrot sceptique;* Adolphe Willette, a notable artist who attended at "Le chat noir," founded a review, *Pierrot,* and his memoirs of the café group were entitled *Feu Pierrot.* Pierrot was indeed ubiquitous, and he was represented in almost every form. Daumier's magnificent "Tête de Pierrot" is perhaps as powerfully disturbing a presentation of the image as any, conveying "the Rembrandtesque force of a man of the people who has known suffering, looked on evil in many forms, and achieved self-respect only despite—or perhaps through—the humiliations of his rôle." Paul Klee has given the twentieth century one of its most sinister images of Pierrot, in the form of a "Pierrot reuig" who figured in many of the images of suffering and death in Klee's compelling paintings from the late 1930s.

From the nineteenth century representations that were available to them, and the genius that transformed their own afflictions into art, Laforgue and Verlaine gave the figure its most exquisitely anguished presentation. Laforgue, especially, who picked up some of his instincts from Paul Bourget, perceived in Pierrot an exquisitely sensitive type of human suffering, in which purity and indecision become representative conditions of a distinctly human pathos; Pierrot becomes both dupe and dilettante, both an insider and an outsider, his individuality intensified in direct proportion to his detachment from the world he experiences. Prufrock and

Mauberly are his successors, for indecision is his signature; he embodies, appropriate to his lunar muse, a "lame reflectiveness," associating the sterility (and sinister inspiration) of the moon with the sterility (and sinister appeal) of art, and celebrating both as effecting the sort of liberation from the will that Schopenhauer among others insisted was necessary for any adequate self-consciousness. Verlaine transformed the figure into a still more disturbing type, that of the almost inhuman outcast haunted by a "nostalgie de la boue," afflicted in his voluntary exile by *Le Guignon*.[39]

This outcast—Pierrot "mort d'un chronique orphelisme"—provided a picturesque embodiment of a human predicament that meant much to late nineteenth-century writers and artists, as it had to the Romantic poets to whom many of them looked for inspiration. The archetype was a figure alienated not only from others but also from himself, and yet paradoxically uniting in himself good and evil, a capacity for action and an inclination towards contemplation, the desires of the flesh and the aspirations of the spirit, in a state of suspended animation. The cause of the alienation that is experienced is an ambiguous self-consciousness which condemns the individual either to a sterile self-questioning (leading to "infinite delay") or to an equally sterile questing after self-fulfillment (leading to narcissism or martyrdom).

The art of Wilde, as that of Arnold and Pater before him and Yeats and Eliot after, was premised upon the single hope that art would both display and create conditions for the development of the realized personality, or what Baudelaire called "the distillation and centralization of the ego." The process necessary for such development, and the experience that must be achieved, involved sorrow and suffering as necessary conditions, and a tragic capitulation of the self as a prerequisite to a joyous discovery of its significance and potential. The great artist such as Baudelaire, as Swinburne declared,

> sawest, in thine old singing season, brother,
> Secrets and sorrows unbeheld of us.[40]

And the great myths such as those of Demeter and Dionysus imaged these sorrows. Parsifal, the pure fool made wise by suffering, is the sublime extreme; but this side of such sublimity there is the wisdom of "the wisest of the Sibyls" (as Wilde once called Elizabeth Barrett Browning), the realization "that, while knowledge is power, suffering is part of knowledge."

There were a cluster of images which represented the way to such knowledge, and together they create a patterned energy that informed much of the art of the second half of the nineteenth century in particular. Gilbert Murray's description of the ritual stages of tragedy as *"agon* or contest, *spargamos* or tearing apart, *anagnorisis* or discovery and *epiphany* or joyous showing forth of the resurrected protagonist" applies remarkably well to the Dionysian processes that Pater was so fond of elaborating (as it certainly should, given the origin of the ritual in the affirmation of the reborn Dionysus), or to the implications of the Marsyas legend that Wilde found so pertinent to and so prevalent in the art of his time.[41]

The contests into which the artists of the age entered were, to use a reasonably Darwinian analogy, for psychic and imaginative survival, which passed through the ritual stages of struggle and disorder to a newly realized order and self-conscious achievement. By the end of the century, almost every self-respecting artist, certainly every Irish one, had discovered the value of the epiphany as an organizing function of experience, if nothing else. In such a scheme, there is no room for external criteria; the process occurs within its own limits, compelled by its own hieratic prerogatives, defiant of all that would reduce the paradox and eliminate the ambiguity of its resolution.

But some Irish artists were less able than others to discover in such a nicely autonomous scheme the consolations and the stability that the structures of art were supposed to offer. There appeared to be a kind of sinister mischievousness even in the most apparently disengaged forms of art, and certainly in the dramatic forms of comedy and tragedy with which the period was especially involved. Life seemed to insist on intruding; and the images which especially appealed to the artists of the time—of Pan and Persephone and Pierrot, of Dionysus and Salomé and Narcissus, of androgynous figures and paradoxical dilemmas—these bear witness to the ambiguous relationships between art and life, and among the categories of each, which fascinated the age of Wilde. The heritage of Oscar Wilde was, as his mother suggested, "grand, misty and Ossianic"; but it passed to him without the design, the *telos,* that his beloved Greeks associated with the highest achievements in art and life. So he gave it one of his own invention; but the result was, like nature, only partly informed by art—with good intentions, but unable entirely to realize them. Terribly improbable, as he said of himself.

Its emblem was the legendary poet Ossian, the redeeming spirit of art in life, and the sustaining idea of Irish culture, but so often becoming the property of the idle fancy, or the plaything of fate and folly and forgery. When Wilde was lecturing in San Francisco in April, 1882, during his American tour, he spoke on "Irish Poets and Poetry of the Nineteenth Century."[42] One of the patriots to whom he drew special attention (and ranked with Charles Gavan Duffy) was the Irish-Canadian writer T. D'Arcy McGee, who had at one time been editor of the *Boston Pilot* (to which Wilde later contributed) and was assassinated in Ottawa in 1868 by Fenian sympathizers whom he had offended. Wilde quoted McGee's famous panegyric on "The Celts":

> Ossian! two thousand years of mist and change
>   surround thy name—
> Thy Finian heroes now no longer range
>   The hills of fame.
>
> The very names of Fin and Gaul sound strange—
>   Yet thine the same—
> By miscalled lake and desecrated grange—
>   Remains, and shall remain!

Oscar lived amidst, and for many he came to represent, the miscalled lakes and desecrated granges of the sentimental nineteenth century imaginative landscape, in an England that Byron had dismissed as "a low, newspaper, humdrum, law-suit country." Wilde used to repeat his father's story about the English landlord who wrote from the Carlton to his Irish agent and said "Don't let the tenants imagine that by shooting you they will at all intimidate me."[43] Wilde was, like the English landlord, blithely determined not to be intimidated . . . and yet there was also a stubborn earnestness in his determination. If (as Kierkegaard suggested) the gods created the world because they were bored, then Wilde would show both that there might be exquisite (or failing that, gross) charm in boredom, and that there was life in the art and art in the life of the world and its creators, whatever the tenants might think. His name Fingal may sound strange—but Oscar remains.

NOTES

ONE.
A GRAIL OF LAUGHTER OF AN EMPTY ASH CAN

1. There are numerous accounts of Wilde's life, and a wide variety of reminiscences of the period which inevitably include mention of Oscar and his circle. Of Wilde's biographers, there were first of all those of his contemporaries who committed their familiarity to a slavering posterity. Robert H. Sherard, Wilde's most numbingly loyal friend, wrote several books of panegyric, filled with invaluable material and astonishing ignorance; Frank Harris wrote exactly the kind of viciously sentimental story that he was most adept at; and Alfred Douglas had someone else help him write all his bitterness into a biography filled with his own shallow sensibility and capacity for adolescent malice, and then added another to modify the picture and perpetuate Douglas's obsession with himself. Short accounts by André Gide and Vincent O'Sullivan provide some valuable insights into the later phases of Wilde's life, and many contemporaries have spoken of Wilde as an aspect of their own autobiographical ramblings. The standard books on Wilde's parents are by T. E. Wilson (1942), Horace Wyndham (1951), Patrick Byrne (1953), Eric Lambert (1967) and Terence de Vere White (1967). The most notable biographies of Oscar leading up to the present have been by Arthur Ransome (1912), Arthur Symons (1930), Hesketh Pearson (1946), Lewis Broad (1955), Vyvyan Holland (Oscar's son) (1954, 1960), Philippe Jullian, trans. by Violet Wyndham (1969), and Rupert Croft-Cooke (1972). There are several recent volumes, in particular by Louis Kronenberg (1976) and Sheridan Morley (1976). The most considerable biography to appear is H. Montgomery Hyde's *Oscar Wilde* (New York: Farrar, Straus & Giroux, 1975). Several essays by Richard Ellmann, in particular, have brought to the subject an imaginative insight not often found in studies

of Wilde. Rupert Hart-Davis's edition of *The Letters of Oscar Wilde* (New York: Harcourt, Brace, and World, 1962) is in many ways the best biographical source of all; it is, without a doubt, a model of intelligent scholarship. Stuart Mason (C. S. Millard) compiled a *Bibliography of Oscar Wilde* (London: T. W. Laurie, 1914), which is still invaluable, though incomplete. Ian Fletcher and John Stokes have completed a recent Review of Research on Oscar Wilde, which is included in *Anglo-Irish Literature*, ed. Richard J. Finneran (New York: Modern Language Association, 1976), pp. 48–137.

2. From one of a series of poems written by W. E. Henley during the Boer War, and included in *For England's Sake* (1900). Henley's lines are quoted in J. A. V. Chapple, *Documentary and Imaginative Literature: 1880–1920* (London: Blandford Press, 1970), p. 167, in which there is also a good brief discussion of the imperial enthusiasms of the time, pp. 157–220. See also Derek Stanford, ed. *Critics of the Nineties* (London: John Baker, 1970), "Introduction," pp. 41–43. For more detail on Henley and his influence, see Jerome H. Buckley, *William Ernest Henley: A Study in the "Counter-Decadence" of the Nineties* (Princeton: Princeton University Press, 1945). A good general study of the period is provided in R. C. K. Ensor, *England: 1870-1914* (Oxford: Clarendon Press, 1936).

3. See Gaylord C. Le Roy, *Perplexed Prophets: Six Nineteenth Century British Authors* (Philadelphia: University of Pennsylvania, 1953), a provocative attempt "to reconstruct the configuration of the [social, political and economic as well as intellectual and aesthetic] environment as it affected" Carlyle, Arnold, Ruskin, James Thomson, D. G. Rossetti, and Wilde.

4. Le Roy, p. 152. As "The Great MacDermott" (whose real name was George Farrell, 1845–1901) was singing his new song, first in 1877, at the Pavilion, William Morris began his ponderous journey towards socialism. For an account of some of the background to these fashions, see *1859: Entering an Age of Crisis*, eds. Philip Appleman, William A. Madden, Michael Wolff (Bloomington: Indiana University Press, 1959). See also Laurence Senelick, "Politics as Entertainment: Victorian Music Hall Songs," *Victorian Studies*, XIX, 2 (December, 1975), pp. 149–180. One of the most formidable influences on the imperialist spirit was provided by John Seeley's *The Expansion of England* (1883).

5. This interpretation was proposed by Noel Annan in an essay on "Kipling's Place in the History of Ideas"; it is discussed in Chapple, pp. 183–84. The widespread interest in sociology was inspired in large part by August Comte and the positivists.

6. Quoted in Jerome H. Buckley, *The Victorian Temper: A Study in Literary Culture* (Cambridge: Harvard University Press, 1969), p. 190.

7. Replying to Arthur Balfour, who had asked him his religion, Wilde remarked "Well, you know, I don't think I have any. I am an Irish Protestant."

8. The period was lively with religious dissent and Roman Catholicism particularly provided a strange and comparatively acceptable fascination. Writing in 1856, Walter Bagehot wrote of Edward Gibbon's conversion that

> it seems now so natural that an Oxford man should take this step, that one can hardly understand the astonishment it created. Lord Sheffield tells us that the Privy Council interfered. . . . In the manor-house of Buriton it would have probably created less sensation if "dear Edward" had announced his intention of becoming a monkey. The English have ever believed that the Papist is a kind of *creature;* some think that the Oxford student is its young. (*The Collected Works of Walter Bagehot: The Literary Essays*, Vol. I, ed. Norman St. John-Stevas [London: *The Economist*, 1965], pp. 362–363.)

9. Liddon, the biographer of Pusey, was appointed Ireland Professor of Biblical Exegesis at Oxford in 1870.

10. *The Letters of Oscar Wilde* (hereafter, *Letters*), p. 17. Wilde's interest was, I think, not unconnected with what might be called the social and political and even the aesthetic, aspect of religious belief; there was, in short, something appealingly un-vulgar, something refreshingly irrational, something almost seditious, about Roman Catholic dogma— so much so that there had been a Public Worship Bill passed in 1874 to curb the ritualism that was infecting the Protestant church (under the terms of which there were several prosecutions and at least one imprisonment of offending Protestant clergy during the following decade).

11. In a short article written in 1886 entitled "To Read or Not to Read," in which he proposed that

> the beautiful poems contained in [the Greek Anthology] seem to me to hold the same position with regard to Greek dramatic literature as do the delicate little figurines of Tanagra to the Phidian marbles, and to be quite as necessary for the complete understanding of the Greek spirit. (*Complete Works*, Vol. 13: Reviews, ed. Robert Ross [London: Methuen, 1908], p. 44.)

(All reference to Wilde's published work, with the exception of *The Picture of Dorian Gray*, will be to this edition, hereafter listed as *Works.*) Lewis Mumford, in a review of A. J. Farmer's *Le mouvement esthétique et décadent en Angleterre: 1873–1900* (1931), was one of the first to draw attention to the importance of the Greek Anthology during this period. (See Helmut E. Gelber, "The Nineties: Beginning, End or Transition," *Edwardians and Late Victorians*, ed. Richard Ellmann [New York: Columbia University Press, 1960], p. 62.) The first posthumous works mistakenly attributed to Wilde were, quite appropriately, translations of Petronius Arbiter's *Satyricon* and of a play by Barbey d'Aurevilly.

12. Quoted in H. Montgomery-Hyde, *Oscar Wilde* (hereafter Hyde, *Wilde*), p. 21; from an article, "Oscar Wilde at Oxford," written in 1929 by G. T. Atkinson. See James Joyce, "Oscar Wilde: The Poet of *Salomé*" (1909) in *The Critical Writings of James Joyce*, eds. Ellsworth Mason and Richard Ellmann (New York: Viking, 1964), p. 201. By 1884, the "Derby

Tip" in the *Illustrated Sporting and Dramatic News* would refer not to a horse, but to Oscar's new hat. By 1894, he was mentioned in dispatches every week, indeed often every day.

13. From Isobel Murray's edition of the novel (London: Oxford University Press, 1974), (hereafter, *Dorian Gray*), p. 41. The nineteenth century was blessed with many gifted conversationalists, and with two who were in different ways undoubtedly unique—Samuel Taylor Coleridge and Oscar Wilde.

14. Wilde's review appeared in the *Speaker* in 1890 (*Works*, Vol. 13, p. 529).

15. See Le Roy, pp. 20ff., and Ensor, pp. 124–128. Positivism contributed to the evangelical spirit through its theoretical advocacy of a "religion of humanity," promoted by Frederic Harrison.

16. "The Decay of Lying," *Works*, Vol. 8, pp. 3–4.

17. "The English Renaissance of Art," *Works*, Vol. 14, p. 276. There were many parodies of this enthusiasm, especially following Wilde's tour in America. Walter Hamilton, who had written a book on *The Aesthetic Movement in England* in 1882, collected a wide group of *Parodies of English and American Authors*, 1884–89, in which Wilde was a prominent subject.

18. "The Critic as Artist," *Works*, Vol. 8, pp. 206–7.

19. For a brief discussion of this aspect of the period, see the chapter entitled "The 'Aesthetic' Eighties," Buckley, *Victorian Temper*, pp. 207–225.

20. See Paul Thomson, *The Work of William Morris* (London: Heinemann, 1967), p. 79. With reference to Whistler's peacock designs, Wilde noted that there was a distinguished precedent (unknown to Whistler) at Ravenna; Wilde's trip there in 1877 had a considerable influence on him. He called Whistler's room "the finest thing in colour and art decoration which the world has known since Coreggio's frescoes" for the Camera di San Paolo in the monastery of San Lodovico at Parma.

21. *Works*, Vol 6, p. 47. "There were times," wrote Walter Pater, when Marius' "life might have been fulfilled by an enthusiastic quest after perfection;—say! in the flowering and folding of a toga." (*Marius the Epicurean: His Sensations and Ideas*, 3rd ed., Vol. 1 [London, 1892], p. 214). Such affectation, like all that provokes humour, had a serious function.

22. It is the transformation of the sense of personality from a particular to a universal quality that, at least for Wilde, defines a true work of art and sustains the paradox that art may both appear purely impersonal and yet give evidence of a determining personality.

23. *Letters*, p. 292; Wilde was writing to one R. Clegg, an uncomprehending reader of *The Picture of Dorian Gray*.

24. From Wilde's review (which appeared in *Woman's World* in 1889) of Caroline Fitzgerald's *Venetia Victrix*, a volume of poetry dedi-

cated to Browning and showing obvious traces of his influence. In the passage quoted, Wilde is discussing Browning's work (*Works,* Vol. 13, p. 482).

25. "Pen, Pencil and Poison," *Works,* Vol. 8, pp. 70–71.

26. From "Picasso Speaks," *The Arts* (New York, May 1923), pp. 315–26; translated from the original interview (in Spanish) with Marius de Zayas. Thus, when Roland Barthes suggests that art is "un système de signification déceptif," or when Vladimir Nabokov or Jorge Luis Borges claims that art is quite literally "illicit," they are following in the footsteps of Wilde.

27. *Letters,* p. 514. Ross was one of Wilde's closest and most loyal friends—they first met in 1886—and after Wilde's death Ross became his literary executor. He was born a Canadian, the grandson of Robert Baldwin, the first prime minister of Upper Canada.

28. Hyde, *Wilde,* p. 22. Lewis Carroll's *Through the Looking Glass* was published in 1871.

29. An article by Wilde on Chatterton was announced in the *Century Guild Hobby Horse* in October, 1886, but never appeared; and Herbert Horne, the editor, was involved with Wilde in a project to place a memorial to Chatterton in Colston's School, Stapleton, Bristol, at which the poet had been a pupil. Wilde did lecture on Chatterton—"the marvelous Boy,/The sleepless Soul that perish'd in his pride" (William Wordsworth, "Resolution and Independence")—at Birbeck College, London in November, 1886. Chatterton's story was well and widely known in Wilde's circle and associated with everything romantic and even vaguely artistic. Wilde proposed that the significant correspondence between imagistic and metric variations which Coleridge and Scott used to such effect came directly from Chatterton. And Chatterton had, in Wilde's later association of the artist with the criminal, the distinct advantage that his poetical achievements were indeed in a real sense illicit (forgeries). More often, Chatterton was seen to be simply adopting a necessary mask in order to show himself more openly.

30. From an excellent essay by A. O. J. Cockshut on "Victorian Thought," *The Victorians,* ed. Arthur Pollard (London: Barrie and Jenkins, 1970), p. 35.

31. See Frank Kermode, *Romantic Image* (London: Routledge and Kegan Paul, 1957), pp. 7–12.

32. Quoted in Stanley Weintraub, *Beardsley: A Biography* (New York: Braziller, 1967), p. 73.

33. This was the only painting of Whistler's marked for sale, though it remained unsold for fifteen years.

34. This story is recounted in Stanley Weintraub, *Whistler: A Biography* (New York: Weybright and Talley, 1974), pp. 323–24.

35. *The Autobiography of Bertrand Russell,* Vol. II (London, 1968),

p. 140. (In his essay on Wilde, "The Poet of *Salomé*," James Joyce suggested in a nice metaphor that "he was to break the lance of his fluent paradoxes against the body of practical conventions.") It is easy to underestimate the unorthodox character of Whistler's celebration of the elitist nature of art; as I. A. Richards has noted in *Principles of Literary Criticism*, "the 'moral' theory of art (it would be better to call it the 'ordinary values' theory) has the most great minds behind it. Until Whistler came to start the critical movements of the last half-century, few poets, artists or critics had ever doubted that the value of art experiences was to be judged as other values are." (Quoted in L. A. Reid, "Beauty and Significance," *Reflections on Art*, ed. Susanne K. Langer [New York: Oxford University Press, 1961], p. 39.)

36. See *Letters*, pp. 45–46, n.4.

37. Yeats recounts Wilde's description of Pater's *Renaissance* as "the very flower of decadence: the last trumpet should have sounded the moment it was written."

38. For a full account of Wilde's relationship with André Gide, with which this parable is itself associated, see Richard Ellmann, *Golden Codgers: Biographical Speculations* (New York: Oxford University Press, 1973), "Corydon and Ménalque," pp. 81–100, esp. pp. 93–94.

39. "About Oscar Wilde," *Other Inquisitions 1937–1952*, trans. Ruth L. C. Simms (Austin: University of Texas, 1964), pp. 80–81.

40. The most scurrilous account of both Miles and Gower is in Rupert Croft-Cooke's *The Unrecorded Life of Oscar Wilde* (London: W. H. Allen, 1972), pp. 40–50. Phyllis Grosskirth, in her biography of John Addington Symonds (London: Longman's, 1964), (pp. 267, 311), speaks of Symonds' disapproval of Gower's "abandoned sensuality"; "Gower," he wrote, "saturated the spirit" by promiscuous attachments which wasted the "adhesiveness" or qualities of Coleridgean "friendism" which the spirit could offer. Symonds' *Studies of the Greek Poets* (1876), which Wilde wrote about in an unpublished review, contained what Grosskirth has described as "in effect an apologia for homosexuality" in its insistence that the concept of "unnatural" behaviour was a pernicious myth.

41. *Letters*, p. 74. George du Maurier, the *Punch* cartoonist, called her one of the three most beautiful women he had met. It was an age that paid homage to feminine beauty; and Wilde's friend Frank Miles did many drawings (as did Whistler and Burne-Jones, among others) of Lily Langtry, one of the most famous of the beauties (or "stunners," as the Pre-Raphaelites termed them) of the day. She was herself a good and close friend of Oscar's and had been given the nickname "The Jersey Lily" after the title of Millais' portrait of her (she was born in Jersey, in 1852). Wilde remarked later in his life that "the three women I have admired most are Queen Victoria, Sarah Bernhardt, and Lily Langtry. I would have married any one of them with pleasure. The first had great dignity,

the second a lovely voice, the third a perfect figure." Wilde had not been without his courtly flourishes. During the summer he met Florrie, for example, he had also managed to agitate a young lady in one of the Kingsford households in Brighton sufficiently to receive delicate correspondence about his intentions. Perhaps he was simply as eligible a bachelor, as much a mark for arrangements, as his brother Willie.

42. Lady Bracknell's response when she is told by Jack Worthing that Cecily Cardew has "about a hundred and thirty thousand pounds in the Funds" is a classic parody of a pervasive theme:

A hundred and thirty thousand pounds! And in the Funds! Miss Cardew seems to me a most attractive young lady, now that I look at her. Few girls of the present day have any really solid qualities, any of the qualities that last, and improve with time. We live, I regret to say, in an age of surfaces. ("The Importance of Being Earnest," *Works,* Vol. 5, p. 161.)

43. *Works,* Vol. 9, p. 21. His regret over Florrie may have inspired the group of poems which were collected near the end of his 1881 volume; most of them appeared in print in the book for the first time.

44. Elton later became a fairly notable critic, writing books on Dickens and Thackeray, Michael Drayton, the Augustan age, the English muse, several volumes of essays, and a monumental *Survey of English Literature* from 1730 to (suitably enough) 1880.

45. First printed in *The Civil and Military Gazette* of Lahore on December 23, 1889. Reprinted in *Turnovers,* Vol. VIII. Collected in *Abaft the Funnel,* 1909. "If you ask nine-tenths of the British public what is the meaning of the word aesthetics," remarked Wilde, "they will tell you it is the French for affectation or the German for a dado."

46. *The Yellow Book: Quintessence of the Nineties,* ed. Stanley Weintraub (Garden City: Doubleday, 1964), pp. 139–146. Miles had been awarded a special silver medal, extra to the annual Turner Gold Medal, by the Royal Academy in December of 1879.

47. Attacks of a much less genial sort had for quite a time been directed against the Pre-Raphaelites and those associated (however tenuously) with them. The most famous bit of vituperation was Robert Buchanan's essay on "The Fleshly School of Poetry," which appeared in the *Contemporary Review* in October, 1871. It was a vicious piece to which D. G. Rossetti—one of the chief targets—responded later in the year with an open letter to the *Atheneum* entitled "The Stealthy School of Criticism"; Swinburne, another of those vandalized, defended his comrades with an article "Under the Microscope." Buchanan replied with "The Monkey and the Microscope"; and Swinburne, in an adolescent rage, wrote a letter to the *Examiner* entitled "The Devil's Due" and signed "Thomas Maitland," Buchanan's pseudonym for the original article. Buchanan sued for libel, and won; while the judge who made the award remarked that "it would have been better if . . . all the poetry of the Fleshly School were committed to the flames tomorrow; the world would be very much the better for it." The chief object of attack of Buchanan's original article was

Charles Baudelaire, who was recognized as godfather to the aesthetic fashions that were deplored. (See Clarence R. Decker, *The Victorian Conscience* [New York: Twayne, 1952], pp. 63–77.)

48. Richard Le Gallienne, *The Romantic Nineties* (London, 1925), pp. 253–54.

49. For a full account of this controversy, see Stuart Mason (Christopher Millard, *Art and Morality: A record of the discussion which followed the publication of "Dorian Gray,"* London, 1912).

50. "In Honorem Doriani Creatorisque Eius," included in *Aesthetes and Decadents of the 1890s,* ed. Karl Beckson (New York: Random House, 1966), pp. 116–17. Iain Fletcher gives the following translation of these lines: "Blessed be to you Oscar! . . . Here are apples of Sodom; Here the hearts of vice; And sweet sins." Walter Pater's welcome review of Dorian Gray appeared in *Bookman* in November, 1891.

51. In the *Nineteenth Century* ("Shakespeare and Stage Costume," later "The Truth of Masks," 1885; "The Decay of Lying," 1889; "The Critic as Artist," 1890); *Fortnightly Review,* ("Pen, Pencil and Poison," 1889). The essays as a whole display an attempt to balance the case for what were called "inductive" and "judicial" forms of criticism, in a manner that has been little noticed.

52. See Hyde, *Wilde,* p. 40.

53. Weintraub, *Beardsley,* p. 60.

54. The law under which Wilde was tried and convicted was the Criminal Law Amendment Act of 1885. In large measure, it was the product of agitation over the spread of organized vice, and in particular the white slave trade in young girls. The inclusion of homosexual acts into the terms of the act, and especially its vague wording, was criticized over the next decade, but Wilde was still caught in the net.

55. *Letters,* p. 430.

56. *Letters,* p. 447.

57. "The Critic as Artist," *Works,* Vol. 8, p. 143.

TWO.
THE AGE OF OSCAR WILDE

1. Wilde's letter to Alfred Douglas from Reading Gaol, which became known as *De Profundis,* is a rich source of his further reflections on his career. For the full text, and a description of its provenance and history, see *Letters,* pp. 425–511. The contemporary was Richard Le Gallienne, and the comment appears in his book on *The Romantic Nineties,* p. 159.

2. "The English Renaissance of Art," *Works,* Vol. 14, p. 245.

3. Froude, who was the Tory successor to the Whig historian Macaulay, and who in 1870 was the editor of *Frazer's Magazine,* was also

responsible for the somewhat acid description of Carlyle. Arnold turned to Celtic panegyric in four lectures he gave on Celtic literature in 1865–66. Quoted in George Watson, *The English Ideology: Studies in the Language of Victorian Politics* (London: Allen Lane, 1973), p. 206. Wilde was, in this as in much else, not shy of speaking his mind; and he confirmed that "the creative instinct is strong in the Celt, and it is the Celt who leads in art." ("The Critic as Artist," *Works*, Vol. 6, p. 203) It became fairly commonplace towards the end of the century to distinguish between the "Celtic spirit," on the one hand, and the Teutonic or Nordic on the other.

4. Hyde recounts the story of how Wilde,

> during his last term at Oxford, had gone to a fancy-dress ball given by Mrs. Frederic Morrell at her house on Headington Hill in the character of Prince Rupert. For this he was dressed in a velvet coat edged with braid, knee-breeches, buckle shoes, a soft silk shirt with a wide turn-down collar, and a large flowing green tie. He would appear from time to time in this garb in London, usually in the evenings . . . jokingly declaring that reformation of dress was more important than reformation of religion. (*Wilde*, p. 46)

Wilde wrote quite extensively and surprisingly earnestly about dress during the early 1880s. Along with vegetarianism, concern about natural modes of dress was much in fashion.

5. See Amy Cruse, *The Victorians and Their Books* (London: George Allen and Unwin, 1935) and *After the Victorians* (London: Allen and Unwin, 1938). One unfortunate corollary of this burgeoning trade was the rise of devastatingly successful societies for the suppression of vice, and moral vigilance associations. The works of Zola provided a focus for their actions in the late 1880s, though Baudelaire, Flaubert, Bourget and Maupassant were also castigated; and more than one book publisher—the most notable being Henry Vizetelly, the founder of the *Illustrated London News* and angel of numerous admirable publishing ventures—went to jail for opposing the iron law established by Smith's and Mudie's and the other circulating libraries. For a more detailed discussion, see Decker, passim; Robert T. Altick, "The Literature of an Imminent Democracy," *1859: Entering an Age of Crisis*, pp. 215–28. Social as well as literary transgressions were zealously proscribed, of course, as Dilke and Parnell and Wilde discovered to their dismay. It was, for example, the unrelenting expression of moral outrage by W. T. Stead of the *Pall Mall Gazette* and others that helped to bring Parnell down.

6. Besides Darwin, there were the more literary sensations: John Stuart Mill's *On Liberty* and Edward Fitzgerald's immensely influential *Rubáiyát of Omar Khayyám*, not to mention Samuel Smiles's *Self-Help*.

7. De Quincey defines "echo-augury," in words that Moore echoes in various places in his *Confessions*, as

> where a man, perplexed in judgment, and sighing for some determining counsel, suddenly heard from a stranger in some unlooked-for quarter words not meant for himself, but clamorously applying to the difficulty besetting

him . . . the mystical word always unsought for—*that* constituted its virtue and its divinity. (*Autobiography from 1785 to 1803*, Vol. 1 [London, 1896], p. 123)
Quoted in George Moore, *Confessions of a Young Man*, ed. Susan Dick (Montreal: McGill-Queen's University Press, 1972), p. 233, n.1.

8. *The New Age*, VIII, 9 (Dec. 29, 1910), p. 204. Quoted in Tom Gibbons, *Rooms in the Darwin Hotel: Studies in English Literary Criticism and Ideas 1880–1920* (Nedlands: University of Western Australia Press, 1973), p. 117.

9. Watson, pp. 166–67.

10. "The Critic as Artist," *Works*, Vol. 8, p. 221. Symons' comment was made in an article, "Tolstoi on Art," which appeared in *The Saturday Review* (Quoted in Gibbons, p. 90). Wilde described the scene at Prince's Hall where Whistler proclaimed his doctrine in 1885 as "in every way delightful; (Whistler) stood there, a miniature Mephistopheles, mocking the majority."

11. See Gibbon, pp. 34ff. Lombroso's book had originally been published as *L'Uomo di Genio*, in 1888. In it, he had argued that "the signs of degeneration are found more frequently in men of genius than even in the insane." In the same year that Ellis' translation appeared, J. F. Nisbet, drama critic for *The Times*, published *The Insanity of Genius*, which claimed to "place upon a solid basis of fact the long-suspected relationship of genius and insanity." Francis Galton, who had introduced the term "eugenics" to the language in 1883, brought out a second edition of his *Hereditary Genius* in 1892, and supported the contention of a close relationship between genius and insanity or degeneration. And Havelock Ellis' own work of criminal anthropology, *The Criminal* (1890), saw even in the vanity of artists a kind of degeneracy, and displayed Verlaine as "an interesting example of the man of genius who is also distinctly a criminal." (The first volume of Ellis' more famous *Studies in the Psychology of Sex*, originally begun in collaboration with John Addington Symonds, came out in 1897.) The important thing to realize, aside from the climate of interest which these studies reflected, is the close and continuous relationship between the study of the psychology of genius and insanity, and the study of creative processes in general. Wilde appealed to "the works of eminent men of science such as Lombroso and Nordau, to take merely two instances out of many . . . with reference to the intimate connection between madness and the literary and artistic temperament" in an appeal for clemency written to the Home Secretary from Reading Gaol in 1896. (*Letters*, p. 402) A variety of articles and pamphlets appeared during Wilde's term of imprisonment, in defense of his inclinations as pathological rather than purely criminal.

12. Hippolyte Taine's comment about Renan—that "il a des impressions, ce mot dit tout"—is among the most succinct. It is quoted by Ruth F. Temple, *The Critic's Alchemy: A Study of the Introduction of French*

Symbolism into England (New York: Twayne, 1953), p. 296, n.3.

13. *Notes on Men, Women and Books* (London, 1891), pp. 327–28.

14. Pater's Marius and Wilde's Dorian provided different versions of this idea. Marius' reading of the *Metamorphoses* of Apuleius "counted" to him with "something more than its independent value" by raising to consciousness and giving coherence to values and instincts for which his soul was ready and anxious. The book that Lord Henry gives to Dorian (the model for which is Huysmans' *À Rebours*), like the story of Tannhäuser, provided imaginative focus for the aspirations and attachments of Wilde himself as well as of Dorian.

15. Wilde remarked, in defense of his reference to *Emaux et camées* in *The Picture of Dorian Gray*, that it was a book "that any fairly educated reader may be supposed to be acquainted with."

16. Swinburne's review appeared in the *Spectator* in September, 1862; reprinted in *Swinburne as Critic*, ed. Clyde K. Hyder (London: Routledge and Kegan Paul, 1972), pp. 27–35.

17. It was Flaubert's dedication of the volume to his advocate in this case that prevented Wilde's obtaining a copy while in gaol. By this time, of course, Flaubert had become fairly accepted everywhere but in prison; and Bourget was invited to Oxford in 1897 to lecture on Flaubert.

18. Richard Howard, "Wild Flowers," *Two-Part Inventions* (New York: Atheneum, 1974), p. 18.

19. *Dorian Gray*, p. 125.

20. Quoted in E. R. Curtius, *Essays on European Literature*, trans. Michael Kowal (Princeton: Princeton University Press, 1973), p. 195. With this reference to encyclopaedic and monumental imaginative accomplishments, it is perhaps appropriate to mention that Russian literature began to be appreciated in England during the 1880s and 1890s. There were translations of Turgeniev, Tolstoy (*War and Peace* and *Anna Karenina*—which were praised highly, though with some reservations by those who did not like melancholy stories), and Dostoievsky during this period. Wilde saw Turgeniev as the "finest artist" of the three, recognized Tolstoy's epic grandeur and simplicity, and praised Dostoievsky for his "fierce intensity of passion and concentration of impulse, [his] power of dealing with the deepest mysteries of psychology and the most hidden springs of life," and his pitiless realism. Scandinavian literature had its special presence with the work of Ibsen, a selection of which was edited in translation by Havelock Ellis in 1887 (see Decker's chapters on "Ibsen in England," pp. 115–30, and "The Russians in England," pp. 131–46 for a more general discussion). Lady Wilde had contributed to early attempts to popularize Scandinavian authors with her *Driftwood from Scandinavia* (1884).

21. See Anthony Ward, *Walter Pater: The Idea in Nature* (London: MacGibbon and Kee, 1966), pp. 43–52 and passim; also *The Eighteen-Seventies*, ed. Harley Granville-Barker (Cambridge: Cambridge Univer-

sity Press, 1929). During this period Jowett was engaged in a continuing debate on matters of educational principle with Mark Pattison, Rector of Lincoln College; and on matters of philosophical issue with T. H. Green.

22. *Letters*, p. 20. Schopenhauer's views had been presented to the English public in the 1870s by the music critic Francis Hueffer, especially in his book on *Richard Wagner and the Music of the Future* (1874). George Moore confessed (in his 1889 preface) that the "philosophy" of his *Confessions* was that of Schopenhauer, "that philosophy which alone helps us to live while in the evil of living." Wilde's more reflective comment (in "The Decay of Lying") was that "Schopenhauer has analysed the pessimism that characterizes modern thought, but Hamlet invented it." The evolutionary determinism of the time certainly reinforced any inclination in that direction.

23. *Affirmations* (London, 1898), p. 16.

24. For a reasonably full account of this question see Robert Blake, *Disraeli* (New York: St. Martin's Press, 1967), pp. 570–628. There were curious alliances formed in this dispute; for example, Carlyle, Ruskin, Froude, Browning, Trollope, Darwin and Spencer supported Gladstone's agitation, while Jowett, Matthew Arnold, and Henry Hyndman opposed the moral crusade, seeing it as an irrelevant diversion. Even Karl Marx, whose application for British citizenship had been recently (1874) rejected, found himself in the unlikely position of writing to Tory newspapers in opposition to Gladstone. The probable model for Wilde's poetic lament was John Milton's magnificent appeal to "Avenge, O Lord, thy slaughter'd Saints" in the late massacre in Piedmont.

25. *William Morris and His Circle* (Oxford: Clarendon Press, 1907), p. 4. In this context, Roger Fry referred (in *Vision and Design*, in an essay, "Art and Life") to the political and religious thought of the nineteenth century as being inspired primarily by aesthetic considerations.

26. Quoted in Kathleen Tillotson, *Novels of the Eighteen-Forties* (London: Oxford University Press, 1961), p. 125. Carlyle's remarks about Froude's novel (from a letter to John Forster written in 1848) are quoted in Tillotson, p. 130.

27. Cockshut, p. 21.

28. See Stanley E. Hyman, *The Tangled Bank: Darwin, Marx, Frazer and Freud as Imaginative Writers* (New York: Atheneum, 1962), p. 58.

29. The obituary notice by Frazer appeared first in *The Fortnightly Review*. Reprinted in *The Gorgon's Head and Other Literary Pieces* (London, 1927). Quoted in Hyman, p. 198. Anthropology had, of course, something of a past as well as a future; and the Société d'Anthropologie had been founded by Paul Broca in Paris in 1859.

30. Alan Willard Brown, *The Metaphysical Society: Victorian Minds in Crisis, 1869–1880* (New York: Columbia University Press, 1947), p. 279.

31. Quoted in Hyman, p. 207. In a similar manner, Wilde's aphorism that "all art is at once surface and symbol" involves a recognition that the aesthetic harmony, the "ordering," which a work of art provides, constitutes only a part of its appeal; its function as a symbol is to satisfy what Morse Peckham has called "man's rage for chaos" as much as his "rage to order." *Art nouveau*, a significant product of the period, also displayed unsettling evidence of "unseen forces" threatening rational order and classical coherence.

32. Ed. J. Max Patrick (Gainesville: University of Florida, 1950). Mallock's comments are taken from his *Memoirs*, quoted in the Introduction. The epigram from the Greek Anthology is one of the epigrams of admonition, a mixture of proverbial wisdom and Epicurean common sense; it is attributed to Glycon. (See *The Greek Anthology*, trans. Shane Leslie [London: Ernest Benn, 1929], p. 194.)

33. See Raymond Williams, *Culture and Society 1780–1950* (London: Chatto and Windus, 1960), pp. 114–27.

34. Quoted in Epifanio San Juan, Jr., "Toward a Definition of Victorian Activism," *British Victorian Literature: Recent Revaluations*, ed. Shiv K. Kumar (New York: New York University Press, 1969), p. 29. San Juan's book on *The Art of Oscar Wilde* (Princeton: Princeton University Press, 1967), is a solid if rather stolid account of the canon. Another critical study worth noting is Edouard Roditi's *Oscar Wilde* (Norfolk, Conn.: New Directions, 1947).

35. Quoted by David Daiches in his provocative discussion of *Some Late Victorian Attitudes* (London: Andre Deutsch, 1969), p. 36. The idea of duty was very much in the forefront. One celebrated anecdote tells of how, in the gardens of Trinity College in 1873, George Eliot, like a "sibyl in the gloom," announced to F. W. H. Myers that of "the three words which have been used so often as the inspiring trumpet-calls of men— the words, God, Immortality, Duty . . . how inconceivable was the first, how unbelievable the second, and yet how peremptory and absolute the third." As Havelock Ellis pointed out when he recalled this story, "what George Eliot proposed was one of those compromises so dear to British minds," the rejecting of Christian theology only "to shore up the superstructure of Christian morality which rests on that theology." There were other theologies, of course—Nietzsche's, for example, which (echoing the uncompromising William Blake) promoted a radically un-Christian sense of duty.

36. Quoted in Cesar Graña, *Fact and Symbol: Essays in the Sociology of Art and Literature* (New York: Oxford University Press, 1971), p. 68. William A. Madden writes of the particular anxiety of the nineteenth-century artist in his essay "The Burden of the Artist," 1859, p. 247, and he refers in passing to Wallace Stevens' remarks (from "The Noble Rider and the Sound of Words") about the "ever-enlarging incoherence" to which the artist is exposed, and the "pressure of reality" which is resisted

or even evaded by "individuals of extraordinary imagination."

37. Quoted in John M. Munro, *The Decadent Poetry of the Eighteen-Nineties* (Beirut: American University of Beirut, 1970), p. xii.

38. There were several "replies" to Nordau, the most notable being G. B. Shaw's "A Degenerate's View of Nordau" (which first appeared in the American Anarchist periodical *Liberty* in July, 1895, and was reprinted in *The Sanity of Art)* and A. E. Hake's *Regeneration: A Reply to Max Nordau*. Hake, the author of a book on *Free Trade in Capital* (1891), had invented a system of banking which Wilde found entertaining.

39. Referred to in Watson, p. 249. In "The Critic as Artist" Wilde recalled that "by the Ilyssus, says Arnold somewhere, there was no Higginbotham." Wilde's own ambition for the art and culture of his time was for a "union of Hellenism, in its breadth, its sanity of purpose, its calm possession of beauty, with the adventure, the intensified individualism, the passionate colour of the romantic spirit." ("The English Renaissance of Art," *Works*, Vol. 14, p. 244)

40. "The Soul of Man Under Socialism," *Works*, Vol. 8, p. 275.

41. These quotations from Engels are from Hyman, pp. 163–164.

42. From his *Economic and Philosophic Manuscripts* (1844). Quoted in Alan Swingewood, "Theory," *The Sociology of Literature*, eds. Swingewood and Diana Laurenson (London: MacGibbon and Kee, 1972), p. 44. By the 1890s, the subject had become matter for parody, though for some there was not much humour in it. Gilbert and Sullivan (in *Utopia Limited*, 1893) had described how

> Some seven men form an Association
> (If possible, all Peers and Baronets),
> They start off with a public declaration
> To what extent they mean to pay their debts.
> That's called their Capital . . .

See Hugh Kenner, *The Pound Era* (Berkeley: University of California Press, 1972), p. 555 and passim.

43. Wilde may have been encouraged in this conclusion by the writings of Kropotkin in particular; for example, in an article entitled "Mutual Aid among Animals" which appeared (in 1890) in the same issue of the *Nineteenth Century* as the second part of Wilde's essay on "The True Function and Value of Criticism," Kropotkin argued from Darwin that co-operation characterizes the "fittest" groups, and quoted Darwin from *The Descent of Man* to describe how "*struggle* is replaced by *co-operation* , and how that substitution results in the development of intellectual and moral faculties which secure to the species the best conditions for survival." The topic was very much in the air; a couple of years later, the distinguished scientist Karl Pearson wrote in the *Fortnightly* about "Socialism and Natural Selection."

44. In this regard, Swinburne wrote an entertaining parody of Tennyson's "The Higher Pantheism," entitled "The Higher Pantheism in a Nutshell," with the instructive lines:

Body and spirit are twins: God only knows which is which:
The soul squats down in the flesh, like a tinker drunk in a ditch.

45. P. 196. One of the most spirited discussions of this notion is by
Robert Langbaum, in an essay entitled "The Victorian Idea of Culture,"
included in his book *The Modern Spirit: Essays on the Continuity of
Nineteenth- and Twentieth-Century Literature* (New York: Oxford University Press, 1970). There is something of this interest in W. K. Clif-
ford's notion of the "tribal self," which intrigued Wilde. For a fuller
discussion of the Victorian "sages," see John Holloway, *The Victorian
Sage: Studies in Argument* (London: Archer, 1962) and Watson, pp.
241–63.

THREE.
THE MOTIVE FOR ART

1. Quoted in Curtius, p. 439.
2. *Complete Works*, trans. F. C. de Sumichrast (New York: Bigelow,
Smith, 1910), pp. 80, 82–3.
3. For a full account, see Dickran Tashjian, *Skyscraper Primitives: Dada
and the American Avant-Garde 1910–1925* (Middletown; Conn.: Wes-
leyan University Press, 1975), esp. pp. 49–62.
4. See Pierre Emmanuel, *Baudelaire: The Paradox of Redemptive Sa-
tanism*, trans. Robert T. Carge (University: University of Alabama Press,
1970), p. 117 and passim, pp. 105–26. See also Barbara Charlesworth,
Dark Passages: The Decadent Consciousness in Victorian Literature
(Madison: University of Wisconsin Press, 1965), p. 136, n. 51.
5. Quoted in Blake, *Disraeli*, p. 212. Balzac called it "smoking enchanted cigarettes"; it was a sign of the times, to be sure.
6. See Michael Hamburger, "Art as Second Nature," *Romantic Mythologies*, ed. Iain Fletcher (London: Routledge and Kegan Paul, 1967), pp.
229ff.
7. From some "Notes nouvelles sur Edgar Poe," quoted in A. E. Carter,
The Idea of Decadence in French Literature 1830–1900 (Toronto: University of Toronto Press, 1958), p. 11. The translation is mine.
8. Included in *The Yellow Book*, ed. Weintraub, pp. 1–16. A later and
more muted version of the same idea is presented by Paul Valéry, with
his insistence that "in all the arts, and this is why they are arts, the
necessity a successfully created work of art must suggest can be engen-
dered only by what is *arbitrary.*"
9. See Curtius, p. 16. J. A. Symonds, in his essay "Is Music the Type
or Measure of All Art?" (first published in *The Fortnightly Review* in
1887, and reprinted in *Essays Speculative and Suggestive*, 1890) spends
a fair bit of time quoting F. W. H. Myers, the noted spiritualist (see

Wilde, "The Decay of Lying," *Works,* Vol. 6, p. 50) and classicist, on the subject of Virgil and his artistic style. Wilde's own heavily annotated copy of the *Aeneid* displays quite clearly his own interest in this aspect of Virgil.

10. This "law" (also called the "biogenetic law"), which stated that the embryological development of the members of any species repeats the evolution of the genus to which the species belongs, had obvious advantages apart from biological theory, and in its sociological or psychogenetic form it was used extensively to justify the habit, that became addictive at the beginning of the century, of seeing in the child the childhood of the race as a whole. The law was further credited, by Herbert Read, with "providing confirmation for the general validity of the generic method in aesthetics" (*Art Now* [London: Faber, 1948], p. 46).

11. Austin Dobson translated these lines under the title "Ars Victrix" in 1876:

> Yes: when the ways oppose—
> When the hard means rebel,
> Fairer the work out-grows,—
> More potent far the spell . . .
>
> Sculptor, do thou discard
> The yielding clay,—consign
> To Paros marble hard
> The beauty of thy line . . .
>
> Even the gods must go;
> Only the lofty Rhyme
> Not countless years o'erthrow,—
> Not long array of time.
>
> Paint, chisel, then, or write;
> But, that the word surpass,
> With the hard fashion fight,—
> With the resisting mass.

There is a distinct line from Gautier's verse to the "imagist" aesthetic of Ezra Pound; and Pound's praise of Lionel Johnson's poems as "small slabs of ivory, firmly combined and contrived," makes the connection even more specific. Donald Davie has suggested in *Ezra Pound: Poet as Sculptor* (New York: Oxford University Press, 1964, p. 98) that Gautier's *Emaux et camées* provided a definite model from which Pound developed his refined artistic style. See also Chapple, pp. 367–68.

12. "The Critic as Artist," *Works,* Vol. 8, pp. 207–8.

13. Quoted by Havelock Ellis in his essay on Huysmans included in *Affirmations* (London, 1899), pp. 178–79.

14. *Ibid.,* p. 180.

15. "Sailing to Byzantium," *The Collected Poems of W. B. Yeats* (London: Macmillan, 1969), p. 218; "The Idea of Order at Key West," *The Collected Poems of Wallace Stevens,* pp. 128–9. Both Yeats and

Stevens, incidentally, set much store by Pater's emphasis on and celebration of the element of style in art.

16. From an interview given by Beardsley to Arthur H. Lawrence, published in *The Idler* in March, 1897. Wilde's Sphinx, that "exquisite grotesque", belongs directly in this tradition.

17. *Autobiographies: The Trembling of the Veil* (London: Macmillan, 1926), pp. 410–11. Quoted in Weintraub, *Beardsley*, p. 132.

18. Canto LXXX, *The Cantos of Ezra Pound* (New York: New Directions, 1972), p. 511. Symons' poem is included in *Images of Good and Evil* (1899); see *Poems*, Vol. 2 (London: Martin Secker, 1924), p. 82. For some further account of Yeats and Wilde, see Richard Ellmann, *Eminent Domain: Yeats Among Wilde, Joyce, Pound, Eliot and Auden* (New York, Oxford University Press, 1967).

19. The complete text of Symons' essay is included in *Aesthetes and Decadents*, pp. 135–51. Richard Le Gallienne, to whose satire and criticism Symons was in part replying, had already referred to the disease of "the euphuistic expression of isolated observations" as a characteristic theme of *décadents*, and to decadence itself as "merely limited thinking, often insane thinking," in a review that he wrote in January, 1892, of a book by Churton Collins entitled *Illustrations of Tennyson* which he felt compelled him "to think out the whole question of literary decadence." (*Retrospective Reviews: A Library Log* [London: John Lane, 1896], vol. 1, pp. 24–6, quoted in Roger Lhombreaud, *Arthur Symons: A Critical Biography* [London: Unicorn Press, 1963], pp. 97–98.)

20. Another side of this kind of interpretation was provided by late nineteenth- and early twentieth-century Marxist critics such as George Plekhanov, with a view that any hermetic art form is the expression of the alienated artist out of accord with his environment. Later writers of this tradition, such as the sociologists of the Frankfurt School and in particular the great critic Theodor Adorno, saw a more positive side to this alienation, *verfremdung* instead of *entfremdung*. (For a discussion of this with relation to Wilde, see J. E. Chamberlin, "Oscar Wilde and the Importance of Doing Nothing," *The Hudson Review*, XXV, 2 [Summer, 1972], pp. 194–218.)

21. There is much written on this group, and their activities and conversations, but most of it is scattered in memoirs and miscellaneous studies of sometimes dubious reliability. Lhombreaud gives what is perhaps the most useful, brief account for present purposes in *Symons*, pp. 83–88, though W. B. Yeats and others have included a discussion of its significance in their autobiographies or reminiscences. Ezra Pound, whose interest in this coterie was substantial, once remarked that "the whole set of 'The Rhymers' did valuable work in knocking bombast, and rhetoric and victorian syrup out of our verse." (Quoted in Gibbons, p. 96.) For a full account of "The Books of the Rhymers' Club," see James E. Nelson, *The Early Nineties: A View from the Bodley Head* (Cambridge, Mass:

Harvard University Press, 1971), esp. pp. 150–183.

22. From the introductory poem "To the Reader," quoted in Lhombreaud, *Symons*, p. 98.

23. At the time of publication, Hichens had just been appointed to succeed George Bernard Shaw as music critic for *The World*. Wilde had referred, in "Pen, Pencil and Poison," to Wainewright's "curious love of green, which in individuals is always the sign of a subtle artistic temperament, and in nations is said to denote a laxity, if not a decadence of morals."

24. Quoted in Weintraub, *Beardsley*, pp. 72–73.

25. *English Poems*, pp. 106–7. See also Lhombreaud, *Symons*, pp. 97–99. Le Gallienne's reference to street lamps perhaps needs a note to recall that electric street lighting was first introduced in London in 1878 (and the London telephone exchange established in the following year). Le Gallienne himself did not escape parody: for example, in 1897 one "Richard Le Lyrienne" (probably David Hodge) appeared as the author of *The Quest of the Gilt-Edged Girl*.

26. *Dorian Gray*, p. 125.

27. *Works*, Vol. 8, p. 134. "One can fancy," suggested Wilde in "Pen, Pencil and Poison," "an intense personality being created out of sin." James Joyce, from a somewhat different perspective, commented of Wilde's aesthetic attitude that "at its very base is the truth inherent in the soul of Catholicism: that man cannot reach the divine heart except through that sense of separation and loss called sin" ("Oscar Wilde: The Poet of *Salomé*", p. 205). It is interesting to note that, as Vincent O'Sullivan has recalled, Wilde liked few American authors with one particular exception being the Hawthorne of *The Scarlet Letter*. C. S. Nassar, in *Into the Demon Universe: A Literary Exploration of Oscar Wilde* (New Haven: Yale University Press, 1974), pp. 120–22, makes much of this, and relates it explicitly to Wilde's fascination with sin.

28. Quoted in John A. Lester, Jr., *Journey through Despair: 1880–1914: Transformations in British Literary Culture* (Princeton: Princeton University Press, 1968), pp. 66–67.

29. *Swinburne's Collected Poetical Works*, Vol. 1 (London: Heinemann, 1924), p. 362. See also Philip Henderson, *Swinburne: The Portrait of a Poet* (London: Routledge and Kegan Paul, 1974), p. 176.

30. *Dorian Gray*, p. 18. *The Chameleon*, the short-lived Oxford magazine of the "new culture" in which Wilde's "Phrases and Philosophies for the Use of the Young" were published in 1894 (in the only issue that appeared), had as its epigraph a phrase from R. L. Stevenson referring to "a bazaar of dangerous and smiling chances." In a sense, active sin becomes in such a frame of reference the inverted opposite of salvation by works, itself a major tenet of evangelicalism.

31. For a general discussion of the reception of *À Rebours*, see Robert Baldick, *The Life of J.-K. Huysmans* (Oxford: Clarendon Press, 1955), pp. 87–91.

32. *Selected Prose,* trans. Mary Hottinger and Tania and James Stern (London: Routledge and Kegan Paul, 1952), p. 303.

33. See A. E. Carter, *The Idea of Decadence in French Literature,* pp. 134ff; also, George Ross Ridge, *The Hero in French Decadent Literature* (Athens: University of Georgia Press, 1961). In Chapter 3, entitled "Nerve-Storms and Bad Heredity," Carter gives an account of the many studies of the psychopathology of genius which led up to the final and most preposterous expression of the idea in Max Nordau's work.

34. Carter, p. 149.

35. See Curtius, pp. 381–82. One section of the *Fleurs du Mal* is entitled "Spleen et Idéal." (Stefan) George translated it as "Trubsinn und Vergeistigung" ("Dejection and Sublimation"). The sense of decadence was a form of modern psychological suffering incident to the age. To succumb to the attraction of forces hostile to life was only possible if one's own vital powers had already been stricken. For the artist this meant the drying up of his creative power. One of the main themes of Mallarmé's poetry is the sterility of his Muse.

36. For a complex reading of *Salomé,* see Nassar, pp. 80–109.

37. Baudelaire sets the stage nicely with his Blakean pronouncement that "the angelic element and the diabolic element function in a parallel manner." For an extended study of the division of the self by which nineteenth-century art was so compelled, see Masao Miyoshi, *The Divided Self: A Perspective on the Literature of the Victorians* (New York: New York University Press, 1969). Several writers on Wilde have focussed on this aspect of his work, among them George Woodcock, *The Paradox of Oscar Wilde* (New York: Macmillan, 1950); Arthur H. Nethercot, "Oscar Wilde and the Devil's Advocate," *PMLA,* LIX (1944), pp. 833–50; Arthur Ganz, "The Divided Self in the Social Comedies of Oscar Wilde," *Modern Drama,* III (1960), pp. 16–23; and Barbara Charlesworth in her chapter on Wilde in *Dark Passages,* pp. 53–80. *The Importance of Being Earnest,* Wilde's other, major and his greatest play, has both structural and thematic ambiguities which are in their way as unsettling. Wilde probably took the name of Bunbury from a family friend named Henry S. Bunbury who had a town house near Monmouth and a country house in West Coleford; but the implications of the scheme of Bunburying, and the confusions that he works into its development, went far beyond what may have been suggested by this reference. The ambivalences in the play may, however, have a significant personal reference to Wilde himself.

38. From "Vesperal," a poem dedicated to Hubert Crackanthorpe. *The Poems of Ernest Dowson,* ed. Mark Longaker (Philadelphia: University of Pennsylvania Press, 1962), p. 78. See also Longaker's biography of Dowson (1968). Wilde, Beardsley and Crackanthorpe were often linked together as representing the various facets of decadent art and life in the 1890s.

39. There is a largely unexamined sense in which Pater's portraits

prepared the way for the fiction of James and Woolf, and for early twentieth-century attitudes towards the techniques of fictional portraiture. For a somewhat different perspective on Pater's work, see G. C. Monsman, *Pater's Portraits: Mythic Pattern in the Fiction of Walter Pater* (Baltimore: Johns Hopkins Press, 1967).

40. Michael Hamburger, p. 230, giving a summation of Hofmannsthal's attitude. (See also Richard Ellmann, "Two Faces of Edward," *Edwardians and Late Victorians,* ed. Ellmann [New York: Columbia University Press, 1960], pp. 205–7.) The final quotation is Wilde's.

41. In the novel (p. 109) Dorian speaks to Basil of Sibyl's suicide in the following words:

> The last night she played—the night you saw her—she acted badly because she had known the reality of love. When she knew its unreality, she died, as Juliet might have died. She passed again into the sphere of art. There is something of the martyr about her. Her death has all the pathetic uselessness of martyrdom, all its wasted beauty.

42. A. D. Nuttall, *A Common Sky: Philosophy and the Literary Imagination* (London: Chatto and Windus, 1974), p. 111.

43. *Appreciations, with an Essay on Style* (London: Macmillan, 1889), pp. 61–3.

44. Quoted in Kermode, pp. 112–13. The idea that all true art is symbolic became by the end of the century quite orthodox; and the descriptions of symbolism that critics such as Arthur Symons provided were the conventional wisdom.

> The Symbolist would flash upon you the "soul" of that which can be apprehended only by the soul—the finer sense of things unseen, the deeper meaning of things evident. And naturally, necessarily, this endeavour after a perfect truth to one's impression, to one's intuition—perhaps an impossible endeavour—has brought with it, in its revolt from ready-made impressions and conclusions, a revolt from the ready-made of language, from the bondage of traditional form, of a form become rigid. (Arthur Symons, "The Decadent Movement in Literature," *Aesthetes and Decadents,* ed. Beckson, p. 137).

45. The nineteenth-century interest in Heraclitus became very much the interest in this particular sort of correspondence, and the ideas that were discovered in Heraclitus informed the work of Pater in particular.

46. "The Critic as Artist," *Works,* Vol. 8, p. 222.

FOUR.
WHATSOEVER THINGS ARE COMELY

1. "The School of Giorgione," *The Renaissance: Studies in Art and Poetry* (London: Macmillan, 1888), p. 140.

2. From Ruskin's *The Elements of Drawing* (London, 1857), quoted in E. H. Gombrich, *Art and Illusion: A Study in the Psychology of*

Pictorial Representation (London: Phaidon, 1962), p. 250. 1874, the year in which Wilde went up to Oxford, was the year of the first, and startling, Impressionist exhibition in Paris. (For a telescoped account of the impressionist scene, see George Moore, *Confessions,* pp. 68–71, and notes 3 and 4, p. 237.)

3. "School of Giorgione," p. 140.

4. *Works,* Vol. 8, pp. 44–45. It is a nice touch, perhaps of some psychological significance, that Cyril and Vivian were the names of Oscar's children. (His younger son was in fact christened Vyvyan and preferred that spelling himself; but it was his parents' habit to spell his name Vivian.) Moreover, it is Vivian who carries the argument in Wilde's essay, though it was undoubtedly Cyril (perhaps simply because he was the eldest and, as Oscar said, a "friend" to his father) who was his father's favourite.

5. "Two Early French Stories," *The Renaissance,* pp. 2, 28.

6. Arthur Symons' translation of these lines went as follows:

> Music first and foremost of all!
> Choose your measure of odd not even,
> Let it melt in the air of heaven,
> Pose not, poise not, but rise and fall.

> Choose your words, but think not whether
> Each to other of old belong:
> What so dear as the dim grey song
> Where clear and vague are joined together . . .

> Let every shape of its shade be born;
> Colour, away! come to me, shade!
> Only of shade can the marriage be made
> Of dream with dream and of flute with horn.

7. See A. G. Lehmann, *The Symbolist Aesthetic in France, 1885–1895* (Oxford: Basil Blackwell, 1968), pp. 136–38. Wilde's poem *The Sphinx* owes much both to "The Raven" itself (especially the fiction of the apparition appearing to a student in his rooms) and to the account of its origins (for it appears from the drafts that Wilde at least in part followed the compositional program outlined by Poe). He had praised it as a model during his lecture tour in 1882, out of more than courtesy to his American hosts.

8. From the Preface to *The Picture of Dorian Gray.* Writing in *The Yellow Book* in July, 1894 (in an article entitled "Reticence in Literature: Some Roundabout Remarks," a response to Arthur Waugh's plea for "Reticence in Literature" which had appeared in April) Hubert Crackanthorpe remarked that

> throughout the history of literature the jealous worship of beauty—which we term idealism—and the jealous worship of truth—which we term realism—have alternately prevailed. Indeed, it is within the compass of these alterations that lies the whole fundamental diversity of literary temper. (*The Yellow Book,* ed. Weintraub, p. 364)

9. Many people did not much like this transformation, of course, and routinely told the chief theoretician of Realism, Emile Zola, "to drive his pigs to some other market."

10. "The Critic as Artist," *Works*, Vol. 8, p. 194.

11. Alfred Orage, attempting to understand Nietzsche, called such moments "both cause and effect of all great art." Most artists and critics of the time would have agreed, with more or less idiosyncratic qualifications.

12. It was in an anonymous review of "Poems by William Morris" (afterwards entitled "Aesthetic Poetry") in the *Westminster Review* for October, 1868, that Walter Pater first published the notorious passage that later appeared as the "Conclusion."

13. See Lehmann, *The Symbolist Aesthetic*, pp. 194–247.

14. Winifred Nowottny, *The Language Poets Use* (London: The Athlone Press, 1965), p. 221.

15. *Appreciations*, p. 65. For a discussion of this aspect of Pater, see Richmond Crinkley, *Walter Pater: Humanist* (Lexington: University Press of Kentucky, 1970). Sir William Hamilton provided Wilde in particular with his first (and very persuasive) introduction to this idea; and Wilde's early notes are filled with its various critical implications.

16. A different version of this idea is presented by Noel Annan in "Science, Religion and the Critical Mind: Introduction," *1859*, pp. 31–50.

17. "The Critic as Artist," *Works*, Vol. 8, p. 178. The idea of personality was, to Wilde as to Pater, absolutely central, for (in Wilde's words) "as art springs from personality, so it is only to personality that it can be revealed, and from the meeting of the two comes right interpretative criticism." ("The Critic as Artist," *Works*, Vol. 8, p. 164; see also "The English Renaissance of Art," *Works*, Vol. 14, p. 251.)

18. "The Critic as Artist," *Works*, Vol. 8, p. 142. The quotation which follows is from a review which Wilde wrote for the *Pall Mall Gazette* in 1886 of some English translations of Balzac. (*Works*, Vol. 13, p. 77)

19. Graña, pp. 187–88.

20. Quoted in Decker, p. 72.

21. See Philip Wheelwright, *Heraclitus* (Princeton: Princeton University Press, 1959), esp. pp. 90–101.

22. From a letter to the *Pall Mall Gazette* (December 11, 1891), in response to a review of *A House of Pomegranates*. (*Works*, Vol. 14, p. 163) Coleridge's definition appears in his *Biographia Literaria* (1817), chapter XII, thesis X.

23. "The Critic as Artist," *Works*, Vol. 8, p. 150.

24. William Wordsworth, "The Excursion," Book IV, pp. 174–78. To be set against this, there is A. H. Clough's apostrophe:

> Staid Englishman, who toil and slave
> From your first childhood to your grave,

And seldom spend and always save—
And do your duty all your life
By your young family and wife.

25. "Prometheus Unbound," Act I, 543–45. (*Complete Poetical Works*, ed. Thomas Hutchinson (London: Oxford University Press, 1965), p. 220.)

26. See Wheelwright, *Heraclitus*, pp. 116–18.

27. *Four Quartets*, in *Collected Poems: 1909–1962* (London: Faber and Faber, 1963), p. 219. For a provocative discussion of the paradox of the fortunate fall, and of the nature of paradox in general, see Philip Wheelwright, *The Burning Fountain: A Study of the Language of Symbolism* (Bloomington: Indiana University Press, 1954), pp. 70–73, 358–60.

28. See Robert T. Peterssen, *The Art of Ecstasy: Teresa, Bernini and Crashaw* (New York: Atheneum, 1970) for the text of the poem and a good analysis of the nature of *ek-stasis*.

29. Hofmannsthal, pp. 304–5.

30. "Conclusion," *The Renaissance*, p. 248.

31. "Il Penseroso," 11. 85–96 from *Complete Poems and Major Prose*, ed. Merritt Y. Hughes (New York: Odyssey Press, 1957), p. 74. For an idiosyncratic but compelling application of this tradition, see Harold Bloom, *Yeats* (London: Oxford University Press, 1972), esp. pp. 1–37.

32. "All Souls' Night," *Collected Poems* (London: Macmillan, 1967), p. 259.

33. Samuel Taylor Coleridge, "The Statesman's Manual," *Lay Sermons*, ed. R. J. White (London: Routledge and Kegan Paul, 1972), pp. 29–30.

34. Wheelwright, *Burning Fountain*, pp. 88–89.

35. "The Statesman's Manual," pp. 64–65.

36. Ibid., p. 62. The quotations from Wilde are taken from his essay on "The Rise of Historical Criticism."

37. "The Truth of Masks," *Works*, Vol. 8, pp. 269–270.

38. "The Critic as Artist," *Works*, Vol. 8, pp. 178–182.

FIVE.
THE CRY OF MARSYAS

1. *Letters*, p. 490.

2. Quoted in Patricia Merivale, *Pan the Goat-God: His Myth in Modern Time* (Cambridge: Harvard University Press, 1969), p. 16.

3. *Works*, Vol. 9, pp. 166–188.

4. *Aurora Leigh* (London, 1857), p. 221.

5. *The Beardsley Period: An Essay in Perspective* (New York: Boni and

Liveright, 1925), p. 113. Burdett takes as his motto Beerbohm's boast that he "belong[ed] to the Beardsley period." Others defined themselves slightly differently; Reggie Turner, for example, liked to be remembered chiefly as a disciple of Oscar Wilde, and a contributor to *The Yellow Book* (See Stanley Weintraub, *Reggie: A Portrait of Reginald Turner* [New York: George Braziller, 1965]; David Cecil, *Max: A Biography* [London: Constable, 1964]; and *Letters to Reggie Turner*, ed. Rupert Hart-Davis [London: Hart-Davis, 1964].)

6. Quoted in Merivale, p. 48.

7. For a discussion of this which touches on the main issues, see John E. Smith, "Nietzsche: The Conquest of the Tragic Through Art" in *The Tragic Vision and the Christian Faith*, ed. Nathan A. Scott, Jr. (New York: Association Press, 1957), pp. 211–37.

8. *Biographia Literaria*, Chapter XXI.

9. *Letters*, p. 490.

10. Ibid., p. 482.

11. Hyde, *Wilde*, pp. 388–89.

12. Quoted in Weintraub, *Reggie*, p. 99.

13. Herman Melville, *Moby Dick* (New York: W. W. Norton, 1967), chapter 96, p. 355. The association of Wilde himself with Job has been a common, if somewhat melodramatic, one; over his first grave at Bagneux, the words of Job (chapter 29) were written: "After my words they spake not again; and my speech dropped upon them." James Joyce suggested that the future would carve a more pious verse, from the Psalms: "they part my garments among them, and cast lots upon my vesture." Wilde's body was moved to the cemetery of Père Lachaise in 1909, and rests under Wilde's own words:

> And alien tears will fill for him
> Pity's long-broken urn
> For his mourners will be outcast men,
> And outcasts always mourn.

For a discussion of Jacob Epstein's monument of the Sphinx for Wilde's tomb, see the sculptor's biography *Let There Be Sculpture* (London: Michael Joseph, 1942).

14. William Wordsworth, "The Borderers," Act III. Wilde (mis) quoted these lies in *De Profundis* (*Letters*, p. 467).

15. "The Critic as Artist," *Works*, Vol. 8, p. 179.

16. *Letters*, p. 481.

17. This and the following passages are taken from "A Study of Dionysus: The Spiritual Form of Fire and Dew," reprinted in *Greek Studies: A Series of Essays* (London: Macmillan, 1895), pp. 10–11, 20–21, 34, 39, 45.

18. This passage is taken from Pater's essay, "The Myth of Demeter and Persephone," *Greek Studies*, pp. 109–10.

19. *Letters*, p. 509.

20. *Kora in Hell: Improvisations* (San Francisco: City Light Books,

1957), pp. 45–46. See Tashjian, p. 94.

21. C. F. Keppler, *The Literature of the Second Self* (Tucson: University of Arizona Press, 1972), pp. 79–80. There is a nice irony in the fact that one of the most startling presentations of the theme that Keppler discusses, James Hogg's *Memoirs and Confessions of a Justified Sinner*, was in a sense rediscovered for English readers by André Gide, who himself (as Richard Ellmann has pointed out) had been involved in a debate with another aspect of himself, a debate in part orchestrated by Wilde.

22. *Miscellaneous Studies: A Series of Essays* (London: Macmillan, 1895), pp. 220–21.

23. For an exhaustive study of this, see A. J. H. Busst, "The Image of the Androgyne in the Nineteenth Century," *Romantic Mythologies*, pp. 1–95.

24. Keppler, p. 1.

25. Busst, pp. 6–9.

26. *From Toulouse Lautrec to Rodin* (London: J. Lane, 1929), p. 151. One of the more sordid aspects of Solomon's career was the reaction to his arrest (in 1876) on charges of soliciting for homosexual favours in front of a public lavatory; his friends all shunned him and he was reduced to destitution. See Henderson, *Swinburne*, pp. 149, 183–84. Robert Ross included a brief but illuminating essay on Solomon and his times in *Masques and Phases* (London: Arthur L. Humphries, 1909). Both Ross and Wilde owned several of Solomon's works.

27. For an extended account of this topic, with specific reference to Yeats but nonetheless of general interest, see Harold Bloom, *Yeats*, passim, and p. 485, n.10.

28. "Leonardo da Vinci," *The Renaissance*, pp. 122–23.

29. *Appreciations*, pp. 216–217. For another perspective on this passage, see Crinkley, pp. 35–67.

30. *À Rebours*, translated as *Against Nature* by Robert Baldick (Harmondsworth: Penguin, 1959), p. 196. The prose translation given by Baldick is as follows:

> Oh mirror! cold water frozen by boredom within your frame, how many times, for hours on end, saddened by dreams and searching for my memories, which are like dead leaves in the deep hole beneath your glassy surface, have I seen myself in you as a distant ghost! But, oh horror! on certain evenings, in your cruel pool, I have recognized the bareness of my disor-
> dered dream!

31. T. S. Eliot, "Burnt Norton," *Collected Poems*, p. 191. Kermode's remark is included in *Puzzles and Epiphanies: Essays and Reviews 1958-1961* (London: Routledge and Kegan Paul, 1962), p. 4. See also Kermode, *Romantic Image*, esp. pp. 49–91; Hamburger, pp. 230–38; and, the source of so many ideas that have been developed since its appearance, Mario Praz's *The Romantic Agony*, trans. Angus Davidson (London: Oxford University Press, 1951).

32. *Dialogues,* trans. William McCausland Stewart (New York: 1956), p. 57.

33. See Nassar, pp. 80–109. Stanford, pp. 55–58, draws attention in a useful way to Rossetti's unfinished poem "The Orchid Pit," and to other work of the period, as exemplifying the fascination with the image of the "darkling" Venus that is so obvious by the 1880s and 1890s, and most particularly in Wilde's *Salomé.*

34. See Helen Grace Zagona, *The Legend of Salomé, and the Principle of Art for Art's Sake* (Paris: Librarie Minard, 1960), p. 94 and passim; and *Against Nature,* p. 68.

35. Quoted in Baldick, *Huysmans,* p. 91; the answer was yes.

36. Quoted in Emmanuel, p. 122; and (below) p. 118.

37. Charles Robert Maturin, *Melmoth the Wanderer* (Lincoln: University of Nebraska Press, 1961), pp. 80, 152, 250, 274.

38. See A. G. Lehmann, "Pierrot and Fin de Siècle," *Romantic Mythologies,* p. 223; and passim, for much of the history of Pierrot which follows. See also R. W. B. Lewis, *The Poetry of Hart Crane: A Critical Study* (Princeton: Princeton University Press, 1967), pp. 54–65.

39. The title of Mallarmé's long poem, published in 1862, and reprinted (by Verlaine) in his *Poètes maudits* (1894), *Le Décadent* (1886), and *La Revue rose* (1887). Gogol's comic masterpiece *Dead Souls,* which was widely read during the latter part of the century, provided an early glimpse at what Paul Klee termed (with reference to Gogol) "the world of visible laughter and invisible tears." "There is a laughter," Gogol himself remarked, "which may be classed with the higher lyrical emotions, and which is as distant as heaven from the convulsions of a common jester."

40. "Ave Atque Vale," *Collected Poetical Works,* Vol. 1, p. 347.

41. Hyman, p. 28.

42. For an edited and reconstructed text of this lecture, with a useful introduction, see *Oscar Wilde: Irish Poets and Poetry of the Nineteenth Century,* ed. Robert D. Pepper (San Francisco: Book Club of California, 1972).

43. See *Letters,*, p. 547.

INDEX